The
GOLD

The
GOLD

THE REAL STORY BEHIND BRINK'S-MAT:
BRITAIN'S BIGGEST HEIST

NEIL FORSYTH and THOMAS TURNER

EBURY
SPOTLIGHT

1

Ebury Spotlight, an imprint of Ebury Publishing
20 Vauxhall Bridge Road
London SW1V 2SA

Ebury Spotlight is part of the Penguin Random House group of companies
whose addresses can be found at global.penguinrandomhouse.com

First published by Ebury Spotlight in 2023

www.penguin.co.uk

A CIP catalogue record for this book is available from the British Library

Hardback ISBN 9781529149524
Trade Paperback ISBN 9781529149531

Printed and bound in Great Britain by Clays Ltd, Elcograf S.p.A.

Imported into the EEA by Penguin Random House Ireland,
Morrison Chambers, 32 Nassau Street, Dublin D02 YH68.

CONTENTS

Introduction

Shortly before 7am on Saturday 26 November 1983, an armed gang burst into the Brink's-Mat depot near London's Heathrow Airport. They expected a significant haul, but what they found was beyond their wildest dreams. Gold bullion worth almost £26 million.

Making off with the gold, the gang committed what was at the time the largest robbery in world history, and unwittingly set off an extraordinary, decades-long chain of events.

The Brink's-Mat robbery took place in a society in flux. Britain was changing. Heavy industries were in terminal decline, with traditional trades becoming little more than folk memories. Old societal bonds were pulled apart as ideas of a new world took shape. Cut loose from tradition, Britain would no longer grow rich from production; instead, money would come from money. The country would derive its wealth from expertise in services. Britain was to become a handler nation. Fortunes would not be made through hard graft but by making a canny investment, cutting a sharp deal, trading with anyone who had the cash. It was a brasher, more individualistic, entrepreneurial world, driven by money.

What was true for society was true for crime. During the 1970s, the cunning burglar and expert safecracker of folklore had been replaced at the top of the criminal tree by the armed robber, whose threat of brutal violence offered a more reliable route to success. But by the early 1980s, the supremacy of the armed robber was beginning to slip, replaced by a new generation of criminal entrepreneurs who operated in the shadows, not committing the crimes themselves but making fortunes from buying and selling stolen goods and investing the profits in further criminal enterprise. In this, they were aided by a small army of seemingly respectable professionals; of dodgy lawyers, accountants, bankers and advisers prepared to turn a blind eye to the sources of their clients' wealth while taking their cut.

The Brink's-Mat robbery happened in the midst of all this change. The loose network of criminals who committed the robbery and handled the gold straddled the old and the new worlds, combining traditional craft criminals with upwardly mobile wheeler-dealers and unscrupulous professionals. Together, they took advantage of the opportunities unleashed by the economic and social forces transforming Britain, in deals done in both shady back rooms and smart corporate offices, and with old codes abandoned in favour of opportunity and greed.

Ranged against the criminals was a police force that had become mired in rumours and allegations of malpractice, and legislation that had not kept up with the changing face of crime or society. The investigation into the robbery was an inquiry under the constant threat of corruption, facing opponents with the money to buy a lot of favours. Just as importantly, it confronted a public and media that was sometimes sceptical about its claims, and which showed a willingness to side with the word of the accused over that of the police officer.

The Brink's-Mat robbery is both famous and unknown. Other than the fact that it occurred, few are aware of the events that followed. By its nature, it is a difficult story to tell. Much of what happened during and after the robbery is known only to those who took part. Very few of those people, and none of those convicted, have ever spoken publicly about it. After forty years, myths and legends have grown around the robbery and those involved which only serve to obscure the reality further. It is a consistently murky tale, where little is what it seems. Including, we will reveal, the popular story of the robbery itself.

This book is our best attempt to reconstitute the events set in train on 26 November 1983. We have worked through forty years of criminal trials, police interviews, media archives, unpublished records and the diligent work of investigative reporters through the decades. We tracked down and spoke to as many people connected to the case as we could find, in Britain and around the world. Some of those we spoke to we can acknowledge, some we cannot. By painstakingly connecting these glimpses of the story from across the decades, we have recreated and told as clear an account of the Brink's-Mat robbery and its aftermath as is currently possible.

Where the story of the Brink's-Mat robbery ends is a matter of debate. Whether it has ended is another. What is unequivocal is where it begins.

On a cold morning, in west London, in 1983.

CHAPTER ONE

Unit 7

It began in the dark. On an early Saturday morning in late November, in a trading estate on the south-eastern edge of London's Heathrow Airport, a group of men huddled outside a nondescript warehouse. This was Unit 7, a modern two-storey, brick and corrugated steel construction. Distinctive orange and white shutter doors stretched from the ground to the roof. Above them, a single CCTV camera looked out over the main vehicle approach. From the outside, there was nothing to indicate what the unit contained and, unlike most of its neighbours, the name of the occupant was not listed on the estate's signs. It was just another unremarkable building set among similarly unremarkable warehouses and small engineering shops.

The building's occupant was Brink's-Mat, a leading security firm. Despite appearances, Unit 7 was among the most secure sites in Britain. It was used to store currency, precious metals and other high-risk consignments as the firm's guards moved them between locations, generally through Heathrow Airport, in dark blue armoured vans. Behind the orange and white shutter doors was a secure, concrete-reinforced vault that contained three of the toughest, most secure safes available. It was where the firm's valuable cargoes were usually stored.

The men gathered outside the building early that morning were the security guards, waiting for a Saturday overtime shift to begin. They stood together by the side door towards the rear of the building. Unlike the main vehicle entrance at the front, it was not covered by a camera. They talked, laughed and clapped their hands to stay warm in the chill November air. The electronic security systems that protected the building overnight meant they could not enter before their shift began. Unit 7 had been unoccupied since 11pm the previous evening, when the late-duty keyman had signed off. The facility was guarded by an infrared detector that reacted to body heat and a microwave system to pick up disturbances in the air. If a key was inserted into the door lock before 6.30am, alarms would start ringing. At 6.30am, an automatic timer switched off the overnight alarm.

While his colleagues waited, Michael Scouse watched from his car, listening to the radio. At 6.30am, he got out and walked to the door. As the supervisor on duty, he inserted his key in the lock and entered the building alone. Inside, Scouse retrieved another key from a safe to turn off the night alarms covering the perimeter walls and windows, and to set the day alarms. Only when this was done did Scouse let his shivering colleagues into the building, locking the door behind them. The building had an 'air-lock' system, with another locked door behind the external door. When all of the guards had passed into the building, Scouse locked the second door behind them and reactivated the alarm. The building was secure. Impregnable.

For the guards, it was another day in the safest building in Britain. They began to prepare for the day's task: transporting a shipment of gold from Unit 7 to Gatwick Airport so it could be loaded onto an 8.30am Cathay Pacific flight to Hong Kong. There were six guards there that day. Or there should have been. Scouse had let in his colleagues Robin Riseley, Ron Clarke, Richard Holliday and Peter

Bentley. One guard, however, was missing. Tony Black. Scouse was happy to have a team at all. It was only the previous afternoon that Scouse had been told to rustle up some staff to work overtime that Saturday. There had been some grumbling before Riseley, Bentley and Holliday agreed to come in. Clarke and Black agreed immediately. But now Black wasn't here.

Scouse started without him. They were used to handling high-value consignments, but today's load was a challenge. When Scouse finished work the previous evening, the vault contained around £750,000 in gold and other metals. Several hundred thousands of pounds in used banknotes were locked in the safes. But more had been delivered after he left. Three tons of gold. It was this that they were to move to Gatwick Airport.

The ground floor of Unit 7 contained the vault and a vehicle loading bay. On the first floor, where the guards convened that morning, there was a radio-control room, a small office and a staff room. Scouse laid out the plan. Riseley would ride in the cab of the armoured van while Bentley drove and Holliday sat in the back with the gold. Clarke would follow behind in a smaller Brink's-Mat Ford Escort van to provide additional security. Black, if he ever arrived, would be on radio duty, maintaining contact with the two vans from his base at Unit 7. But there was a problem. Their Mercedes van only had a payload capacity of two and a half tons. They would have to chance it.

Some of the men were nervous at the prospect. After all, it was while travelling that they faced danger. Security van robberies were an established subset of British crime. A cashless society was a long way off in 1983. Security vans were used to move huge quantities of money between banks, post offices, large employers and big stores. Successful robbers could make off with hundreds of thousands of pounds at a time. Brink's-Mat's vans were a common target. They were hit while on the move, in brazen, fast, often highly violent attacks. On the road and outside the safety of Unit 7 was where the guards were vulnerable. And to go out there with an overweight van seemed an unnecessary risk. As nerves grew, the doorbell rang.

Scouse walked down the stairs and opened the two doors. Outside was a dishevelled Tony Black. It wasn't unusual for Black to be late; he offered his apologies, explaining that he had overslept, as Scouse led him upstairs. As Black entered the staff room, Riseley glanced at his watch. It was 6.40am. Black appeared pale and apprehensive. He disappeared to the toilet, then joined Scouse in the radio-control room and began rolling a cigarette.

Back in the staff room, the guards chatted while Bentley stood at the sink, preparing tea for his colleagues. And then, a harsh Cockney voice filled the air.

'Get on the floor or you're fucking dead!'

The safest building in Britain had been breached. In the doorway stood a masked figure, pointing a semi-automatic pistol at the guards. He pulled the top of the gun back to cock the weapon. Riseley, Clarke and Holliday dived from their chairs to the floor. Bentley hesitated, thinking it was a practical joke. That was a mistake. Rushing into the room, the intruder raised his pistol and smashed it down on Bentley's head. The guard fell to the floor, hitting his head on a table on the way, two bloody gashes opening up on his scalp.

From the floor, Riseley could make out the gunman: a white man, about five feet, eight inches tall, clean shaven. He had on a dark anorak or car coat over a black blazer, black trousers, white shirt and black tie. On his head, he wore a trilby hat. He had hitched up a bright yellow ski mask that covered all but his eyes as he entered the room, giving Riseley a split-second glimpse of his face. Holliday could also see him and noted the crispness of his starched shirt and the herringbone pattern of his hat. He saw a lock of fair hair protruding from beneath the hat. Bentley thought the man looked a little like Inspector Clouseau, the comical French detective played by Peter Sellers. Not that he told him at the time.

The man waved through the open door and more armed masked men rushed into the room. It all happened too quickly for the guards to be able to tell how many there were: three, maybe four. Riseley was an army veteran and to him it looked like a well-planned military operation, with each man knowing where he needed to be and what he needed to do. Speed, aggression and surprise were used to overwhelm and terrify the victims, giving them no chance to fight back.

The four guards were immobilised quickly. Drawstring cotton bags were pulled over their heads, their hands were tightly cuffed behind their backs and their legs were bound with duct tape. Holliday began thrashing on the floor, finding it difficult to breathe. A man rolled him onto his back, loosened the drawstring and moved the bag above his lip so he could breathe more easily. After being hooded and bound, in an odd glimpse of compassion, Clarke was asked if he was in any distress.

Another voice was heard. It was a well-spoken man, clearly used to giving orders. 'Get that radio tuned in,' this new voice said. 'If you hear anything, tell us.' The guards all later agreed that this man was in charge. They heard several men leave the room but could tell they were not alone. The radio was tuned to a police frequency.

From the control room, where he sat with Black, Scouse heard what he later described as 'a commotion'. When he looked out the room, he was confronted by a masked man running at him with a pistol in his outstretched hand, yelling at him to get down on the floor. Scouse flashed a look at Black and mouthed, 'Who the fuck's that?' Black immediately dropped to the floor; Scouse joined him. He felt a pistol pressed into the back of his neck as the gunman ordered him to put his hands behind his back. A bag was put over his head, and he was handcuffed and kicked a number of times before a voice asked, 'Are you Scouse?' When he confirmed he was, Scouse was lifted to his feet.

Scouse was told to breathe deeply, then felt a knife slicing through his belt and the waistband of his trousers. A can was placed under his hood and he was asked if he recognised the smell. It was unmistakeable: petrol. Scouse felt the liquid being splashed all over him, soaking his genitals, stinging and burning his skin. A voice told him that they knew where he lived, above a television rental shop on Ruislip High Street, and that they had been watching him for nine months and planning the operation for twelve.

Scouse, terrified and fearing for his life, was dragged downstairs and told to open the vault. One of the masked men told him, 'If we don't get what we want, if the alarms go off or the police turn up, I'll put a match to you and a bullet to the back of your head.' Scouse believed it.

Back in the staff room, other gang members asked Robin Riseley to identify himself. Riseley knew why they wanted him but he did so anyway. He was dragged to the office, where he was subjected to the same treatment as Scouse. His trousers were cut open and fell to his ankles, and petrol was splashed all over him. The effect was terrifying. 'Right, Riseley, what's your job?' someone asked. He answered that he opened the safes. What neither guard knew at this point was that the petrol had been watered down. It did not matter. The fear was enough. Scouse and Riseley, the two guards needed to open the vault, had been identified, terrorised and were being escorted downstairs within minutes of the masked gang's arrival.

The security systems at Unit 7 were unbreachable. The contents of the vault were protected by several layers of security, both physical and electronic. Getting into the building through the foot entrance required passing through two locked doors. The outer shutters that allowed vehicles to enter and exit could only be operated from inside.

The vault itself was the secure core of a secure building. Behind the shutters, there was first a large outer door from the loading bay into an inner loading area. It was secured by a padlock and an electronic alarm that could be switched off with a number code. Behind the outer door was the main vault door and another alarm that needed a key to switch it off. The vault door was protected by a combination lock that required two number codes. Inside the vault, the inner section was within a locked cage. Once the cage had been opened, two more alarm systems had to be deactivated. At the very heart of the vault were three safes protected by magnetic shields and locked with keys and number combinations.

The only weakness with the technology lay in the humans who had to operate it. Even then, Brink's-Mat security protocols were stringent. Knowledge of the various code numbers and passwords, and access to the keys, was highly restricted. It was impossible for a single person to gain access to the contents of the vault or the safes. Two people were always required. On this Saturday, that was Scouse and Riseley. Scouse was the designated 'keyman', responsible for the keys. He also knew some of the codes and the passwords for the different alarms. Riseley, as the crew leader and next in command, had codes for the main vault and for the safes.

In the radio-control room, the gunman pressed a gun to Scouse's chin and asked for his combination for the main vault. Scouse did not hesitate in telling him. The gunman then demanded the keys. Scouse told him where they were and the gunman retrieved them.

The bag was torn from Scouse's head and he saw the gunman had the leather pouch that contained every key for Unit 7.

As he was hustled downstairs to the vault, Scouse was shocked at how well the gang knew the security systems. Later, he would say: 'To be honest, I could have written down the combination numbers, given them the keys and sat upstairs and had a cup of tea. They told me how to get into my own vault.'

Meanwhile, in the office, Riseley was asked for his combination. He offered it up and tried to give instruction on the combination lock, only for a gunman to tell him he would be opening it himself, the alternative being that he'd be burned alive. Soon Riseley was being rushed down the stairs too.

The masked gang passed through the outer door and first alarm systems quickly. When they came to the vault door, they ordered Scouse and then Riseley to each enter their halves of the code. With the vault opened, the gang made their way rapidly through the remaining security systems and came to the three safes protected by magnetic shields. Riseley had the codes for all three safes. Or at least, he should have done.

A few days before, the codes had been changed. Riseley had not yet committed them to memory but had noted them in his diary. The diary was at home. As he travelled through the security measures, Riseley knew what was coming. Him, standing outside the safes, unable to open them. He did what he could, desperately racking his brain while the masked men shouted at him and thrust a gun into his face. As he tried and failed to remember the numbers, one robber was later said to have suggested they give Riseley a moment to compose himself, but was overruled by others who threatened him with such aggression that Riseley concluded he would shortly be killed.

It appeared that he was right to do so. The yellow-masked gunman turned to his colleagues and said, 'It looks like we've got a hero.' One of them replied, 'It's a shame we're going to have to do him in.' Someone began to strike matches. A knife was produced and Riseley was stabbed in the hand. He was told he would be castrated if he did not open the safes.

The hooded Scouse listened on from a corner, where he had been made to sit on a metal box with a man holding him down with a gun in his ear. Scouse could hear his workmate being tormented as he attempted to remember the combinations. He stood and intervened. 'Leave him alone,' Scouse called out into the darkness, with a desperate attempt at humour. 'He's like that during the week.' The joke failed to land. Scouse was shoved back onto the box and told to shut up. A voice from the gang declared, 'I'm going by 7.30 and if they're not open by then, you're a dead man.'

In frustration, the masked gang turned their attention away from the three safes and to the rest of the vault. A gang member is said to have pointed to a small barrel and asked Scouse – his hood briefly removed – what was inside. 'Scrap,' replied Scouse. It was, but it was scrap silver and highly valuable. Another gang member pointed to a different barrel. Scouse told him it contained palladium sponge, another valuable metal. The gang are said to have become agitated, their desperation growing. They were drifting from the promise of the locked safes and were now clutching at straws. One gang member's attention had been caught by two pallets of neatly stacked grey cardboard boxes. Each was about the size of a shoe box, secured with a metal strap, a handwritten code on the outside. The robber asked what was in them. Scouse looked at the pallets that were, right now, supposed to be on their way to Gatwick Airport. Then replied …

'Gold.'

In 1983, about twenty tons of gold passed through the United Kingdom per week – much of it going through Heathrow Airport. Brink's-Mat carried almost all of it. Most of that Saturday's unusually high load of gold, due to be flown to Asia, had arrived from Johnson Matthey, a London-based gold and precious metals refiner that could trace its origins to 1817, which supplied gold to the Bank of England. It had been ordered by Johnson Matthey's customers in Asia, Europe and the Middle East. Each customer had ordered a different amount and each wanted their gold in different sized ingots. The Republic Bank of New York in Singapore had ordered 1,000kg, packed into twenty boxes with fifty 1kg bars in each. The Sumitomo Corporation in Tokyo wanted 500kg, packed into ten boxes with fifty 1kg bars in each. The DG Bank in Frankfurt had asked for the same. The Mitsubishi Corporation in Japan had ordered 200kg but wanted it in half-kilo bars, packed one hundred to a box, four boxes in all. The Eastern Trade Corporation of Dubai wanted 470kg, but it asked for even smaller bars: 4,000 of them packed into sixteen boxes.

When all these orders were put together, the result was sixty boxes, or 2,670kg of pure gold, arriving at Unit 7 from Johnson Matthey. A Brink's-Mat van had been forced to make two runs the previous evening to transport the cargo from the Johnson Matthey vault in Hatton Garden in central London to Heathrow. Another sixteen boxes of gold had come from Engelhard, the American precious metals company, with each box containing twenty-five 1kg bars. By the end of Friday night, there were seventy-six boxes of gold, each about the size of a shoebox and each bound with a metal securing strap, in the vault at Unit 7. Loaded onto two pallets, they were similar in size to a large domestic freezer. Each ingot was about the size of a chocolate bar. The total weight, three tons, was about as much as two family cars.

There was a moment of silence before the gang grabbed at the boxes. One of the robbers slid a knife through one of the straps and opened a box. The atmosphere in the vault turned on a dime. Jubilation, excitement and frantic planning immediately ensued. It was the first time that people would be confronted and seduced by the Brink's-Mat gold without knowing what to do next. It would not be the last.

The gang debated how to remove the boxes. Scouse was asked who could open the shutters to let in their van. Tony Black, he told them. Black was still upstairs, lying handcuffed in a pool of petrol that had dripped from Scouse. He was moved into the radio-control room. The other guards heard the sound of the shutters being opened and of a vehicle being driven in. A robber shouted, 'We're going to need another van!' The shutters were opened again and the guards heard what they presumed was another vehicle drive in.

The robbers began to load the gold, making use of the depot's own forklift. As the gold was hurried from the vault, Scouse observed to one of the robbers: 'You load it quicker than we do.' Once again, Scouse's joke received a difficult reception. He was taken upstairs, where he was hooded again, with his legs bound with tape. He was handcuffed to pipework and locked in an office. Before Scouse's mouth was taped shut, one of the robbers asked him, 'Are you all right, Mick?' Scouse asked that water be poured over his shirt and trousers; he still feared he could go up in flames.

Riseley was also manhandled upstairs and pushed into a cupboard, where Black was already cowering, and punched violently in the stomach. Amid the pain, Riseley felt only relief. They wouldn't have put him in the cupboard, he hoped, if they still planned to kill him. This appeared to be confirmed when he heard a robber tell him, 'It's a good job it's Christmas.'

From the loading bay, there came the sound of an engine being started. One of the robbers went round loosening the guards' bonds and hoods, casually threatening them with death if they tried to raise the alarm. Clarke heard one of the robbers shout, 'Thanks ever so much for your help and have a nice Christmas.'

With that, the shutters were closed and the robbers were gone.

The ordeal had lasted little over an hour.

Outside, it was only just getting light.

CHAPTER TWO

The Inside Man

After the chaos came silence. Scouse gave it a few minutes, to ensure the gang really had left, before calling out to check whether his colleagues were still alive. They shouted back, one after another, to confirm that they were. Bentley set to work freeing himself. Handcuffed to the staff room's pipework, with his head throbbing from a pistol whipping, he used his teeth and a set of keys to tear through the tape that bound his hands and legs. He then lifted his feet against the wall and, by pushing himself backwards, managed to snap the chain between his handcuffs.

Bentley rushed to the office where Scouse was locked in and kicked a hole in the door. Inside, he is said to have found Scouse dripping with petrol, handcuffed to a pipe and demanding that Bentley hand him the phone. While Scouse dialled 999, Bentley freed Riseley and Black from the cupboard. Meanwhile, Scouse was battling trauma. He was aware enough to call for help and to switch the phone to an outside line when it failed to connect. But he was also viscerally terrified by the ordeal. When the emergency services operator fired standard questions at him, Scouse was unable to answer coherently. He struggled to make himself understood, then slammed the phone down. It rang with an incoming call. Scouse picked it up.

A few miles away in Hayes, Alan Bullock, the workshop manager at Norman Reeves Trucks, phoned the Brink's-Mat depot shortly after 8.20am. His mechanics had been servicing a Brink's-Mat Ford Transit security van when its sensitive alarm system had been triggered. It was a common occurrence and Bullock knew the routine. With the van's siren ringing in his ears, he had to call the depot at Heathrow, ask for help and then wait for one of the company's keyholders to drive round and deactivate the alarm. Bullock first received no answer, then the engaged tone and now he got Scouse. This time, Scouse spoke with clarity: 'Phone the fucking police! We've been turned over!'

Bullock hung up and dialled 999. 'I've just called the Brink's-Mat warehouse at Heathrow,' he shouted at the operator. 'They've been robbed.' As he spoke, behind him in the workshop, the siren on the Brink's-Mat van continued to shriek in warning.

The alarm was raised around 8.20am. At the depot, Bentley had freed his colleagues. The six stunned guards gathered in a daze. Bentley used a handkerchief to mop blood from his head. Scouse tried to get into the radio-control room to activate the panic button but found the robbers had locked the door. It did not matter. Within minutes, the first police arrived on the scene.

In the early morning of 26 November 1983, Detective Sergeant Bill Miller of the Flying Squad had been on a surveillance job in east London, watching a post office van that police believed would be the target of an armed gang. His radio had crackled with new instructions and, for Miller and others, a new destiny. They were to make their way across London to the scene of the robbery at Heathrow. With him was Detective Inspector Tony Brightwell, a young, ambitious detective, known among his colleagues for being upright and thorough.

Brightwell and Miller were among the first police to get to Unit 7 following the robbery, arriving around thirty minutes after the alarm had been raised. To Brightwell, the ground floor of the depot appeared simply as an ordinary warehouse. Upstairs, it was a different story. He found total disarray – upturned furniture, abandoned hoods and ropes, and an overwhelming stench of petrol. It was a scene that spoke of violence.

Back at Scotland Yard, news of the robbery spread through the offices of both the Flying Squad and the Criminal Intelligence branch. With its emblem of a swooping eagle, the Flying Squad was regarded as an elite force within Scotland Yard. As a result of various corruption scandals, its remit had been changed in 1978 from investigating any serious crime to focusing on the growing issue of armed robberies. Its members were tough, streetwise detectives. Their approach was to mix with the criminal underworld, talking to criminals on a daily basis, gathering intelligence and information about crimes. Flying Squad officers needed to be self-motivated, skilled at interviewing suspects and running informers, and excellent thief-takers. They also needed to be brave, as the squad specialised in pavement ambushes of armed robberies in progress. Officers had to be prepared to tackle armed criminals face to face.

The Flying Squad were supported in their battle against armed crime by the Criminal Intelligence branch, known internally as C11. Set up in 1960, it was a small unit of around fifty officers. Once a criminal had been targeted, detectives from C11 would be brought in to keep them under surveillance, monitor their movements, and watch their acquaintances. Any important information would be passed on to the officers of the investigating squad. Most of its work was clandestine and highly secret, with its detectives deliberately shunning the limelight.

By the time the Flying Squad's commander Frank Cater had arrived at Unit 7, a well-rehearsed investigative machine was already at work. Scene-of-crime specialists began gathering what evidence they could. The hoods, handcuffs and industrial tape that had been used to secure the guards were collected. A fingerprint officer dusted surfaces, a photographer captured the aftermath of the robbery, and an illustrator drew a map of the depot's layout. David Stickland, the depot manager, arrived to take an inventory of what remained and what, therefore, had been taken. The final haul taken by the robbers would be detailed as: seventy-six boxes of gold bars and ingots, one pouch of platinum ingots, one pouch of diamonds, one box of palladium sponge, one pouch of travellers' cheques and one box of assay certificates. The total value of the stolen goods was £26,369,778, of which the gold was worth a dominating total of £25,911,962.

It was immediately obvious to the police that the robbers had left little evidence at the crime scene. Besides the contents of the safes that they had not been able to access, there were some empty pouches and three drums of precious metal waste. Everything else had been taken.

The next few days saw a flurry of activity. Statements were taken from anyone the police could find across the Heathrow trading estate and environs. An appeal for witnesses prompted calls from all over the country from people who claimed to have seen vehicles that might have been carrying gold. Through the private investigations firm, Robert Bishop and Co., the gold's insurers offered a reward of £2 million for information that led to its recovery. The police made sure word of the reward went out to their network of criminal informants.

The informant system was fragmentary and shrouded in secrecy, but many Scotland Yard detectives worked with registered informants who received payment if they passed on information that led to arrests. Detectives were encouraged to meet informally, even to socialise, with known or suspected criminals as a way to gather information. Cater asked his men to squeeze their informants as soon as the inquiry into the robbery began and the offer of a record, no-questions-asked reward was designed to encourage criminals to talk. Newspaper reports hinted that information had been received as a result of the offer and that it had 'loosened underworld tongues'.

Some leads came in from the public. There were reports of one or possibly two suspicious blue vans seen near Unit 7 around the time of the crime. At a press conference at Scotland Yard on Tuesday 29 November, Cater told around sixty reporters that one was thought to be a box-shaped faded light blue work van, possibly a Commer, probably ten to fifteen years old, with the letters XKS or YKS as part of its numberplate. It had been seen near the depot with two men inside at around midnight on the Friday night, six and a half hours before the robbery, and again between 7.55am and 8am on the Saturday morning, just as the robbers were leaving the area. It was spotted turning out of Green Lane, the location of Unit 7, onto the main road towards Feltham. It had 'appeared very heavily laden and was riding low upon its suspension' and its engine was 'very laboured and under stress', Cater told reporters. The driver was said to have had a light-coloured moustache and was thought to be wearing a beret. The second van was thought to be a dark blue Ford Transit or Bedford and had been seen on the trading estate between 6.15am and 6.30am on the Saturday morning. At the press conference, Cater also showed the boxes in which the gold had been stored and the canvas drawstring bags that had been used to hood the guards.

This was the type of public-facing activity to be expected in the wake of a high-profile crime. More significant was the immediate actions of the detectives on the ground, skilled operators who looked at the Brink's-Mat robbery and knew what they were seeing. To the experienced officers of the Flying Squad, several things were immediately obvious. This was clearly the work of a group of professional criminals. The job had been quick and organised, and they had left very little evidence. However, what the detectives also immediately suspected was that the criminals might have left something else behind.

An accomplice.

• • •

For an unbreachable building to be breached, it has to happen from the inside. Unit 7 showed no signs of forced entry; the robbery had happened on a Saturday, when the building was manned by a skeleton crew, and had coincided with the vault being unusually full. In addition, the robbers had detailed knowledge of the depot's security systems. Right from the start, Miller and Brightwell sensed an inside man. It could have been someone on duty, someone who worked elsewhere in the company or someone who had recently left. On this occasion, though, with no sign of forced entry, the detectives started with what was in front of them: six terrified guards, one of whom might be equally terrified at the prospect of the discovery of their hidden role.

For the Flying Squad team, steeped in knowledge of London's criminal underworld, there was only a handful of criminals capable of mounting a raid of such scale and audacity. By 1982, Criminal Intelligence had developed a secret 'Top 100' list of serious criminals operating in the capital. The job, as ever, was to find the links. When someone from a non-criminal background is corrupted, it is invariably through a social or familial link to someone of more committed criminal intent. The Flying Squad's attention, therefore, turned to the guards. And who they might know.

Having victims of a horrific armed robbery as suspects was not easy. The detectives had to balance a respectful approach to traumatised individuals with applying enough pressure to establish whether a guilty party was hiding among them. One by one, the guards faced extensive questioning by detectives accustomed to interrogating hardened professional criminals. They were asked to repeat everything they could remember about the events of the morning: whether they had seen anything suspicious when they arrived for work, where they had been in the building, what they had seen and heard. They were asked for descriptions of the robbers' voices, clothes and weapons. As the questioning continued, it became more forceful. The guards were asked about when they had learned they would be working overtime that Saturday, when they had discovered what was in the vault that morning, and whether they had any reason to be suspicious of their colleagues. Detectives probed for holes and inconsistencies in their answers.

From the outset, Scouse and Riseley were regarded as the prime suspects. Both men were clearly rattled by their experience, and both had suffered blistering from the petrol that was poured over them, but only they had access to the codes and keys needed to access the vault. Their houses were searched and their interrogations were the harshest. 'They were put through the hoop,' Brightwell would later recall. After several days of investigation, the police had seen enough. Scouse was arrested on suspicion of being involved in the robbery.

For Scouse, his trauma had reached a new level. Exhausted and scared, he blamed his erratic performance under police interrogation on shot nerves. 'One would ask me a question and I would answer it,' he later recalled, 'then one of the others would jump in and say, "Five minutes ago you said …" so my brain would start to backtrack, what did I say five minutes ago? Somebody had set me up. And that was what was at the back of my mind: who's done it?'

A breakthrough came when Cater gave the go-ahead for a video reconstruction of the raid to be made after the idea was suggested by a young detective sergeant. It was a novel approach, taking advantage of the spread of new home-video technology, and nothing like it had been tried before by Scotland Yard. Each guard would be individually recorded walking the police through their memories of the robbery. The plan was to find a story that didn't add up.

The prime suspect, Scouse, went first, gradually taking Brightwell, Miller and their Flying Squad colleagues through his movements from arrival at the depot, pausing to answer questions and check his statement. His story was flawless. It was either well rehearsed or true. The other guards followed. Some were nervous, some were angry, but no one tripped up.

And then came Tony Black. Visibly nervous and with a cigarette in his hand, Black took Brightwell through his version of events. Even though he had been singled out by the robbers to operate the shutter doors, he claimed to have seen very little: 'I can remember sort of seeing someone in the background, you know, it wasn't clear, but, but he was someone in the background,' he told the detectives. When asked if he had seen the vehicles that had been used to carry away the gold, he claimed he had seen nothing, even though the switch that operated the shutter doors was in the radio-control room beside a window looking out over the loading bay below. 'From where you were standing, could you see the shutters open?' Brightwell asked him. 'No, I was looking in the corner.'

At this point, Black was in various levels of danger. Increasingly nervous, his screen presence was becoming a difficult watch. 'It was obvious,' said Bill Miller, in dry understatement, 'the man wasn't right.' More pressingly, Black's story was presenting him quite the physical challenge. There was simply no way he could have opened the shutters without having a clear view, through the window, of the robbers' arrival and departure. When Miller asked him to show how he opened the shutters, Black was under pressure.

Panic does strange things to a man. In the case of Tony Black, standing in the Brink's-Mat depot with stern detectives watching his every move and a camera whirring, it sent him briefly into the world of physical comedy. He demonstrated opening the shutters while contorting himself into the corner of the room, his arms stretched out and his face pressed into the wall. The overriding challenge for the detectives, aware of the camera's presence, was to refrain from laughter. Back at Scotland Yard, there were no such restrictions. That afternoon, the film was shown to the rest of the Flying Squad officers. Several times. Every time Black came on screen, the room jeered as though he were a B-movie villain.

The police had one good reason to suspect Black. Soon, they had another.

• • •

Through their detailed inquiries into each of the guards' backgrounds and family lives, detectives discovered that Tony Black's sister Jennifer lived as common-law wife with a man called Brian Robinson. It was the link they had been looking for.

To combat the increase in violent armed robbery in the capital, during 1980 and 1981, Scotland Yard's Criminal Intelligence branch had run an operation to increase their knowledge of the gangs and individuals responsible. It was codenamed Operation Kate, after one of the secretaries working on it, and sought to build up a detailed picture of the small hardcore of south-east London professional criminals who specialised in highly organised, spectacular armed robberies, and who supplied weapons to other, lesser gangs who focused on smaller targets.

The operation was top secret, with the officers involved reporting directly to the commander of Criminal Intelligence, Brian Worth, and was one of the biggest undercover intelligence-gathering operations ever undertaken by Scotland Yard. For nearly a year, the Scotland Yard surveillance teams placed suspects under observation, tapping phones and analysing businesses to establish the sources of the money behind them.

The surveillance work yielded a mass of intelligence on the suspects and the connections between them, all of which enabled the police to put together an accurate picture of which individuals were likely to work together. By the end of the operation, the police had information on about 200 individuals, with about twenty identified as the hardcore. Worth said, 'We discovered that we had confined in south-east London twenty or so of the most adept, enterprising, violent, ruthless robbers in the entire country.' In the immediate aftermath of the Brink's-Mat robbery, the Operation Kate files and photographs provided a ready-made list of suspects for the Scotland Yard investigators.

So, when Black's link to Brian Robinson was established, the Flying Squad were elated. They knew that Robinson was a major figure in the south London criminal underworld and believed he was an armed robber; in the past three years he had beaten two armed robbery charges because there was not enough evidence against him. They also knew he was closely linked to a number of other suspected criminals. They were closing in. Black's account of the robbery had collapsed. Furthermore, the detectives were now focusing on Black's trip to the toilet shortly after his late arrival at the depot on the morning of the robbery. The toilet was downstairs. Near the pedestrian entrance.

And then they discovered a photo among the intelligence files. Taken by a Criminal Intelligence surveillance officer a few weeks before the robbery, it showed six men coming out of a south-east London block of flats together. Of the six, five could be identified. They were all significant criminals of a type that tended to come together for one reason. Brian Robinson, Micky McAvoy, Tony White, John Fleming and John Lloyd. On 28 November, the *Evening Standard* reported that detectives believed the raid had been master-minded by a criminal they nicknamed 'the Colonel'. The same man was thought to have been behind Britain's biggest cash robbery, the £7 million raid on the Security Express depot in Shoreditch, east London, in April 1983. That won't have helped Tony Black's frame of mind. The Colonel, as half of south-east London knew, was Brian Robinson.

The police had their suspects, but they needed evidence. They needed to break the inside man.

• • •

At 8am on Sunday 4 December 1983, Flying Squad detectives arrived unannounced on the doorsteps of the six guards. The target was Black. The others were taken in as cover, including the increasingly unfortunate Scouse.

Black was asleep when the police began banging on his door. Like the others, he was taken to Hounslow police station. While the others were questioned methodically, Black was interrogated. Brightwell led the questioning, supported by Detective Sergeants Alan Branch and Nicholas Benwell. It was to go on for more than six hours. They walked Black through his statement. He insisted it was true. Brightwell pointed out various discrepancies and suggested Black might want to reconsider. When Black insisted on his innocence, he was charged with armed robbery. Still, he stuck to his story. The detectives revealed they had found Black's work diary, where he had written '6.30' against the date of the robbery. Black said this was the time he was due to start work. Brightwell pointed out Black had not written his start time in any other day. Black didn't have an answer for that.

After a day of toying with the suspect, it was time to move in for the kill. Brightwell casually asked the question the officers had been building toward: 'What does your brother-in-law, Brian Robinson, think about the robbery?' Black was immediately unsettled. Brightwell then played the second part of his plan. He knew Black was unfamiliar with a police cell. They told him that he was being detained until the morning and sent him back to the cells, with the Robinson revelation for company.

The interrogation resumed the following morning, Monday 5 December 1983, at 11.32am. Brightwell and Branch walked through Black's growing list of inconsistencies. But the battle had already been won. Black asked for a cup of tea. When it arrived, he sat for a moment with the mug steaming in front of him and a heavy silence settling in the room.

Then Tony Black looked up and asked, 'Where do I start?'

Brightwell answered. 'Let's start at the beginning, shall we?'

CHAPTER THREE

The Colonel and Mad Micky

Tony Black was, in the words of one of the Brink's-Mat detectives, 'a very average type of guy'. He had been brought up in south-east London, growing up close to the docks in Deptford. He escaped London for a life in the army and was posted to Northern Ireland, Cyprus and West Germany. Alongside his military career, Black embarked on a dramatic romantic odyssey: marrying a woman from Northern Ireland, with whom he had a daughter; having an affair with a German woman; returning to mend bridges with his wife; settling in London and taking work at a Brink's-Mat depot before being caught exchanging letters with the German woman; moving to Germany to live with her and, finally, being thrown out by the German, forcing him to move back to London to live with his parents and return to work, as a single and perhaps bewildered man, at Brink's-Mat on 29 January 1979.

Back in London, Black began to reconnect with his family. His older sister Jennifer helped him find a place to live closer to his work in central London. Brian Robinson, her partner of the past twelve years, let him live in a flat above a shop on a council estate on Ben Jonson Road in Stepney, in the East End. When he moved in, Robinson and another man, who was introduced as Tony, drove him there in a powerful Rover. Black rebuilt his life, summoning the strength to move past his traumatic relationship history. He married a local bank clerk, bought a maisonette two miles from Heathrow Airport and applied for a fateful transfer to the Brink's-Mat depot at Heathrow, which had recently acquired the popular moniker 'Thief Row' because of the high levels of crime associated with the airport.

Black often visited his sister's home in Chilham House, Rollins Street, New Cross, not far from the old Surrey Dock and close to where he had grown up. Doing so, he gradually became close to Robinson. Black thought a friendship was growing between them. In fact, it was something else entirely.

Robinson had also grown up in south-east London and experienced military life, but that's where his similarities to Black end. While Black was feckless, a practical joker who failed to stick at anything for long, Robinson was a quiet, serious man with a cunning intelligence and a violent streak. He had worked for a time as a painter and decorator, and gave his occupation as a motor trader, but for most of his adult life he earned a living through crime.

Robinson had served several prison sentences, for a range of offences that included robbery, but they had not been a deterrent. Among his peers, Robinson was known for having an eye for detail – it was his planning and organisational abilities that had earned him the nickname 'the Colonel'. Yet, despite his success and high standing among other criminals, he lived a modest, unpretentious life and kept a low profile. He shared a ground-floor council maisonette with Black's sister and drove an unassuming Renault. Black may not have known all the details, but he was impressed by his brother-in-law's reputation, and drawn to the apparent glamour of the criminal world. Little did he know, he was already within it.

The grooming began. Black gave Robinson his cheque book and card then reported them stolen, an easy fraud that Robinson regularly practised. Robinson returned later having signed twenty-six cheques. Rather than giving Black the £5 he had promised for each one, he gave him a series of presents: a lawnmower, a portable television, some groceries and some spirits.

Black had passed the test. Robinson's attention turned to Black's job. He told Black that he wanted photographs of the inside of the Brink's-Mat vans. It was for a friend. Black borrowed Robinson's Polaroid camera and took three images. He met with Robinson a few days later. The two men left Robinson's flat and walked around the corner, where they met another man, who Robinson introduced as Mick. The man asked if a Land Rover with a ram welded to its front might break open the rear doors of one of the Brink's-Mat vans. Black said he didn't think that would work. Mick left with the Polaroids. Not long afterwards, in December 1980, a Brink's-Mat van was stopped and robbed in Dulwich, south-east London. Its armoured doors were rammed open with the jib of a mobile crane. The police had been tipped off and the gang were arrested, though the informant was allowed to escape. A few days later, Black asked Robinson if he had been involved. 'I wasn't on that job. I had a feeling it was a set-up,' he answered. Robinson had done the groundwork; now he waited more than two years before going to work again on Black.

The planning of the Brink's-Mat robbery began in July 1983, four months before the raid, when Robinson began asking Black about security arrangements at Heathrow. Were there any easy targets they could 'walk in on', he wondered? Black told him about a regular currency shipment from Dublin to London on Aer Lingus that he collected once or twice a week. The two men began to meet, going fishing together on the Thames at Laleham, on the outer edges of west London. Robinson weighed up the possibilities Black suggested, drawing him in with talk of how they might profit from Black's job at Brink's-Mat. On one occasion, the two men drove through Heathrow's sprawl so that Black could point out the Aer Lingus buildings where he collected the banknotes. A few days later, they met again at Robinson's flat. Aer Lingus was too risky, Robinson said. The building was next to others used by a Middle Eastern airline that was more likely to be monitored by the police. 'It's no good,' Robinson said. 'Don't you get anything back at your base?'

For more than an hour they talked about the routines of the Heathrow depot. Black told him how the patterns of his work were dictated by customers' office hours and flight schedules. He could predict with some accuracy when shipments of cash, travellers' cheques, diamonds, gold and other valuables would be stored in the vault and for how long. Black told him that Fridays were the best night to hit the depot, as there were often large shipments stored overnight ready for delivery to Asia on Saturday morning.

A few weeks later, Robinson called and told Black he needed to introduce him to two associates. They met on a Sunday morning at the Gibbs Garage, a car dealership close to Heathrow. When Black arrived, Robinson was already there with two men Black had met briefly before. The one he knew as Tony. And the one he knew as Mick.

• • •

Michael McAvoy was born in 1951 and grew up as part of an Irish immigrant family in working-class Camberwell, south-east London. Driven by a desire for easy wealth, he became involved in crime at a young age, organising illegal road races of stolen cars, and by the time he left school was already committing burglary and stealing from the nearby docks. He boxed at a local club and, as a teenager, developed a reputation for a ferocious toughness and the accompanying nickname 'Mad Micky' that he would carry into adulthood.

McAvoy enjoyed being a criminal. He was fiercely loyal to those around him and to the traditional criminal codes, and proud of his south-east London roots. As a young man, he first went 'across the pavement', underworld slang for armed robbery, and became a participant in violent raids on banks, post offices and cash-in-transit security vans. He started working as an enforcer for the gangsters who ran West End protection rackets and began to meet older, more experienced criminals. Men like Brian Robinson.

By the mid-1970s, McAvoy had made a name for himself in the London underworld. He became known as a good man to have on a robbery, the first out of the car and the first to get the money. It is said that in 1976, McAvoy and Robinson were asked by a couple of older, well-respected armed robbers if they would be prepared to put together teams to commit robberies outside the capital. They would receive cash up front in exchange for a share of the takings from every robbery. McAvoy and Robinson took on the job along with their friend and fellow south-east Londoner, Anthony 'Tony' White. As one detective would later say, White looked 'like your stereotypical film extra of a robber; he's a heavy'. He had gone to school with Robinson and was good friends with McAvoy. The group achieved considerable success. By the end of the decade, McAvoy was one of the capital's leading armed robbers and, police believed, also an underworld 'armourer', someone who supplied weaponry to other gangs.

One lesson Robinson had taught McAvoy was to keep a low profile. McAvoy was a militantly guarded man. He trusted few people, gave little away in conversation and was said to be paranoid about police surveillance. He maintained a quiet home life, living with his wife, Jacqueline, and children in a small flat in an Edwardian house on Beckwith Road in Herne Hill, south London. He worked occasionally as a painter and decorator, and for a time ran a grocery shop with his wife. It was all part of the façade.

McAvoy was a committed, high-level criminal ever watchful for opportunity.

And his friend Brian Robinson had found one.

• • •

Robinson, McAvoy and White quizzed Black in minute detail on the security arrangements at the Brink's-Mat Heathrow depot. Black told them everything he knew and gave them instructions on how the alarm systems worked, who held the keys and combinations, and how the building was laid out. It was the first of many meetings. During the summer of 1983, Black met about once a week with Robinson, often with Mick or Tony there too. Sometimes the men got together outside Hatton Cross tube station; on other occasions they met in the car park of the Bulldog pub or at the Gibbs car dealership on the main A30 road outside Heathrow. One time they met on the riverbank at Laleham. Over the course of the meetings, Black gave up everything he had. The others wanted more.

Robinson gave Black a camera and instructed him to photograph the shutters at the premises, the vault doors, the vault and parts of the security system, including the panic buttons and alarm box. Black agreed and took the photographs secretly when he was given the job of painting the inside of the vault. A few days later, Robinson drove Black to a terraced council house on Tarves Way in Greenwich, south-east London. Mick and Tony were already there. On the floor, they had laid out large blow-ups of the photographs with a plan that Black had drawn of the depot. Black answered yet more questions, then Robinson drove him home.

The gang knew what to do once they were inside the building; now they had to work out how to get in. At the end of October 1983, Robinson asked Black to get him the key to the depot's pedestrian door so a locksmith could make a copy. One lunchtime, when the depot manager was off sick, Black stole a set of keys from his desk. He drove to a meeting with Robinson, Mick and Tony in the car park of The Beaver pub near Heathrow and handed over the keys. He waited in his car while Tony and Mick went to get copies made. When they came back, they handed three copies to Black and told him to mark which one fitted best. The duplicates, Mick mentioned, cost £4.50. The following afternoon, Black tested them. None worked at first, so he got a piece of emery cloth and smoothed the rough spots on one of them. He tried it again. It worked. He wrapped a piece of tape around it and gave it to Robinson.

It was agreed that Black would use code to tell Robinson whether or not he was going to work on any particular Saturday. If he was asked to work, he would call Robinson from the depot payphone on the Friday afternoon and tell him, 'I'm going fishing tomorrow.' Black later said that the question of what he would receive in exchange for his help with the planned robbery was never properly discussed, at least, not in specific detail. He said, 'I was told whatever was stolen would be put in a safe place and left for five years until things quietened down. I got the impression it would be put locally in a safe in the ground which would be covered with concrete.'

While McAvoy and Robinson probed Black for detailed information about the depot, they also put together a team to commit the robbery. The reputation of both men and their high standing in criminal circles meant they could recruit some of London's top armed robbers to the job. The group they eventually assembled became known in professional robbery circles as 'the meatiest team in the business'. A detective who worked on the case later described them as 'the cream of robbery teams'. Among them was John Lloyd, a well-known robber from Stepney in the East End, whose name had been linked to some of the most serious robberies of the 1970s. He was in a relationship with a woman called Jean Savage, the ex-wife of another armed robber, and had recently set up home with her in West Kingsdown, a small town in the Kent countryside to the south-east of London. They also included John Fleming, a robber from south London with a home in Denmark Hill and a string of convictions. They were joined by Brian Perry, a major south London criminal fixer who ran Blue Cars, a minicab firm that was used to launder the proceeds of various illegal enterprises. Perry had convictions for burglary and robbery, and had started his criminal career as a runner for the Arif family, the notorious Turkish-Cypriot gang from south-east London.

Perry was one of McAvoy's oldest and closest friends. They had known each other since the early 1970s, when McAvoy and his wife ran a grocery shop near to Perry's minicab office. Perry was not someone known to 'cross the pavement' but was thought by police to have helped with the logistics of the robbery, principally transportation. Behind the robbers who would do the job stood the shadowy figures from organised crime who provided the financial backing necessary to plan and execute it. One was a man known only as 'the Fox'. He had been a top robber in the 1940s and had been one of the most senior figures in the London underworld for three decades. There were rumours that he had helped finance the Great Train Robbery in 1963. McAvoy and Robinson are said to have approached him to help finance the raid.

By November 1983, everything was in place.

• • •

Black called Robinson every Friday to tell him whether he would be working the following day. On 25 November 1983, he called close to midday. The message was the same as it had been for the previous weeks. There was no big shipment scheduled and he would not be working overtime. Black rang off and had his lunch. Two hours later, Scouse asked him if he could work after all. He agreed straight away and, when no one was looking, Black later claimed that he made his way downstairs to the payphone and called Robinson. The plan was on; he was going fishing.

Robinson was unsure if the team, which had been stood down for the weekend, could be reassembled. He asked Black to meet him later in the Bulldog car park. When Black got there, he saw Robinson, Mick and Tony in a black Ford Escort near the entrance. The door was open. As soon as Black got in, Mick handed him a tissue and said, 'Use this. Don't touch the motor.' He was asked what he thought would be in the vault the next day. Exactly what Black told them is unclear.

Black ran through the security procedures and told them that Scouse and Riseley would have the keys and combinations. Mick told him that they would be doused with watered-down petrol to scare them into opening the vault. He asked Black if he thought they might be likely to 'have a go'. Black was assuring him that they would do as they were told, when a voice came from the back of the car, 'It doesn't matter, we have a right nutter on the team.' It was a reference to Mick. Black asked who would do the robbery; he was concerned that his connection to Robinson might be discovered afterward. He was assured that Robinson would not be required and that the guards would not be harmed.

The only thing left to discuss was the timing. Black would be starting at 6.30am. He said he would come downstairs, unlock the inner door, and wave through the window to let the gang know he was ready. He told them they should wait a couple of minutes to let him get back upstairs before making their move, letting themselves in through the outer door with the copied key he had tested. With that, he was allowed to go, getting out of the car using the tissue to hold the door.

Later that night, Black and his wife ate takeaway food and watched television. They went to bed but Black found it hard to get to sleep. His mind was racing. He woke with a jolt at 6.20am. He had slept through his alarm. He was going to be late for his own armed robbery. He frantically washed, dressed and drove at speed to the depot. As Black ran into the building, the robbery gang sat waiting in a van parked outside, watching their inside man enter the building. Not long after, he waved from a window, they left their van and the robbery began.

• • •

It took eight hours for this story to emerge from Tony Black's interview with the Flying Squad detectives. The statement Black finally agreed to covered everything. It even said that, towards the end of the raid while he was lying on the floor, McAvoy had come up to him, raised his mask, and whispered, 'It's all right. We've got the lot.'

When he was finished, Black met with Commander Frank Cater. No one else was present, so what was discussed is not known. Shortly before midnight, after Cater had finished with him, Black is said to have been shown a collection of police mugshots and from them to have picked out Michael McAvoy and Anthony White as 'Mick' and 'Tony', the men he met with Robinson.

In the small hours of Tuesday 6 December 1983, just over a week after the robbery, Black returned to a holding cell with his life collapsed around him. He was formally charged later that day, appearing at Feltham magistrates court and accused of robbing Brink's-Mat of gold bullion, diamonds and travellers' cheques worth £26,369,778. Standing alongside a uniformed police sergeant, wearing a blue anorak and black trousers, heavily bearded, Black did not object to being remanded in custody. He did not have a lawyer but said he might want one at a later date. The hearing lasted two minutes.

Black was moved to a bomb-proof police cell at Paddington Green station normally reserved for terrorists. His wife was driven from her home in the back of a police car and was given round-the-clock protection. When Black was outside his cell, he was made to wear a bulletproof vest. Police intelligence had picked up that there was already a price on his head.

But the police had already moved on. It was time to bring in the gang.

CHAPTER FOUR

The Round-Up

They went for Tony White first. At 6.30am on Tuesday 6 December 1983, Detective Sergeant John Redgrave, a ginger-haired, six-foot-five Flying Squad officer, banged on the door of 45 Redlaw Way, White's second-floor flat in a rundown council estate near the Old Kent Road. Several other Flying Squad detectives and uniformed officers, some of them armed, covered the front and back of the building. White came to the door in his pyjamas. He was shown a warrant and arrested. For the next two hours, Redgrave and the other detectives methodically searched the house. They demanded to know where White's car was kept, as a witness reported seeing a similar car to his near the scene of the crime on the morning of the robbery, but he refused to tell them. White was put into a police car in handcuffs and driven to Heathrow police station. He arrived at 9.50am and was put in a cell.

While Redgrave and his team handled White, a short distance away, their colleagues were preparing to arrest Micky McAvoy. At 6.50am, Flying Squad Detective Inspector Tom Glendinning banged on the door of McAvoy's flat on Beckwith Road, Herne Hill. The house was covered front and back by armed police, given police suspicion that McAvoy supplied weapons to other gangs. On hearing that he was being arrested on suspicion of involvement with the Brink's-Mat robbery, McAvoy reacted in disbelief: 'Leave it out! Where did you say you are from?' He was taken to Chiswick police station.

At Chilham House, less than a mile from White's flat, Detective Chief Inspector Ken John led the team that arrested Brian Robinson. Detective Sergeant Bill Miller was with him. The raid began at 6.55am. Robinson answered the door to the police team in his underpants. 'Come in, look around,' he said. 'I've been half expecting you.' As with the other suspects, his home was searched and, at 9.30am, he was arrested and taken to West Drayton police station.

Detectives began questioning the suspects later that day. None of them were given access to a solicitor and none of the interviews were tape-recorded. This was entirely normal for the time. Police were not required to allow solicitors to be present during interviews, and in many cases prevented suspects from speaking with their legal representatives while they were being questioned. The officers doing the interrogating would usually write notes afterwards, then ask the suspect to sign a copy to confirm their agreement with the content. Many refused. Some drew lines in any blank spaces on the statement in fear that police would make later additions. Others accused police of 'verballing' – talking them into vague comments that could later be construed as confessions – or of simply making up statements that were then attributed to the suspect.

On the other hand, loose regulation in the interview room meant secret deals could be thrashed out without lawyers present and information traded in exchange for lesser charges or a good word with a judge when it came time for sentencing. Suspects could speak knowing their words could be retracted and denied in court if a deal was not forthcoming and they did not sign the notes. With no objective record, there was simply no way of knowing what really had been said. It all meant that the accounts that emerged could be ambiguous and contradictory, with a fog of uncertainty cloaking what really went on. The interviews with the three men suspected of the Brink's-Mat robbery were no exception.

• • •

At 2pm, Tony White sat down with two detectives (who cannot be named). What followed was later disputed. According to the police account, one of the detectives told White why he was being held and asked him to explain his part in the robbery. White, they said, aggressively denied being involved. The detective then suggested that White had been preparing to flee and that he had cleaned his house to remove forensic evidence that could tie him to the robbery. At this, they said, White told them: 'All I'm saying is that if I sit here with my mouth shut, you haven't got fuck all. I know that.'

The detective took another approach, revealing that Tony Black had confessed to his role in the robbery, and had identified White, McAvoy and Robinson. At this, White was said to be incredulous. The detectives later claimed they had then shown him a copy of Black's statement. White was allowed to see the front page but was prevented from reading any further. According to the police, he asked if they thought he was 'another Tony Black' and claimed he would 'die for his mates before I'd shit on them'. A note was taken and was allegedly shown to White, but police said he refused to sign it. The first interview was said to have ended there.

The police said White was taken from his cell later that afternoon for further questioning by Redgrave. In their account, White now mulled over his position. At how old his child would be when he was released after a possible thirty-year sentence, at what 'the animals on the outside' could do to his family to get hold of the gold, at the conundrum he faced in potentially giving up the gold without being seen as a grass. 'Robbo has been my buddy for years, we went to school together for fuck's sake, and Micky is my best mate,' the police claimed White said. 'If I do a day less than them, then they'll know I've grassed and I'd rather do the whole thirty than have them think that.' When they tried to get him to relate his part in the robbery, he refused to cooperate. 'I've never pleaded guilty in my life and I don't intend to start now,' the police noted White as saying. 'I've got to sort out what's best for my family. I can't do that in an hour; you'll have to give me more time.' The officers ended the interview and White, they said, refused to sign their notes.

The officers spoke to White again the following morning, 7 December 1983. The interview began, they said, with White still apparently weighing up whether to confess or not. According to the police, he asked to see a copy of Black's statement. The detective passed one to him and allowed him to read it through twice. After White had completed his second read, the detective said he asked him whether he had understood it. According to the police, White answered, 'How many times are we going to go over this? What do you want me to fucking say? Yes, it is fucking right and, yes, I went on it but that's it. I've told you, no more fucking questions about that thing. What I want to talk about is the gold and what can be done for me, all right?'

They claimed that the conversation then centred on what White called 'a right catch-22 situation'. He wanted to discuss what giving up his share of the gold might gain but didn't want to 'grass anyone up'. He explained that he wanted to get the 'best deal for me, Micky and Robbo' and that if lighter sentences could be agreed for the three of them, then he could consider giving up the gold. The detective told him he could not arrange a lighter sentence. White replied:

'Right. That's it. I'm saying no more. I've given you what I want. Come back when you've made your minds up.' The interview ended at 12.40pm and police said White again refused to sign their notes of the conversation.

White later claimed that he had said none of this and that he had made repeated requests to see his solicitor, none of which was recorded in the police version of events. He denied that he had ever been shown Black's statement or that he had even heard of him until his name was mentioned by his police interviewers. His version of events was very different. According to White, the officer said, 'Look, I'm not going to insult your intelligence. I know you will not tell us anything, nor will the other two. You've never nicked Old Bill before so I know you won't nick your own. We want that gold back and we don't care how we get it. It can be left on a motor or anywhere or even on a rubbish tip or anything. We don't care if we don't nick anyone else; as long as we get it back we don't care.' White replied, 'I've told you. I don't know nothing about it.' The officer continued, 'Let me tell you, you three will be nicked for this and fitted up. We'll make sure you get a long sentence. That's why we're not making any notes at all. Because if we get any help from you, or the other two, we can write this up how we like. You know what we can do, you know the power we've got.'

• • •

While White was being interviewed, Ken John started work on Brian Robinson at West Drayton police station. The experienced Robinson politely refused to answer any of John's questions unless his solicitor was present, saying, 'I don't wish to be rude, but I'm entitled to have a solicitor present. I don't wish to say anything at this stage.' John eventually gave up and returned Robinson to his cell. At 5pm, the interview resumed. John told Robinson that Black had told the police 'certain things that incriminate you', but Robinson claimed to have no idea what those could be. He agreed with much of Black's story about their relationship but said nothing about the planning of the robbery. He also confirmed his friendship with White and McAvoy and provided a persuasive alibi.

On the day of the robbery, Robinson claimed to have risen at 6.10am and driven to visit his mother on the Isle of Sheppey in Kent. He said he stopped for breakfast at the Little Chef on the M2 at around 6.50am and arrived at his mother's at 8am. He said he stayed until late afternoon, and left for home around tea-time. During the visit, he also saw his brother who lived with his mother, who refilled the radiator on his car. It was a convincing, and possibly partly true, story.

Nevertheless, detectives were confident Robinson had been involved. The search of his house had found tape similar to that used to bind the guards, a knife in a bedside drawer and a Polaroid camera like the one Black said he had used to photograph the Brink's-Mat van. Robinson was dismissive, saying he never gave the camera to Black, that he kept the knife for fear of intruders and that the tape was used for decorating. The interview ended at 6.20pm. Like White, Robinson refused to sign the note taken by the detectives.

Robinson was interviewed again on the Wednesday afternoon, 7 December 1983. This time, he was shown Black's statement. After reading for a few minutes, he placed the statement on the table and asked detectives if Black had turned supergrass. Since the 1970s, the Metropolitan Police had been pressuring suspects detained for armed robberies to name their co-conspirators in exchange for more lenient sentencing. The criminals who agreed became known as 'supergrasses'. It was devastatingly successful. The police quickly discovered that there was little honour among thieves and that most criminals put their own interests above those of their mates. Consequently, the supergrass system was used with great success against armed-robbery gangs, cracking bonds of criminal loyalty and destroying supposed codes of honour. By the early 1980s, it had made armed robbery an increasingly risky venture.

John confirmed to Robinson that Black would be giving evidence and asked Robinson to continue reading. Robinson did so but was eager to know if McAvoy or White had cracked, repeatedly pausing to ask questions. He alighted on the part of Black's statement that detailed how he had asked Robinson not to take part in the raid and told detectives he never went into the depot, only that he had introduced Black to 'some blokes'. He said he had nothing to do with the petrol; that that was someone else's idea. According to police, he eventually finished with, 'I can't say anything about the Saturday, guv. Believe me, I wasn't there. The vans and all that, I can't help you with. Look, guv, if I could get the gold back, I would help you. I'm looking at a thirty-year stretch. Do you think I wouldn't help you if I could? It all adds up against me but, honestly, I was only helping some others who were hard up. They never expected to get all that gold. We expected a good haul but nothing like all that gold. My share was just going to be a drink for the introduction, that's all.' John was unconvinced. He suggested that Robinson was on the robbery and had lined up a cast-iron alibi because he knew he would be identified from his family ties to Black. According to police, Robinson replied, 'I've told you my part and if you don't believe me, forget it. You've told me you can't do me any favours, only I can help myself, so that's what I'm going to do. I don't want to discuss this any more until I've seen my solicitor.' At 4.32pm Robinson was returned to his cell. As before, he refused to sign the note of the interview taken by the police.

• • •

McAvoy's questioning began at Chiswick police station at 3pm on the afternoon of Tuesday 6 December. Detective Inspector Tom Glendinning led the interview, if it could be called that. For the police, perhaps predictably, McAvoy was the hardest opponent of all. Question after question brought forth no response. When McAvoy was finally told that Black was helping police, he made no reply. Eventually he spoke, but only to say: 'I'm completely innocent of these allegations put to me. I've had nothing to do with the Brink's-Mat job and I would like my solicitor present during these interviews.' Glendinning refused and the interviewer continued to ply the suspect with questions, which McAvoy resolutely continued to refuse to answer. Eventually, the interview was brought to a close and McAvoy was returned to his cell.

Glendinning questioned McAvoy again the following afternoon. Once again, McAvoy refused to answer any questions. When Glendinning tried to get him to recount his movements on the days before and after the robbery, McAvoy told him he had an alibi and would tell it to his solicitor. When it was suggested that he might be picked out in an identity parade, he told the detectives that it would be a mistake and maintained his innocence. He told Glendinning that he had considered the potential sentence: 'For £26 million I'll get thirty years. On a normal robbery it would be eighteen but for that one, it will be topped up to thirty.' When he was told that Black had described his role in planning and executing the robbery, McAvoy was disdainful: 'Downstairs, I'm reading Harold Robbins,' he said, referring to a paperback he had with him in his cell, 'Black should start writing stories like that.' The interview was stopped at 3.36pm.

Glendinning decided to try again later that evening. At 8.30pm, McAvoy was again told of the evidence against him and that because he had not worn his mask for part of the raid, two of the guards would be able to identify him in a parade. He was then shown Black's state-ment. McAvoy refused to read it and so it was read to him. McAvoy's response, according to the police, was only, 'He's got some memory, he has.' He refused to confirm whether the statement was true but asked what the others were saying and whether they had also seen Black's statement. He was told that White had accepted his role in the robbery and was keen to meet with McAvoy and Robinson to discuss the return of the gold. The police claim that McAvoy then asked to see Commander Cater. Asked why, he explained that he had spoken to him four years ago and that if White had seen Cater, he wanted to as well. Glendinning pounced: 'Do you mean you were on the robbery?' McAvoy would later deny this, and claim that he was taken to Cater, who said if they got the gold back he would get a more lenient sentence.

Here, the murk descends again. According to police, but in a statement that McAvoy later refused to sign, the following exchange took place:

MCAVOY: It looks like it or I wouldn't be here, would I?
GLENDINNING: Mick, were you on the robbery?
MCAVOY: Yes!

McAvoy refused to answer any more questions until he had seen Cater, who he said he trusted more than any of the detectives. Shortly before midnight, Cater and one of his deputies came to the room and waved the others out. He informed McAvoy that there was no possibility of a meeting between the three prisoners to discuss the recovery of the gold, and told him: 'McAvoy, you are wasting my time. You asked to see me. If you want to indicate where the gold is, then do so. All I will tell you is that whatever you say about the gold will be dealt with at the highest level. Now it is up to you.' McAvoy did not dispute his answer to Cater. 'I can't help you,' he said.

The police were frustrated but confident. They had the gang, now it was about gathering evidence and wearing them down. Traditional detective work that would ultimately bring traditional results. But what the police didn't appreciate at this time was that the Brink's-Mat story would be about more than that: it would be about a break with tradition. This was a story that would start with cops and robbers, but become something bigger, different and unique. It would be about other people. Shadowy figures that flitted between criminality and conventional society, who would be seduced by the prospect of £26 million of gold looking for somewhere to go. While the police interrogated the robbers and moved carefully and slowly towards convictions, outside the police stations, some of these other people had entered the story, and they were moving fast.

Buried in the disputed police notes of the White interviews is an intriguing nugget. While considering the return of the gold, White's phrasing was that he 'might be able to get the gold back'. When the detective pressed on why he said 'might', White explained that the robbers no longer had control of the gold.

If White did say this, then he was right.

CHAPTER FIVE

Kenny and John

If you are going to commit the biggest robbery in world history, it helps if you know that in advance. Because with a robbery of that scale, and a haul of that glaring magnitude, it is not about how to steal it. The challenge is what happens next. Plans must be prepared. A network must be created for the criminal gains to be quickly passed on, their monetary value realised in an untraceable manner. With a steal that hot, the heat must be passed through many hands, cooling as it goes.

Robinson and McAvoy had no such plan. Exactly what they expected to find in Unit 7 on the day of the robbery is a matter of debate. Some believe the robbers expected several hundred thousand pounds of used banknotes; others that they predicted a haul of around a million pounds' worth of foreign currency, while Tony Black claimed to the police that he told the robbers they could expect between £1 and £2 million worth of gold. Among these competing theories, what is accepted is that the robbers did not expect to find three tons of gold. The debate is over how far short their estimation fell. Ultimately, a smaller haul would probably have been a better result for the robbery gang. It would have been a profitable operation that would have made the previous six months of painstaking planning worthwhile. Police attention would have been considerable but not overbearing, and they could have moved on their gains through normal, traditional criminal channels. Instead, they found themselves with three tons of gold, media attention and a Flying Squad highly motivated to solve the biggest robbery they had ever encountered.

While measures had been put in place to deal with stolen cash and valuables before the robbery took place, they were not sufficient. It is rumoured that while they were planning the raid, McAvoy and Robinson had been introduced to the Adams brothers, heads of a notorious north London crime family and among the capital's most proficient money launderers. Controlling a patch of London that included Hatton Garden, the traditional gold and diamond district, the Adams' connections would be essential when dealing with large sums of cash or fencing any stolen gems and precious metals.

'The Garden' is a network of narrow streets on the edge of the City of London that has been linked with the jewellery trade since the medieval period. In 1822, Percival Norton Johnson moved his gold assaying business – the company that eventually became Johnson Matthey – into 79 Hatton Garden, attracting other jewellers and precious metal dealers to the area. In the 1870s, the De Beers diamond company set up in the area. A century later, most of its tall, late-Victorian buildings had garish jewellery shops on the ground floor, while upstairs there were warrens of rooms, interspersed with heavy security doors, where dealers and craftsmen worked. It was a place where legitimate and illegitimate business rubbed together, and was awash with fraudsters and unscrupulous traders. Among them was Saul Solomon 'Solly' Nahome, an Iranian-born jeweller who bought and sold large quantities of gold, paying always in cash, and who was a close associate of and launderer-in-chief to the Adams family.

McAvoy's old friend and close associate Brian Perry was another who was waiting in the wings to help handle the robbery's proceeds. Others made their own arrangements to deal with the anticipated profits. A few days before the robbery, John Lloyd and a number of his associates incorporated two companies ready to handle and conceal any illicit money.

With their van labouring under the weight of the haul, the gang made off from Unit 7 in a state of shocked silence. Perry is said to have told an associate years later: 'We just couldn't believe we had pulled it off and we kept looking in the back of the van where the gold was, as if it might disappear and we'd wake up from a dream.' When the immediate buzz of the robbery had worn off and the haul had been taken to a safe location, the problems it created became more apparent.

What the press dubbed 'the Great Bullion Robbery' dwarfed previous major robberies. The gang had taken 6,800 bars of gold, each of them individually marked. The way to monetise stolen gold was simple: disguise it and sell it back into the legitimate gold market. As Peter Knight, a bullion dealer interviewed by ITN on the day of the robbery, said, 'It doesn't require an awful lot of skill to heat the metal up to a certain temperature which will make it liquid. One only needs then a reciprocal to pour it into and you've changed the form and the shape, you've eliminated the numbers, the marks and everything else, and nobody can prove that it was the original bar.' But, with a haul of this size, conducting that operation without detection by either police or other criminals was an intimidating task.

The gang's apparent plan – to divvy up the expected currency haul between them and sell any gold or precious metals through relatively small-time fences, someone who bought and sold stolen goods – suddenly looked woefully insufficient. For some of the robbery gang, with the buzz of the raid fading, a new clarity emerged. The real difficulties had only just begun. They were the first of many who would face the challenge of the Brink's-Mat gold. Seduced by what it offered, entrapped before they knew it, they were now facing the fight of their lives to back out of its orbit. To do so, they and their associates needed help.

They needed Kenny Noye.

• • •

Kenneth Noye was an associate of John Lloyd and Brian Robinson. He was a similar age to the robbers but had been born and raised in suburban Bexleyheath, a small town on the south-eastern fringe of London. His parents had joined the post-war exodus from London, leaving behind the grimy inner-city neighbourhoods that McAvoy, White, Robinson and Black called home. Noye grew up in relative comfort. His father was a post office manager and his mother worked at a greyhound racing track as a manager. At fifteen, Noye left the local comprehensive school with a clutch of GCEs and went to study commercial art at the London College of Printing in Elephant and Castle, south-east London. He had a series of jobs as a teenager, working early-morning paper and milk rounds, selling programmes at his mother's dog track, working in a London department store on Saturdays and occasionally selling newspapers in the Strand. After college, he got an apprenticeship as a Fleet Street printer and once that was completed, he worked nights in Fleet Street. Driven by the desire to make money that would shape his life, for good and bad, Noye took a second job driving a tipper truck during the day.

Noye's life become one of smoke and mirrors. Publicly, he was an ambitious, hard-working young man, keen to get on in life and full of entrepreneurial endeavour. Behind the façade of respectability, he was developing a parallel career as a criminal. This duality had begun in early life. While he was doing well academically at school, he was also a bully and extortioner, running a protection racket and stealing dinner money from other pupils. As a hard-working print apprentice, he developed a lucrative sideline stealing cars and scooters and selling them on. When someone tipped off the police, he was arrested and in June 1967 convicted of ten charges of theft. Aged nineteen, Noye was sentenced to a year in borstal. On his release, he reconnected with other ex-borstal boys and began to frequent the south London pubs and clubs where the capital's top criminals congregated. Soon he had carefully placed himself on the fringes of major crime, becoming an associate of some of the most significant players in the London underworld.

In 1970, Noye met Brenda Tremain. She was a secretary in a barristers' chambers; they met while Noye was waiting to discuss a prosecution he faced. The couple married that year and moved to a modest bungalow on Hever Avenue in West Kingsdown in Kent, near to where John Lloyd lived. Noye gave up his work as a printer, bought a lorry and set up his own haulage company. In a yard behind a garage, he set about building his business, at first using a battered old caravan as an office. The fleet eventually grew to a dozen lorries. Noye branched out into property development in Kent and the outskirts of London, and put money into investments in Florida and the Netherlands. Meanwhile, using the haulage business as cover, Noye developed a reputation as a fence, buying and selling stolen goods. He ended up in court on a number of occasions for petty offences and was questioned several times by the police. At one point, he got into trouble because the Rolls-Royce he was driving was still registered to a merchant bank in London. Many of his activities were criminal but many were not. He made substantial profits by mixing legitimate with illegitimate business.

Noye also realised that success in the murky London underworld of the 1970s and 1980s meant cultivating links with people in positions of power and authority. During this time, it is rumoured that he began corrupt relationships with police officers in Kent and London, and in the mid-1970s, he is said to have earned several thousand pounds for tipping off police about a gang who had tried to sell him stolen goods. In 1977, he received an eighteen-month suspended sentence for handling stolen goods and for unlawful possession of a shotgun. Also that year, he was registered as an informant by Ray Adams, a rising detective inspector on the Flying Squad, after Adams questioned him about a case. Later, internal investigations suggested that Noye provided no meaningful information. It is alleged Adams protected Noye from prosecution and that Noye used his police connections to build his criminal business at the expense of his rivals.

Noye's cultivation of influence also led to him joining the Freemasons. On 10 January 1980, he was accepted into Hammersmith Lodge No. 2090, which met at the Star and Garter Hotel in Brentford, west London. Membership brought Noye into social contact with influential, well-connected and powerful men. Freemasonry was rife in the Metropolitan Police at the time. It has been said that Noye's Lodge included several serving police officers and bullion dealers among its membership, though this has been denied by a Freemason and retired police officer. Noye was also rumoured to have a close relationship with an MP.

In 1981, Noye faced his first serious criminal charge. He had bought a Smith & Wesson pistol in the United States and asked another person to smuggle it back to Britain for him. That person reported Noye to Customs and Excise, who monitored the gun as it moved by post to an address at a farm in Kent. Noye was charged with the offence and received another eighteen-month suspended sentence and a fine of £2,500 at Canterbury Crown Court. It is claimed that Adams prevented him receiving a more serious punishment.

In 1980, Noye acquired Hollywood Cottage, a rundown listed building on School Lane in West Kingsdown. Named after the local holly, it was set back from the road in twenty acres of grounds surrounded by woodland and bordered by a reform school. In December 1980, Noye submitted an application for an extension but it was refused by the district council. An alternative scheme was permitted in January 1981 but a few weeks later, the original house was severely damaged by an unexplained fire. It was not the first time property linked to Noye had been consumed by flames: a few years previously there were two mysterious fires at buildings occupied by a woman who owned a parcel of land that had originally formed part of Noye's haulage yard.

To replace the original, modest house, Noye built a large, executive-style home complete with outbuildings and a swimming pool. The bewildered local council repeatedly refused planning applications but Noye just kept building anyway. By the time he was finished, the new house was seven times larger than the original. West Kingsdown residents referred to Hollywood Cottage as 'Fort Knox' due to its overt security measures. Noye installed high, electronically operated gates and closed-circuit television cameras. Rottweiler dogs patrolled the grounds.

The Noyes kept themselves to themselves, building few friendships in the village. After moving to their new house, Hollywood Cottage, Noye built homes in Hever Road for his parents and his sister and brother-in-law, upsetting locals by felling a number of trees and building over a well-used footpath. Noye did, however, let the local Cub pack use his swimming pool and was friendly towards the boys from the reform school next door, whom he allowed in to do odd jobs in the garden for generous reward.

Behind Noye's affable demeanour lay a savage temper that could see his mood switch in an instant. A well-related story about him concerned a man who had spilled his drink on Noye in a Peckham pub. Noye demanded that the man buy him a new drink. The man refused and his friends taunted Noye. Noye left the pub only to return a few moments later brandishing a shotgun. He threatened the man and his friends before letting off a shot into the ceiling, showering the men with dust, then calmly walking out.

By the time he received the call from the Brink's-Mat robbers, Noye was a significant figure in the criminal underworld and an associate of some of London's most notorious criminals. But while Noye respected those men, and enjoyed associating with and working with them, he had long ago had an epiphany. The best returns came not from carrying out the big crimes but by being a high-class middle man, buying and selling stolen goods, and laundering the proceeds of crime for huge profit. If you wanted a long and profitable criminal career, don't be the one that commits the initial crime. Don't be the one that 'crosses the pavement'; be the one the robbers turn to once they've done the job.

As a result, Noye was, in the words of a detective, 'a money mover, a fixer'. By the early 1980s, he was registered on the intelligence files as a major criminal player, though his determination to stay out of the limelight and preoccupation with secrecy meant his significance was known to only a small number of detectives. Noye had become a top receiver of stolen goods, gaining admiration and respect in the process. One journalist would describe him as a 'criminal yuppie'. He was in tune with the times. As Britain shifted from the old heavy industries into a service economy dominated by financial services, where money was made from handling other people's money, Noye took a similar approach. He was a criminal entrepreneur, not a criminal craftsman. He was an enthusiastic embodiment of 1980s morality. There was money to be made and the old rules, regulations and establishments that got in the way were to be worked around or ignored. Criminality was no longer black and white. There was, after all, profit to be had in the grey.

It was an outlook that Noye shared with one of his few close criminal associates, a jeweller based in Bristol in the south-west of England. The two were close in age and shared a burning ambition, an exhaustive work ethic and a desire to make serious money.

Noye's associate was called John Palmer.

• • •

John Palmer was one of seven children born to Irish immigrants in Olton in Solihull. His father was absent from an early age and his young life was scarred by poverty and deprivation. He suffered with dyslexia and scarcely attended school, preferring to associate with the young criminals in his neighbourhood. Like Noye, his criminal career started in his teens, when he coordinated gangs of teenage shoplifters and began selling goods stolen by other criminals. In 1968, aged eighteen, he set up a shop to move stolen jewellery. He enjoyed considerable success for a couple of years but was arrested for fraud aged twenty-three and placed on remand in a Birmingham prison. Shortly before his twenty-fourth birthday, Palmer pleaded guilty to the charges and received a suspended sentence. Rival criminals took over his business while he was in jail, making Birmingham a challenging place for him to live once he got out.

In the early 1970s, Palmer moved to Bristol and gradually re-established himself as a major fence, handling millions of pounds' worth of stolen goods. He went into partnership with a local man called Garth Chappell and developed links with local crime families, using a carpet shop, second-hand car sales and a furniture business as cover for criminal activities. The pair teamed up with Terence Patch, another local criminal face. Palmer and Chappell opened a precious metals and jewellery business, called Scadlynn, in Bedminster, a suburb of Bristol. Like Noye, Palmer protected his criminal interests by cultivating contacts on the local police force.

Around 1979, Palmer had a smelter installed in the garden of his home. He used it to smelt scrap and stolen jewellery brought into Scadlynn so it could be sold back into the legitimate market or through his three jewellery shops around Bristol and Bath. As one of the few people in England with access to a sizeable private smelter, Palmer handled gold and other precious metals for a network of contacts in south-west England, which led to him gaining the nickname 'Goldfinger'.

Palmer met Marnie, a local model and hairdresser, in 1972. They married in 1975. In 1981, as Palmer's success grew, the couple moved to the Coach House in the grounds of Battlefields, a gothic mansion in Lansdown, near Bath. Dating to the early nineteenth century, it had been designed by the notable local architect John Wood the Elder. In the years that followed, Palmer gradually bought up the surrounding land and buildings, eventually amassing an estate that encompassed thirty-three acres, including eight stables, several outbuildings, a summer house, a swimming pool, gardens, woodlands and a lake. As at his previous home, Palmer installed a smelter in a hut in the gardens of the Coach House. This one was even better. It would need to be.

Like Noye, Palmer was comfortably wealthy. Like Noye, that was not enough to dull the attraction of quick, criminal profits. Noye and Palmer began working together around 1980, after Noye asked Palmer to smelt some stolen gold. Soon, Palmer was handling large amounts of stolen high-end jewellery for Noye. The pair also enthusiastically joined the criminal ranks that had landed upon a new, easy crime, unwittingly created by Margaret Thatcher's Conservative government.

Thatcher's 1979 election victory delivered unexpected – and unintended – gifts for Britain's criminal underworld. One of the new Conservative administration's very first acts was to scrap value added tax (VAT) on gold coins like the South African Krugerrand and the Canadian Maple Leaf. The British government had imposed VAT on the sale of gold – and almost all other goods – in 1973, and through the rest of the decade the supply of gold to the public had been tightly controlled. The changes in 1979 were designed to give private individuals the freedom to trade in gold. But VAT was retained on gold bullion, and at the same time the tax rate was increased from 8 per cent to 15 per cent. The move coincided with a leap in the price of gold. For those of a criminal disposition, overnight the use of gold for VAT fraud became a highly attractive proposition.

It was a simple swindle. The first and most basic form was to buy a batch of gold coins from a dealer, melt them down and cast them into bullion bars, then sell them back to a dealer and collect the market price plus an additional 15 per cent in VAT. A VAT certificate was required before the bullion dealers would hand over the tax, so fraudsters simply registered for them in false names. It was an easy 15 per cent profit on every transaction. As one fraudster explained in 1992: 'You go and buy from one of the big bullion houses, say £100,000 of Krugerrands, paying a small premium. The coins were then melted down and sold back to another bullion house for slightly under the price of gold. So the team might get £98,000 plus 15 per cent VAT; that's £112,700. After expenses, their profit was £10,000 (although they still owe the VAT of £15,000). The next day, the team would buy £110,000 of Krugerrands. And so it would go on.' It could be six months before Customs caught on, by which point the team would have either disappeared or started again under a different set of names.

Professional criminals learned of the scam from dealers and associates in Hatton Garden. They were quick to make the most of the new opportunities, and in the early 1980s VAT gold fraud boomed. Unscrupulous gold dealers, armed robbers, mafiosi, the IRA and other criminals began purchasing gold coins in bulk, melting them down into bars, and selling them back to the big bullion houses, so they could pocket the VAT. Much of the fraud went through Hatton Garden, the heart of the gold business and home to both major bullion houses and less scrupulous small-time dealers. It was not unusual for the large bullion dealers to buy back the bullion gold they had initially sold as coins. As a financial crime Scotland Yard largely ignored it, leaving it to HM Customs and Excise to deal with the mess.

By the end of 1981, Customs were aware that there was a serious problem. One of the first indications that something was wrong was when a notorious Hatton Garden character was picked up by police driving a gold Rolls-Royce while disqualified. Many VAT-registered businesses were disappearing without paying their taxes. Even those who did get caught faced a maximum of only two years in jail. Parliament was told that at least £40 million had been stolen since 1979, but the real total was probably much greater. In early 1982, the government hastily reimposed VAT on gold coins. Fraudsters were not deterred. They began smuggling gold in from abroad where VAT rates were lower or non-existent. In 1983, Customs moved to stop this, threatening to seize anything they suspected to be fraudulently traded gold. A system was devised that would allow bullion houses to protect themselves by paying VAT direct to the Inland Revenue, rather than to their suppliers. Smugglers were not put off, with one group smuggling gold in from Belgium and Switzerland and smelting it with copper and zinc to disguise its provenance, making £1.5 million in criminal profits.

Some of London's armed robbers were among those attracted to the easy profits offered by VAT fraud. With a number of armed robbers being shot by police in the 1970s and others being taken down by the supergrass system, VAT fraud offered a safer career path. Armed robbery had also become harder, with the Flying Squad refocusing solely on catching armed robbers, and the security industry becoming far better at protecting valuables, whether in transit or at their intended location. So, tax fraud was an alluring exit strategy for armed robbers looking for an easier life. By the early 1980s, gangs of former armed robbers had become adept at avoiding border controls and were operating between London and locations where gold could be purchased with little or no questions asked, like Jersey, Guernsey, Liechtenstein and Switzerland.

By the mid-1980s, it was estimated that between £100 million and £500 million had been stolen from the government through these criminal methods. Hatton Garden was said to be thick with gangs engaged in tax fraud, buying, smelting and reselling vast quantities of gold. Noye and Palmer are said to have been among them, and in the early 1980s they are thought to have generated considerable wealth by defrauding the taxman in this way. Some of the proceeds are thought to have been used to buy the Coach House and Hollywood Cottage.

When the Brink's-Mat robbery happened at the end of 1983, everything was already in place to handle the gold and turn it into vast amounts of cash. What was required was someone willing to take it on.

Noye and Palmer had formed a connection that was perhaps not strictly a friendship – more an association based on respect and financial opportunity. But they had also learned criminal lessons and methods that others lacked. And now, in November 1983, they found themselves in an advantageous situation. They were connected to the Brink's-Mat robbers but, unlike the robbers, they knew what to do with the gold.

• • •

As news of the robbery filtered out, Noye is said to have contacted John Lloyd and made it clear that he and Palmer would be willing to help handle the gold. Some of the robbery gang are said to have been wary of accepting assistance from outside the tight criminal networks of south-east London. But the reality is that they had no choice. The record £2 million reward had done its job, making it risky to sell on the gold in small batches. As one insurance broker said, 'What would you do, risk eight years for receiving stolen gold or turn them in and get a reward?' Instead, the gang needed someone willing to take on massive amounts, who was personally known to them and who was vouched for by other criminal associates. That wasn't a long list and Kenny Noye was at the top. Even then, he was imperfect. His background in Bexleyheath and home in West Kingsdown marked him as an outsider who would be hard to manage and there were rumours of his involvement with police officers. It's unlikely that the London-based gang knew anything about John Palmer.

In the days after the robbery, two members of the Adams family may have visited Palmer in Bath to inspect his smelter and discuss possible terms. What happened at these meetings, and indeed, whether they even took place, is not entirely clear. However, it is said that the brothers arrived unannounced at Palmer's home, told him they had helped finance the raid and that they wanted to get the best possible deal for fencing the gold. It was subsequently agreed that Palmer and Noye would take a 25 per cent fee on everything they smelted. Palmer and Noye did not tell the gang that they planned to pocket the additional 15 per cent VAT they would make when selling the gold on the legitimate market. It was an audacious plan that would make a fortune for both men, leaving them better off than most of the robbers. Two further meetings between the two parties are said to have taken place at the Savoy hotel in central London. Noye and Palmer assured the Adams brothers that they had a water-tight plan to handle the stolen bullion.

It was just a few days after that meeting when police arrested McAvoy, Robinson and White. And just a few days after that when White allegedly told the police that the robbers no longer had control of the gold.

While Noye and Palmer got to work on the gold, the men who had stolen it faced justice.

CHAPTER SIX

Old Bailey, Court Two

The news that Micky McAvoy and others had been arrested soon reached his solicitor. Henry Milner had attended boarding school in Oxfordshire and studied at the London School of Economics before pursuing a career in the legal profession. His big break came in 1976 when he represented one of the men accused of robbing the *Daily Express* newspaper offices on Fleet Street at gunpoint. It led to a successful criminal defence practice, specialising in representing people charged with serious crimes such as armed robbery. Soon, Milner's tiny office in Hatton Garden, usually filled with the smoke of his favourite Cuban cigars, played host to some of London's most powerful criminals. He started by representing McAvoy and Tony White, and was to become one of the key players in the multiple Brink's-Mat legal sagas.

On the morning of Tuesday 6 December 1983, Milner made a series of calls to police stations around London. He asked to be allowed to see his clients but in every case was refused. The standard justification from the police was that they feared information would be leaked to others involved in the case. Speaking not of Milner but more generally, Flying Squad detective Bill Miller said, 'In some cases, there were some solicitors that you'd refuse to let in because you knew that if you let a solicitor in, he'd be straight out and telling everybody else what was going on.'

The law did not specify how long police could hold a suspect before making a charge. It stated only that for serious offences a person should be brought before the court 'as soon as practicable'. Milner knew that if any of his clients were charged, it was almost certain the evidence against them would include a confession said to have been obtained in a police interview. His only option was to try to speed up the process and reduce the amount of time the police had with his clients.

The legal battles over the Brink's-Mat robbery would rage for many years with dramatic victories for both sides along the way. The first engagement came with a salvo from Milner. Enraged at the treatment of his clients, Milner issued a writ of habeas corpus. Translated from the Latin as 'show me the body', this is an ancient legal mechanism to protect against unlawful and indefinite imprisonment. It required that the person under arrest be brought before a judge and that lawful grounds be shown for their detention. It was effectively a demand that suspects should be charged or released.

The following day, Wednesday 7 December 1983, Milner made an emergency application to the High Court stating his clients were being unlawfully detained. It was heard by Mr Justice Taylor. Representing the detained suspects, Victor Durand QC told the judge that Milner had repeatedly asked the Flying Squad for access to his clients but that 'access was refused again and again'. Durand told the judge, 'The seven are being denied their right to legal advice despite the grave nature of this inquiry.' The judge acknowledged that the police could refuse access, 'if it was going to hinder their inquiries or if it was shown to be contrary to the interests of justice that access should be given at that time,' but made it clear these were exceptional circumstances. The counsel representing the police told the judge that the charge against them would be defended and that they would seek his permission to hold the suspects longer. The case was adjourned for a planned second hearing the following day. It was not needed. At 9.30pm that evening, Robinson, McAvoy and White were charged. Four other people swept up in the police raids were released. The next morning, they were brought before Feltham magistrates court and formally charged with committing the Brink's-Mat robbery 'with others' and remanded in custody.

The Flying Squad detectives continued gathering evidence against the three men. They had Black's confession and the guards' testimony; now they moved to identity parades. For the guards, it was a daunting process. There were no screens, no two-way mirrors. It was just them, in a room, with a succession of three of south-east London's most intimidating criminals. Robinson came first. Robin Riseley recognised him; Robinson stared back at him silently. Then came Micky McAvoy. Three guards – Holliday, Bentley and Riseley – all identified him. McAvoy said only that they had made 'a terrible mistake'. White came next. None of the guards could positively identify him.

Then came a nervous Tony Black. He was also asked to identify the men he believed were the robbers. Black identified Robinson and White quickly and without trouble. It was a different story with McAvoy. He walked along the line of men assembled at Ealing police station then placed his hand on McAvoy's shoulder and declared he was the man he had met. McAvoy responded by hitting him, hard, full in the face, and shouting, 'You fucking slag!'

The case built. The police found the robbers' van in Hilborough Road in Dalston, east London. It had been abandoned at 1.30am on 27 November by two men who were driven away in a Mercedes. The police made a further discovery that the van had been seen with false numberplates outside Blue Cars, the taxi firm in Peckham owned by Brian Perry. The Flying Squad already knew of McAvoy's friendship with Perry and so Perry was placed under close surveillance, most likely with intercepts on his phone lines. In the coming months, the intelligence gathered was to prove very useful.

• • •

The first Brink's-Mat trial took place at the Old Bailey on 17 February 1984. It was a brief affair. A sorry-looking Tony Black sat in the dock wearing a bulletproof vest with an armed guard on either side of him. He had spent the previous months in police custody at Paddington Green police station, guarded at all times for his own protection, in a special bullet- and bomb-proof cell. The price on Black's head, police intelligence had now identified, was £50,000.

Black pleaded guilty, so the proceedings were something of a formality. Commander Frank Cater told the court that Black had confessed and was prepared to give evidence against those he had implicated. He said he would prefer Black to remain in police custody rather than go to prison, as he feared he may come into contact with men who might be extremely dangerous and influence his evidence: 'I would like him in my charge where I know I can properly protect him,' Cater said. Black's barrister, James Rant, read out what Black had told the police: 'I didn't have any promise of a reward. I don't know why I did it. I just seemed to go along with it. It's weird.'

After just forty-five minutes, Black was put out of his misery, with Judge David Tudor-Price sentencing him to six years imprisonment and offering a chilling warning: 'Never again will your life be safe.' As Black was led away, a woman shouted from the public gallery, 'Tony, see your mum. It's killing her!' Black's wife was later taken to a police safe house.

The press reports of the trial gave the public their first glimpse of the violence used during the robbery. The following day, the Home Secretary, Leon Brittan, authorised Black's removal from the prison he had been taken to after the trial back into police custody. He was collected by a team of twelve armed Flying Squad detectives and driven in a bulletproof van back to a specially prepared cell in a central London police station, where he was watched over constantly by armed detectives. The police were taking no risks with their most valuable witness.

After the initial skirmishes of December 1983, the first major legal battle linked to the Brink's-Mat robbery started on 1 May 1984 with the committal hearing of McAvoy, Robinson and White at Lambeth's heavily fortified courthouse. Tony Black gave evidence in a bullet-proof vest while the three accused sat quietly in the dock, occasionally shaking their heads, whispering denials or smiling at friends in the public gallery. On the second day of the hearing, a major problem with the prosecution case became apparent. The detective who inter-viewed White claimed that after White had read through Black's statement, he had taken the document and entered it as an exhibit, marking it R/S 1. The police claimed that after he had read the state-ment, White had said, 'Yeah, it's more or less right.' White denied having said the words or having ever seen the statement.

Milner had arranged for White to be represented by John Mathew QC, one of the country's leading – and most expensive – criminal defence barristers. Mathew had represented one of the team behind the Great Train Robbery and been appointed first senior prosecut-ing counsel at the Old Bailey, where he prosecuted the Krays, before making a decision to revert to the more highly paid defence work. Mathew now asked to see the statement, exhibit R/S 1. If White had read it, as the police claimed, then his fingerprints would be all over it. The defence asked for access to it so they could have a fingerprint expert check for White's prints; it was the only way to corroborate what the police officers claimed, Mathew said. On the third day, the prosecution admitted that the document could not be found. By the end of the hearing, the magistrate was satisfied that the case could proceed to a jury trial and the three defendants were committed to trial at the Old Bailey. Mathew, however, had found a key weakness in the case against White that could be exploited later.

Soon after the committal hearing, police learned that McAvoy hoped to avoid trial altogether. The intercepts on Perry's telephone were said to have revealed that an audacious plan was being hatched to break McAvoy from Brixton prison, where he was being held on remand. It would involve smuggling a weapon to McAvoy and using a helicopter to carry him out of the prison yard. As Brightwell recalled later, 'On one occasion, they actually did a dry run when the helicopter flew very close to Brixton prison but it was warned off by a police helicopter because it was in airspace that it shouldn't have been in.' McAvoy was moved overnight to the high-security Winchester jail, where he was placed in solitary confinement. His daily visits were severely restricted and his conversations were monitored by prison guards. In protest, and possibly inspired by media coverage of IRA prisoners, McAvoy went on hunger strike, demanding that he should be returned to Brixton. After McAvoy had gone seventeen days without food, his brother Anthony spoke to a reporter. He claimed his brother was being treated like an animal. 'He has lost two and a half stone and he is having trouble seeing out of his left eye,' he said. 'He is determined to die rather than remain at Winchester.' According to him, McAvoy's daily visits had been cut from fifteen minutes to ten minutes, except on Sundays, when he was allowed to speak privately with his sister and his girlfriend, Kathleen Meacock.

His conversations were constantly monitored and frequently interrupted by prison officers.

McAvoy instructed his solicitor to apply for a judicial review on the basis that he would not receive a fair trial if he had to prepare in such conditions. An application was made and on 6 July 1984, David Lederman, representing McAvoy, argued in the High Court that McAvoy's legal right to visits from his family and lawyers was being unlawfully restricted. 'There is no doubt that, although it is not impossible, it is extremely difficult for his lawyers to visit him at Winchester,' he said. Outside the court, McAvoy's brother told reporters, 'He is determined, if he loses this case today, to stop taking liquids. He could be dead by next week. He has already lost three stone in weight and has considerable trouble seeing.' The Home Office rejected McAvoy's right to seek judicial review, saying the Home Secretary had discretion in prison rules. McAvoy's application was unsuccessful, but two weeks later, he was moved back to Brixton prison in his native south London, where he quickly put back on the weight he had lost.

The first major trial linked to the Brink's-Mat robbery finally got underway in the Victorian splendour of Court Two of the Old Bailey at the end of October 1984. Court Two is both the largest in the building and offers the greatest security, as jurors' faces cannot be seen from the public gallery. The jury of five men and seven women were given round-the-clock guards and warned by Judge David Tudor-Price that they may face intimidation. They were escorted by a special police team and telephone calls to their homes were intercepted and vetted. The police had heard rumours that an attempt would be made to either silence Black or 'spring' one of the defendants from the court.

The prosecution case rested on Black's statement, the testimony of the guards, the police interviews with the three defendants and the identity parades in which McAvoy and Robinson were identified.

Black spent two and a half days in the dock, marked by angry shouts from the public gallery during his testimony, and ferocious attacks from the defence barristers. Black's mother took the stand and said, 'Until his father died, he was a good boy. After that he was unreliable and untruthful.'

The guards gave evidence, with the trial being yet another gruelling ordeal. Riseley had come to believe his phone was bugged and was increasingly paranoid that he was being watched when he was outside his home. Unlike the jury and Black, he was offered no protection, despite being a key prosecution witness. At the end of his first day of evidence, Riseley's mother and girlfriend had letters pushed through their doors. Both letters read: 'If Robin doesn't tell the truth, Oscar will leave him.' His mother had no idea what it meant; his girlfriend did. It was a reference to his pet name for his penis.

This was not, understandably, a pet name that Riseley used outside his home. When Detective Sergeant Bill Miller went and spoke with him at his house, Riseley, he later recalled, 'was in a terrible state' about what was, after all, the second threat of castration he had recently received. Whoever wrote the letter, Miller said, 'had to be in his house to know this. And he was really, really unnerved by the whole thing and on the verge of not giving any more evidence […] When I explained to him that if he did that we could possibly lose Robinson altogether he was quite adamant that he would go ahead, and a very brave decision he made.' Belatedly, Riseley was provided with police protection and continued with his evidence.

When the officers who had conducted interviews with the suspects took to the witness stand, Mathew challenged their claims mercilessly. He was particularly fierce with the detective who interviewed White, who claimed to have allowed White to read Black's statement, which had gone missing. Mathew attacked the police as liars and suggested they were verballing the defendants.

Finally, Commander Cater took to the witness box. A week before the trial started, he had admitted that exhibit R/S 1, the copy of Black's statement supposedly read by White, could not be found. He claimed that after the robbers had been charged, he had ordered the destruction of all copies of Black's statement for 'security reasons' but that he had realised afterward that this was a mistake. With the prosecution unable to produce the crucial document, Mathew took his attack further. He asked to see the Occurrence Book from Heathrow police station, where White had been held and questioned. It should have included a record of the interview. This key piece of evidence was also missing. The case against White was disintegrating.

The third week of the trial began with White on the witness stand. He read out his version of the events that had taken place after he was arrested. A further twenty defence witnesses were called. White's wife said he had been at home at the time of the robbery; two family friends said White and his wife had been with them the night before, when Black said he had met with Robinson, McAvoy and White. White's probation officer testified that White had worn a full beard at times when Black had described him as clean-shaven.

McAvoy also gave evidence in his defence. There was no forensic, photographic or telephone evidence that placed him at the scene of the crime, and there was nothing at his home that linked him to the robbery. He said he had never met Black and that the guards' identification of him as one of the robbers was mistaken. He denied making the statements police attributed to him and claimed that he, too, was a victim of police verballing. He made clear that he thought the police had it in for him after several previous acquittals. He said he had taken a minicab from Blue Cars on the morning of the robbery, to collect his car from being serviced in Chislehurst. He said he had witnesses and paperwork to prove it. He also claimed to have paid £300 to a painter and decorator working on his house that morning and that he had a receipt to prove that too. The decorator appeared in court but under examination was forced to admit that the notepaper on which the receipt was written had been produced in May or June 1984, six months after the receipt was supposed to have been issued. Robinson declined to give evidence himself but produced evidence that suggested he was miles away at the time of the robbery. With his family connection to Black, the case against him was much stronger than it was against McAvoy and White.

In all, the jury spent almost four weeks under armed guard and listened to seventeen days of evidence. This was followed by sixteen hours of summing up by the prosecution and defence, before the judge presented his summary and, on Wednesday 28 November 1984, asked the jury to come to their decision. The jury deliberated the case for the next four days, spending nights in a secret London hotel. For the first time in the history of the Old Bailey, the court was allowed to sit over the weekend.

On Sunday, the judge instructed the jury that if they could not come to a unanimous decision he would accept a majority verdict. He and others began preparing for the prospect of a mistrial and discharging the jury, but, shortly after 3pm on the afternoon of Sunday 2 December 1984, the jury said it had reached a conclusion. Their deliberations had lasted 26 hours and 46 minutes. They found White not guilty. McAvoy and Robinson they found guilty by a majority of ten to two in each case. The court was adjourned until the following day as the Lord Chancellor, who had authorised the special weekend sitting, thought it disrespectful to issue sentences on a Sunday. White whispered 'thank you' to the foreman of the jury, then hurried from the court in the back of a white Mercedes.

On Monday morning, a buoyant White spoke to a reporter at his home in Bermondsey. He didn't hold back. 'I'm no angel,' he admitted, but continued: 'None of the three of us were involved.' He claimed police had been waiting for an opportunity to stick something on himself and the others. 'If I'm innocent, then the other two are innocent. The evidence was the same for all three of us.' White said he was looking forward to spending Christmas with his family and that it would be 'one to remember'. His plans for the future were modest. 'At the moment I'm unemployed,' said White. 'Before this all came up, I was planning to buy a shop. Now I'll get straight on with that.' His barrister Mathew would later speak with contempt about the claim White had made a confession after reading Black's statement, describing it as 'typical, bloody Serious Crimes Squad verballing'.

While White celebrated, his associates were in more challenging circumstances, as the court reconvened for sentencing. The judge told McAvoy and Robinson that their sentence 'must be sufficient to indicate to all that a robbery of this kind is not worth it', before giving them twenty-five years each. Robinson shook his head. McAvoy said, 'Thank you.' The jury pleaded for a continuation of police protection. It was granted.

For the police, media coverage was a mixed bag. While they had secured convictions over the robbery's two masterminds, one of their prime suspects had been acquitted and the rest remained at large. And there was a more pressing question. It had been a year since the robbery.

Where was the gold?

CHAPTER SEVEN

The Gold Chain

Exactly what Kenny Noye and John Palmer did with the Brink's-Mat gold and its criminal proceeds has never been fully revealed. Those who know have never spoken about it, at least not publicly or on the record, and the evidence gathered by the police provided only glimpses of what really went on in the year after the robbery. But although detail of the operation remains hazy, by putting together different accounts and pieces of evidence, a picture of how three tons of stolen bullion was transformed into huge amounts of cash slowly becomes clear. The most surprising aspect is how simple it was.

A lack of oversight and regulation allowed what is likely to have been the largest money-laundering operation ever conducted by British criminals to take place with the proceeds of the Brink's-Mat gold. And it began with a process that, as the prosecution later put it, 'smacked of simplicity'. After the robbery, the stolen gold is thought to have been hidden across south-east England. It was first melted and recast, either by Noye or others close to him, to remove the identifying marks and take on a different appearance to the ingots stolen from Unit 7. This was probably done using a new smelter purchased from Charles Cooper Ltd in Hatton Garden and, when the work was complete, it was all but impossible to identify the gold as being part of the robbery's haul.

Once that initial recasting was complete, the gold is thought to have been handled by what the police called the 'gold conduit' but what others came to know as the 'Gold Chain'. This was a loose collection of trusted associates who assisted Noye, Palmer and Palmer's business partner, Garth Chappell, in their illicit work. Some of these individuals were suspected by the police of being serious professional criminals; others were shady figures who, like Noye, straddled the line that separated legitimate and illegitimate business. They were responsible for moving the gold from the south-east of the country to Scadlynn Ltd, Palmer and Chappell's gold and precious metals business in the south-west. There, the gold was melted again, either at Scadlynn or in Palmer's garden. This time scrap jewellery, copper coins and other lesser metals were added to the mix. This changed the chemical composition and meant that when they cooled, the bars that emerged could no longer be identified as the pure gold taken during the robbery.

The adulterated gold bars were then taken in small consignments by Scadlynn employees to the Assay Office in Sheffield, one of four historic offices established by an Act of Parliament that have the power to hallmark gold, silver and platinum. The Sheffield office determined the purity levels of the gold and gave it a hallmark that meant it could be sold on the legitimate gold market. Once this had been done, it was sold by Scadlynn to a series of bullion dealers.

To conceal the origins of the gold coming into Scadlynn, Chappell took out local newspaper advertisements offering to buy unwanted jewellery and prepared fake paperwork that showed the company had bought large quantities of scrap gold.

The change in the company's fortunes was scarcely credible, and the amounts involved could barely be believed. Order books were prepared that showed Scadlynn had bought £1 million worth of gold from BC Gold, a Dorset company that had ceased trading two years previously.

The company's owner had no idea its name was being used. More false invoices were obtained from Shimmerbest Ltd and the International Precious Metals Company. Both businesses were owned by Matteo Constantino, an elderly London jeweller long known to the Metropolitan Police and HM Customs and Excise as a top fence suspected of links to organised crime. He operated his business from a small office in Greville Street, Hatton Garden. More false paperwork was obtained from another associate in the north-east named Hammond.

One of the principal buyers was Johnson Matthey, the dealer that sold most of the stolen gold in the first place. It was an ironic twist, though perhaps not entirely unexpected given Johnson Matthey's significance in the gold market. Others included the precious metal wholesalers Dynasty Metals and TVA Silver. The money from selling the gold flowed into Scadlynn's account with Barclays Bank. In his dealings with the bank, Chappell used the alias Charles Cooper, referencing the business that sold the smelter used by Noye. As soon as the payments were credited, Chappell and others linked to Scadlynn withdrew huge sums of cash from the small Bedminster branch. The money, tens of thousands of pounds at a time, was taken from the bank, occasionally in cardboard boxes and plastic carrier bags.

The cash was then carried back to Noye in Kent, who distributed it among the various parties, taking a large cut for himself. Noye and Palmer also pocketed the tax that was paid to them when the gold was sold. The entire operation was, obviously, conducted in utmost secrecy. Before embarking on it, Noye and Palmer are thought to have agreed that they should not meet, and in March 1984, as the scheme got under way, Palmer officially resigned as a director of Scadlynn in an effort to distance himself from the business. He nevertheless continued to direct the operation and personally smelted the gold at his home. The operation seems to have begun in early 1984, shortly after Tony Black was jailed for his role in the robbery. Starting in March, Scadlynn began receiving regular payments from Johnson Matthey. Each one was for tens of thousands of pounds and represented a few kilos of gold. The payments continued to flow into Scadlynn throughout the year. In July, Scadlynn also began selling to Engelhard Sales Ltd, an American corporation that was the largest precious metal refiners in the world and which had also supplied some of the stolen gold. Chappell ensured that the gold sold to them was less than 10 per cent pure, so that under the regulations then in force the VAT payment went from Engelhard to Scadlynn, rather than direct to HM Customs and Excise. This was one of the restrictions brought in by Customs as part of their attempts to prevent VAT fraud on gold.

Flower-pot shaped lumps of reddish metal arrived at Engelhard on an almost daily basis. As McAvoy, Robinson and White were tried at the Old Bailey, the gold they had stolen was now a model of perpetual motion, a cash generator that they had no idea existed. In September, after doing almost £500,000 worth of business with Scadlynn, staff at Engelhard became suspicious that the gold it was receiving came from smuggled Krugerrands and stopped buying from Scadlynn. Chappell found another buyer: a bullion dealer in Leeds called Dynasty.

Dynasty collected the ingots direct from the Assay Office in Sheffield and sold them on to a company in Staffordshire called TVA Noble Metals Ltd. Dynasty did business worth just over £3 million with Scadlynn but on 5 December, two days after McAvoy and Robinson were sentenced, its owner, Neil Solden, wrote to Chappell saying he would no longer do business with Scadlynn. He too had become suspicious. Chappell's response was simply to start selling direct to TVA Noble Metals, with transactions now registering in hundreds of thousands of pounds at a time.

Solden at Dynasty was not the only person to suspect that everything was not quite above board at Scadlynn. Staff at the Assay Office in Sheffield were suspicious that the quantities of gold coming from Scadlynn could not realistically have derived from scrap. Their analysis had shown that much of it was fine, or pure, gold. Their suspicions were also roused by the state of the gold ingots they received. It all had to be remelted to conduct an analysis. Assay Master Shirley Carson later described it as 'very crudely melted indeed'. There were times, she said, when they offered to do the melting for Scadlynn, as they were obviously doing such a bad job. The offer was turned down. The Assay staff nicknamed one particular ingot that came from a melting pot as 'The Skull, because it looked like a skull, and we melted it and carried out an analysis and it was virtually fine gold.' They later likened the ingots received from Scadlynn as being like a badly mixed cake. Staff at the office were prevented from saying anything because they offered a confidential service: 'We thought it was very strange. We did think things. But customers registering with us, it's completely confidential, and everything that comes through us is confidential and, as such, nothing was said about it.'

Staff at the Barclays branch in Bedminster were also concerned about the sudden transformation of Scadlynn's fortunes. The withdrawals being made from this small, local branch became so great that it was forced to make special requests for money from the Barclays Cash Centre, which had to obtain bank notes from the Bank of England. Angus Leng, the office manager at the branch, later described how, 'In the early days, the cash went in small amounts and in cardboard boxes and even on an occasion or two, a polythene bag!' On 9 July 1984, one of the managers at the bank wrote: 'We have seen evidence that Mr Cooper's bookkeeper has been less than honest following which we have spoken to Mr Cooper about the whole matter. If we are to believe him, he is making very substantial profits at this time from the company and indeed has diverted funds to purchase properties valued at £152,000. Our immediate thought is that there is a tax problem and we are by no means convinced that Mr Cooper is being entirely frank with the Authorities.' Senior managers at the bank discussed the matter and decided that henceforth Mr Cooper would need to be present at the bank to cash any cheques, though the decision was not enforced.

In August, a member of staff at Barclays, Bedminster, wrote: 'I am writing this report not because of any particular difficulties but by reason of certain unusual characteristics which I have never met before on the present scale ... we are dispensing large sums of cash over the counter. For example, this week cash has been withdrawn totalling £205,000 ... It is difficult to pinpoint any risk to the bank but I must admit to a certain unease, particularly with the insistence of cash withdrawals of ever increasing amounts. When the company first opened the account drawings were around £30,000 per week and have been increasing ever since. A number of cheques are issued but in value they are small in comparison to the cash withdrawals.'

The concerns were passed on to local managers, but nothing was done. In December, as the withdrawals increased to over £200,000 a time, the branch manager noted, 'The turnover through this account is phenomenal, with substantial cash being passed over the counter.' The area manager agreed that 'The activity on the account is quite exceptional and the closest of control will continue to be required.' As with the Assay Office, the bank was under no legal obligation to do anything about its concerns. As Leng recalled, 'In those days, you couldn't disclose to the authorities, to the police, any details of a customer's account. The only time one could do that was under the order of a court or the signed authority of the customer, and we certainly had neither of those.'

The Barclays branch in Bedminster was not the only bank seeing, and largely ignoring, suspicious activity. Noye paid his cut into several different banks, moving it through various offshore accounts. He and others working for him deposited huge sums of cash over the counter, bringing the money into the banks in suitcases and plastic carrier bags. On 16 January 1984, just as the operation got going, Noye deposited £95,000 into the Dartford branch of Barclays Bank. He used the money to buy a squash club in Dartford, which was then registered in his wife's name. By early spring, the money had escalated. On 14 March 1984, Noye was back, this time with £300,000 in cash. He returned on 30 April 1984 with another £300,000. On 24 May 1984, he paid in another £47,322.50 in cash to cover the purchase of gold from Charterhouse Japhet in Jersey. On 21 July 1984, he paid £200,000 cash into another account at the Royal Bank of Canada in the City of London. The money was to be transferred to an account held at the Mercantile Bank, with a cashier flown over from Jersey to meet Noye outside the bank. In August, he deposited £91,000 in £50 notes at a branch of Lloyds Bank.

And so it went on. In September, Noye started paying cash into the Bank of Ireland in Croydon with money transferred into another account held under an alias and his wife's maiden name, Tremain. Over a four-month period, Noye paid £1.5 million into the Croydon bank, often arriving with the money in a suitcase. In October, Noye paid £150,000 into the Barclays Bank in Dartford and transferred it to the Union Bank of Switzerland, before visiting Zurich to collect the cash and pay it into a Swiss account. He stayed at the luxurious Dolder Hotel and travelled on a passport stolen from an Essex lorry driver called Ian Bottom.

Noye was not the only person depositing vast sums of cash at high street banks. Money was also flowing to John Lloyd and being paid across the counter by his partner, Jean Savage, and other associates of his. A few days before the Brink's-Mat robbery, a company had been created with Savage listed as one of the directors. Lloyd's associate Patrick Clarke and his son Stephen were also listed. At the end of December 1983, the company purchased Reflections, a dingy back-street nightclub in a Victorian pub in Stratford in the East End of London. It was bought with a loan from the Bank of Ireland secured with guarantees from Clarke, his wife and Lloyd. Ownership was later transferred to a company incorporated in Jersey linked to Lloyd and Clarke. As a cash business, the nightclub was acquired to conceal the origins of the money being received from the robbery.

Between December 1983 and March 1986, Lloyd paid almost £4.5 million to Clarke and an associate who deposited the cash at Bank of Ireland branches in Ilford, Finchley, Jersey and Dublin. When the manager of the Ilford branch asked about the origin of the money, the Clarkes asked him to introduce them to the manager of the Finchley branch in order to open an account there. The introduction was made and the deposits continued. The money was periodically withdrawn in large amounts from 1985 until 1988, when the account was finally emptied, and transferred to other off-shore accounts or distributed in cash.

Lloyd's partner, Jean Savage, was similarly busy. Between March and November 1984, Savage paid over £2.5 million into the Bank of Ireland account in Croydon, the same branch used by Noye, and transferred it to a Dublin account. Savage ran the Silk Cut newsagent on Walworth Road in south-east London. When she deposited money in heavy-duty shopping bags, she was said to have jokingly told bank staff, 'I've had a good day at the shop.' It has been said that on one of these cash drops, Savage visited her daughter in Chislehurst and somehow dropped £12,500 cash in the high street. She only realised when she got to the bank in Croydon and the clerk announced a figure that was short of what she expected. It is claimed that Savage rushed back to Chislehurst and asked at the police station if any cash had been handed in. Remarkably, and perhaps apocryphally, it had.

In the vacuum of regulation, the Gold Chain's operation thrived. But smelting and selling thousands of bars of stolen gold was an ambitious undertaking. Noye seems to have been kept busy melting the gold and moving it between secret locations. During 1984, neighbours of the house he built for his parents in West Kingsdown saw Noye regularly carrying packages of what looked like very heavy batteries from his pick-up truck through to the garage. An hour or so later, he would re-emerge with another package of heavy items, which he would place in the pick-up before driving off. The routine went on for several months. It is possible that this is where Noye was melting and recasting the original bars.

Palmer, meanwhile, had to keep his smelter in almost constant operation. His wife, Marnie, wrote that he began working at it as soon as he came home, and that gold was dropped off at their home for smelting on an almost daily basis. Palmer brought in staff from his jewellery shops to help him deal with the vast quantities of gold. The amounts were so great that he began to worry it was too much.

Palmer's associate Terence Patch asked Roger Feltham, a Scadlynn employee, to take the smelted gold to the Assay Office in Sheffield. The system ran without hitch until 17 December 1984, when the van he was driving was hijacked on the outskirts of Bristol. It was later found at a motorway service station with Feltham blindfolded and bound hand and foot in the back. Chappell told police the van had contained £97,000 worth of gold. In reality, stolen Brink's-Mat gold worth £250,000 was taken for a second time in the raid.

The robbery raised levels of paranoia and forced a change in the operation. A series of telephone codes were devised to signify different pick-up points for gold; these included railway stations in Bristol and Swindon, a pub close to Swindon, hotels in London and a motorway service station. Palmer arranged for a professional security company to carry the smelted gold from Bristol to Sheffield. The guards were shocked when Palmer calmly handed over in the street gold that was still warm to touch. They were equally surprised when they delivered cash to the Scadlynn offices and were told to dump the money – £320,000 and £500,000 – in sacks on the floor.

The operation was not slick. They made mistakes, veered close to discovery and aroused suspicion. But Noye, Palmer and the Gold Chain weaved their way through the worlds of gold trading and banking and emerged unscathed and vastly wealthy. Towards the end of 1984, a year after the robbery, Scadlynn was receiving around £200,000 almost every day. Soon, payments of over £300,000 and £400,000 began to arrive. By January 1985, around £13 million worth of gold – roughly half the total haul – had been sold by the company to major bullion dealers. Between September 1984 and the end of January 1985, over £10 million was withdrawn in cash from Scadlynn's account at the small Barclays branch in Bedminster, with £5.4 million paid out in January 1985 alone.

Noye and Palmer knew that a criminal fortune is mostly at risk from other criminals. They became increasingly concerned about security, worried that rival gangs might attempt to steal the gold or its proceeds from them. What they were less concerned about was the police. And for good reason.

• • •

Right from the start, the police had managed expectations. In the days after the robbery, newspapers reported that Cater believed that those responsible had 'already disposed of the loot' and that the gold 'has probably already been melted down and smuggled out of the country'. It was entirely plausible. The gold might have weighed close to three tons and have been worth almost £26 million, but neatly stacked, the 6,800 ingots would have fitted into a container that measured just six feet by three feet by three feet. As a newspaper noted at the time, it was the size of three coffins.

Privately, Cater and the detectives on the inquiry thought it was unlikely that the gold would have been moved so quickly. They believed it was unlucky that the raid had coincided with such a large gold shipment, and that the robbers had not expected to make off with anything like as much gold. They also knew that in its original state, the stolen gold was effectively worthless to the robbers. All of the ingots taken from Unit 7 carried a series of identifying marks. Most of them bore an oval hallmark with a hammer and pick in the centre that indicated that they had been refined by Johnson Matthey. Many of them were stamped with serial numbers. They also bore a set of figures, either 9999 or 999. Those with four nines were 99.99 per cent pure gold, the highest level of purity that can be reached in the refining process, while those with three nines were 99.9 per cent pure. These were investment grades, of much greater purity than would be found in scrap gold derived from melted-down jewellery and other trinkets. Anyone attempting to sell large quantities of fine gold soon after the robbery would immediately come under suspicion.

The police knew that to convert it into useable cash, the stolen gold had to be sold on the legitimate gold market. And to do that without detection it first needed to be disguised. This meant removing the identifying marks but also reducing the purity levels. This transformation could only be achieved with specialist equipment that would allow the gold to be smelted and mixed with other metals. Only a handful of shops in Britain sold the necessary kit, most of them in and around Hatton Garden.

Scotland Yard knew that without assistance a group of armed robbers would struggle to put together the operation required to sell the Brink's-Mat gold back into the market. They were correct. But they did not expect an operation of that nature to be put in place by others so rapidly. The full extent of the Gold Chain would elude them for several months, and yet, remarkably, could have been caught almost before it began.

• • •

In the days after the robbery, Flying Squad detectives made the rounds of the jewellery shops in Hatton Garden. The popularity of gold-based tax fraud meant staff in the shops were periodically asked to be on their guard against anything suspicious. They were asked now to be especially vigilant and to report anyone who bought or ordered any smelting equipment. The offer of a large reward for information about the gold meant police files quickly filled with reports of all manner of claimed sightings and suspicious behaviour from the public, many of them of little use to detectives of the case. But in mid-December 1983, just a few weeks after the robbery, Detective Sergeant Bill Miller received a call with what sounded like a very promising lead.

On Tuesday 13 December 1983, seventeen days after the robbery and a week after McAvoy, Robinson and White were arrested, two men visited Charles Cooper Ltd, one of Hatton Garden's leading jewellers. They were served by Allan Duncan, a company director. One of the visitors was a friendly, stocky man in his late thirties. He introduced himself as Mr Fielding and said he wanted to buy a large smelter and would pay with cash. Duncan explained that the largest they sold was the Alcosa GF080/2 WPG, a gas and air device capable of melting up to 36kg of gold at a time, that cost £1,047.71. The only problem was that it was not available off the shelf and would have to be ordered specially from the manufacturer. It would be ready in about a week, he said. Mr Fielding said he could not wait and would try elsewhere. After buying a heat-resistant pot, four bottles of acid for testing precious metals and a small set of scales, he and his companion left the shop.

The following day, the two men returned. Mr Fielding explained that he had not been able to get a smelter from another supplier. He placed an order, paying in cash, and said he would collect the machine direct from the manufacturer to avoid any further delays. He gave an address in London Road, Sidcup, on the outskirts of London. The two men were told that the smelter would be ready for collection on 22 December 1983 from its manufacturers in Stourport-on-Severn, a quiet Worcestershire town 130 miles north of London. Duncan was suspicious. It was unusual for a customer to pay such a large amount in cash and Mr Fielding's impatient haste was out of the ordinary. Duncan was also slightly suspicious of Mr Fielding's pronounced Cockney accent. He called Bill Miller and reported the incident.

Flying Squad detectives took down Duncan's description of the men and showed him a selection of police photographs. He helped them identify the man who had introduced himself as Mr Fielding as Michael Lawson, a suspected associate of McAvoy and Noye. The address he had given was fake. Police knew he lived on Top Dartford Road in Hextable, Kent. Lawson described himself as a car dealer.

Detective Chief Inspector Ken John decided to set up surveillance on Lawson and to monitor the collection of the smelter from Stourport. He used only Flying Squad teams, rather than calling on specialist help from the Criminal Intelligence branch, partly because he was afraid information might leak out to the criminals who were handling the gold. Miller thought it was an ideal opportunity to use electronic surveillance equipment and lobbied for a tracker to be inserted into the smelter while it was at the factory. As Miller noted, a smelter was 'full of electrical equipment so a tracking device would never have been noticed by the criminals even if they had looked'. The devices were then being used with great success against the IRA in Northern Ireland. Fitting one to the smelter would make it easier to follow it to its final destination and to then monitor what happened to it thereafter. It seemed like the best chance yet to locate the gold. But the bugging devices were expensive, and required expert personnel to install and monitor them and specially equipped vehicles to track them. They were also not always reliable. For whatever reason, whether it was due to costs or high demand in Northern Ireland, the request was turned down. If that decision had gone the other way, the story of the Brink's-Mat gold would have been a short account of brilliant policework.

Instead, when the day of collection arrived, Bill Miller and his colleague Detective Sergeant Daniel Conway sat in an unmarked police car outside the Alcosa Works of William Allday and Co., a firm that had produced metalworking equipment and furnaces since the eighteenth century. At 3.35pm, under darkening midwinter skies, a white Ford Escort van turned up. A radio call identified it as belonging to a local family firm. The detectives watched the smelter be loaded into the van. When it drove off, they followed in pursuit. It headed towards the market town of Evesham, pulling up at the rear of a local agricultural finance company on the high street half an hour later. Miller and Conway parked and waited. At 4.27pm, they saw a gold Rolls-Royce, registration HPW 977P, arrive. Lawson got out and went into the premises. Miller and Conway sat patiently for almost two hours. At 6.17pm they watched as two men lifted the crate containing the smelter from the van and transferred it to the boot of the Rolls-Royce. The smelter was too big for the boot to shut, so one of the men went inside and returned with a length of rope, which he used to secure the boot lid. The two men shook hands; Lawson got in the Rolls-Royce and drove off. Miller and Conway followed.

The two cars drove south through the darkness towards London. On the way through the Cotswolds, the Rolls-Royce stopped at a house, a petrol station and a pub. At times, it powered along at over 100mph, while the detectives in their police Ford struggled to keep up. Finally, at 1.57am, the car drew to a halt on Lawson's driveway in Hextable. Lawson got out and went inside, leaving the smelter in the boot of the car. Miller and Conway radioed control and were told to sit and wait. It wasn't the smelter's journey that they needed. It was the destination. The detectives settled in for a night in the car, happy that they were to be relieved at 7.30am.

The following morning, four unmarked Flying Squad vehicles arrived in the area and took up positions in the roads around Lawson's house. Miller and Conway finally clocked off at dawn. The replacement surveillance teams had matching orders: follow the Rolls-Royce until it arrived at its ultimate destination.

Shortly after 8.30am, Lawson came out of his house and got back in the Rolls-Royce. He drove off along the main A20 road in the direction of Swanley village and then towards the large roundabout at the junction of the A20 and M25. A few miles before the motorway, he pulled off suddenly into a country road that led to a small village called Crockenhill. Then, after a short distance, the car turned sharply right into the driveway of a large house. It was a classic move to avoid surveillance. Flying Squad detective Chris Colbourne was in pursuit. He knew he could not follow the Rolls-Royce into the drive without detection, so he sped past and turned into a nearby farm. He turned his car around and raced back towards the house, but when he got there the Rolls-Royce had vanished. He drove back along the country lane towards the main road and got there just in time to see the Rolls-Royce and the smelter disappearing into the distance. Colbourne tried to catch it but lost it in the morning traffic.

Twelve hours later, Detective Inspector Tom Glendinning, who two weeks before had interrogated Micky McAvoy, was on the doorstep of Lawson's home. The smelter was nowhere to be seen. Lawson was taken to Bexleyheath police station and questioned about the smelter. Lawson was calm and resolutely unhelpful. He claimed to have bought it for a man, whose name or address he did not know, who said he wanted the smelter to take it out of the country. He said he met the man as part of his business buying cars at auction and that he had been paid £1,500 to buy and collect the smelter. He said he had driven to Crockenhill to spend a few minutes with a friend and had then driven to a rendezvous with the man in a layby near the motorway. Lawson happily admitted that his story sounded 'very dodgy' and helpfully alerted the police to the possibility that the man might have been involved in gold smuggling and tax fraud. If the police had wanted to track down this mysterious man, it would have been a difficult task, seeing as Lawson first recounted that the man was dark-skinned, then decided that he was, in fact, 'a Turk'. The detectives, to put it mildly, were unconvinced. However, other than the crime of offering a muddled narrative, Lawson had done nothing illegal. He was allowed to go. All trace of the smelter vanished and Miller was freshly furious that his tracker request had been denied.

The police had missed out on the chance to stop the Gold Chain before it got started. It would be a long time until they succeeded, and their eventual success would come with tragedy attached.

CHAPTER EIGHT

Something Going on in Kent

After McAvoy, Robinson and White were charged in December 1983, the police inquiry was gradually scaled back. With three of the suspected robbers caught and the insurers having paid out, for some it seemed like the case had reached a reasonable conclusion. The focus moved on to putting together the prosecution and securing the conviction of the three charged men. Resources were allocated elsewhere and the bulk of the Flying Squad returned to fight the armed-robbery epidemic.

A small team of detectives stayed on the Brink's-Mat case through 1984: Detective Chief Inspector Ken John and a handful of officers, among them Detective Inspector Tony Brightwell and Detective Sergeant Bill Miller. They continued investigating and interviewing possible suspects, scouring London pubs and clubs for information, but their proposals for action received little support at Scotland Yard. As time passed, the trail began to grow colder, with little progress made for most of the year.

For the detectives left on the case, there was an increasing sense of frustration. The work of Criminal Intelligence branch, especially

Operation Kate, and routine police surveillance on suspected criminals had given them a detailed understanding of the south-east
London criminal underworld, while informants provided further
intelligence and gossip on individuals' activities. By the summer of
1984, they had a shortlist of men they thought were on the raid and
had identified several others who they thought could have helped
dispose of the gold and handle the proceeds of the robbery.

In July 1984, the Spanish news magazine *El Tiempo* splashed with
the names of five men living in Spain that Scotland Yard wanted
to question in connection with the Brink's-Mat robbery. They were
Clifford Saxe, Ronnie Knight, Freddie Foreman, John Mason and
John Everett. Detectives suspected they were also involved with the
raid on the Security Express depot in Shoreditch in April 1983, in
which £7 million in cash was stolen. The two robberies bore a striking
similarity and in both the guards were doused with petrol and threatened with being set alight. Saxe had been the landlord of The Fox
pub in Dalston and was thought to have masterminded the Security
Express raid. All five had fled to Spain, where they invested in property on the Costa del Sol. There they had smart homes guarded
by security systems and 'magnificent views of the coast'. The men
'enjoy a pleasure-loving but reclusive existence combining the good
life with sport and sunbathing', the *Sunday Times* reported. The
source of their wealth was unexplained. Many suspected their life-
styles were funded from the proceeds of armed robberies. Detectives
were reported to have been keeping watch on the men but without
an extradition treaty with Spain, there was little Scotland Yard could
do to reach them.

In all, the detectives thought as many as fifteen men had taken
part in the preparations and aftermath of the raid. That summer,
they also wrote secretly to the police on the island of Jersey naming

thirteen men who they said were 'known to have been involved in the robbery [and] have also visited the island and opened accounts or deposited money in existing accounts at a number of banks'. The journalist Andrew Jennings saw the letter two years later and wrote about it in the *Observer*, giving clues to the identities of the men concerned. The prime suspects were all south Londoners who had long been associated with Robinson and McAvoy. The list included a 'south London video shop proprietor who lives in Kent', 'a scaffolder from Bermondsey' and a butcher from the south-eastern London suburbs. Three were 'members of a wealthy Turkish Cypriot family' – probably, though Jennings did not name it, the Arif family. The piece also named a north London associate of the Knight brothers – Ronnie, John and James – who had carried out the £7 million Security Express robbery and a Kent man, well known to the Flying Squad, who Jennings implied was George Francis, a former enforcer for the Krays who had moved out to the Kent stockbroker belt. A 'long-time criminal from Stepney who for a while moved out to live in the Kent village of West Kingsdown' was almost certainly John Lloyd. A 'Peckham businessman known to be close to the convicted robber McAvoy' was likely Brian Perry. Jennings wrote that the majority of the suspects had been raided repeatedly by detectives, who had been unable to find sufficient evidence to bring charges.

Kenneth Noye was also named on the list. He was identified 'as one of three men known to have visited the island to deposit "gold and monetary proceeds" from the Brink's-Mat vaults'. The detectives had worked their way to Noye after the fiasco of the lost smelter in December 1983. He was a known friend of Michael Lawson's and the smelter had last been seen heading towards West Kingsdown. Noye was already on the Criminal Intelligence files as a major player in criminal circles. This was an early mention of his name in the inquiry's records, bundled in with the others in the detectives' trawl of suspects.

Scotland Yard had received intelligence from HM Customs and Excise that on 22 May 1984, Noye had travelled to Jersey with a suitcase containing £50,000 in £50 notes. He walked into Charterhouse Japhet (Jersey) Ltd bank – a major supplier of bullion, often used by those engaged in gold VAT fraud – in St Helier and told staff he wanted to buy £100,000 worth of gold. It worked out at eleven 1kg bars. He was told that references would be required, that he would need to open an account with the bank and that a cash deposit had to be made before the purchase could be arranged. Noye provided the necessary documentation and opened accounts in his and his wife's names. He agreed to deposit the £50,000 he had brought with him into the bank's account and said he would arrange the transfer of the remaining £47,322.50 when he returned to Britain. The gold, he said, was an investment for his son and more purchases, possibly a kilogram a month, might follow.

The bank staff were shocked when Noye waved away their concerns about security and said he would collect the gold personally. He also made a point of asking whether the serial numbers of the bars would be shown on the receipts and was told they would not. Eight days later, on 30 May 1984, Noye returned to Jersey. He went to Charterhouse Japhet to collect the eleven bars of gold, this time saying it was to minimize his tax liabilities at home. He dismissed warnings about removing it from the bank and asked staff if they could give him something to take it away in. Someone produced a plastic carrier bag, which he deemed ideal. After putting the gold bars in the bag, he picked it up and walked out onto the streets of St Helier.

Staff at the bank were stunned by Noye's casual attitude and taken aback by what they thought was his vulgar manner. They would have been even more perplexed if they'd known what he did next. Noye strolled to the nearby Trustee Savings Bank (TSB) and acquired safe-deposit box number 246. He put the gold bars in it and left the bank. Noye's actions were curious and seemed to defy logic: why, when Charterhouse Japhet offered their own secure storage facilities, would he take £100,000 worth of gold onto the street in a plastic bag, only to place it in a safe-deposit box at another bank a few minutes later? It seemed like a needless risk.

The staff at Charterhouse Japhet were not alone in being confused by Noye's behaviour. Earlier in the day, Detective Chief Inspector Charles Quinn, the Glasgow-born head of the Jersey police CID, had received a call from Criminal Intelligence at Scotland Yard. He was told that Noye would be arriving on a flight from Gatwick airport and was asked to put him under surveillance. So as Noye went about his business in St Helier, he was monitored by officers from the Jersey CID. They watched him from the airport to Charterhouse Japhet, and from there to TSB. After Noye left TSB, the officers followed him on foot but eventually lost him in a crowd. Noye, like many of his criminal associates, was always vigilant and was adept at anti-surveillance techniques designed to shake off anyone watching him.

An hour later, Noye reappeared at the airport to catch a flight home. After walking through security, he was stopped by a Jersey Special Branch officer and asked to complete an embarkation form. Looking nervous, Noye filled out his name and address, but did not produce anything to confirm his identity. He showed the officer his ticket, which was made out to K. Swan; he said it had been bought for him by a friend who worked for an airline and was able to get cheap tickets. When he was asked what he was doing on Jersey, Noye was evasive, saying simply that he had been on business. Noye's behaviour was suspicious, but he had done nothing illegal. The officer had no choice but to let him continue on his way.

Noye did not return to Jersey for his gold bars. If he had, he would have walked into a trap. After he left TSB, a notice was placed on Noye's safe-deposit card with a warning. If Noye or his wife returned, staff were instructed to avoid acting suspiciously but to contact Quinn and delay Noye for as long as possible.

Detectives later came to believe that the gold Noye bought in Jersey was intended as cover for the melted stolen gold he and others were then moving in small batches across the country. If the authorities caught Noye or any of the other couriers with a package of bullion, then they could be referred to Charterhouse Japhet for an alibi. If that was the case, then it was an insurance policy that was not needed. None of the couriers were ever stopped.

In the summer of 1984, Noye was simply one of several figures Scotland Yard thought might be somehow involved in moving the stolen gold. The authorities in Jersey were warned and asked to remain vigilant, but Noye's actions were not in themselves deemed sufficiently interesting for further action to be taken. After all, police were looking for someone who wanted to dispose of 6,800 gold bars, not someone who was buying eleven more. Noye's Jersey visit was logged on to the police computer database and largely forgotten.

Later in 1984, Noye's name came up again. Towards the end of the year, Detective Inspector Ian Brown was posted to Criminal Intelligence. Brown was a seasoned detective. He had served on the Flying Squad in the 1970s and had a detailed knowledge of south-east London's crime networks. He had dealt with Robinson and McAvoy years before. He was told to find himself a sergeant and that his job was to locate the missing gold. Working with Detective Sergeant Tony Russell, Brown began by going through the case files. He found the photograph of the suspected robbers leaving a south London flat shortly before the robbery. Several years later, Brown described what happened next. Needing to submit a report on another case, he and Russell visited Brixton police station, where they chanced upon an old colleague, a detective who had worked the south-east London patch for years. Over coffee in the canteen, they chatted about their current cases. Brown said he was trying to find the Brink's-Mat gold but was struggling to come up with any leads. His former colleague asked who they thought was responsible. Brown listed the men who had been charged and the others who were suspected of being on the raid, including John Lloyd. If Lloyd was on it, Brown's former colleague said, then 'his mate' will be deeply involved too. Unwilling to say more, the old colleague suggested lunch at Brown's expense.

The detectives retired to a local Indian restaurant. There, the former colleague offered a little more. He suggested that if Lloyd had been one of the robbers, then it was likely that his associate Kenneth Noye would be handling some of the stolen gold. Lloyd lived with Jean Savage, the ex-partner of a jailed armed robber, in a bungalow previously owned by Noye in West Kingsdown, Kent. Brown and Russell were told that Noye was one of the best criminal middlemen doing business, a seasoned handler of stolen gold and other valuables. But there was a reason why it had taken a few hours and a curry to elicit Noye's name. The problem with Noye, cautioned the detective, was that his connections did not end with the criminal underworld. His reach extended into the police. Noye had friends on the local Kent police force, including senior officers, and was said to be a member of a Masonic lodge that included police officers among its members.

Noye was back on the detectives' radar, but he would be a challenging target. Like all serious criminals, Noye was a careful man, always alert to the possibility of police attention. But if he became a focus of the inquiry into the Brink's-Mat gold, then information would have to be closely guarded to avoid the possibility that it might be leaked back to Noye himself. It was obvious that in looking at Noye, the detectives would have to tread very carefully.

Brown and Russell decided to investigate further. In a police surveillance vehicle disguised as a telecoms engineers' van, they drove out of the Metropolitan Police district and into Kent to investigate the address in West Kingsdown their old colleague had given them for Noye. They pulled up on School Lane outside the gates of Hollywood Cottage. One after the other, the two detectives climbed a nearby telegraph pole to get a better look into the grounds of the house. They could make out very little and knew that if they stayed too long they would attract attention. For more sustained observation a better location was required. Across the lane from Hollywood Cottage was Stacklands House, a religious retreat for Anglican clergymen.

Brown and Russell spoke with the retreat's managers and were installed in a room looking out over the road, and supplied with tea and biscuits by their hosts. From this vantage point, they watched a car pull up at the gates, pause while the driver spoke into the intercom, then enter the grounds after the gates had opened. They noted the car's registration number and took some photographs, including one of the driver, and returned to Scotland Yard. There, the driver was identified by another officer as Brian Reader. And that got everyone's attention.

Reader was a notorious underworld figure with extensive connections in Hatton Garden. He specialised in burglary and handling stolen goods, and was part of a loose federation of top-class burglars and robbers who had been active since the 1960s and 1970s. The group was responsible for several major burglaries worth millions of pounds, focusing on the jewellery warehouses and workshops around Hatton Garden. Reader was thought to have sold stolen jewellery back to some of Hatton Garden's less honest dealers.

In September 1971, Reader had been part of the gang that robbed Lloyds Bank at 188 Baker Street in central London. Over a weekend, the gang tunnelled from a neighbouring basement into the bank's underground vault, cleared 268 safety-deposit boxes and got away with more than £8 million. It was Britain's biggest bank raid. Only £250,000 was ever recovered and Reader was never arrested.

Reader managed to avoid convictions through the 1970s by 'going on his toes' – fleeing the country whenever police got too close. His run of luck came to an end in 1980 when he was named by a super-grass and arrested. In 1982, he was set to be tried at the Old Bailey for a series of bullion and jewellery robberies worth £1.2 million. On bail of £40,000, he managed to escape on the day he was due to appear with a plan of impressive simplicity: he told a clerk, 'I'm off to park my car', and disappeared from the court. A friend drove him to Dover, where he caught a ferry to France. He met up with his wife, Lyn, and children and moved to Spain, where the family lived in hiding. In 1983, he was said to have slipped back into Britain aboard a private yacht to carry out a £3 million burglary at Lloyds Bank in Holborn Circus, at the corner of Hatton Garden and where many jewellers stored their valuables. After the raid, Reader is said to have slipped out of the country again. If so, Reader would have read about the Brink's-Mat robbery in sunnier climes.

In summer 1984, Reader returned to Britain. His wife was unhappy with life in Spain and wanted to be closer to her sick mother. The family began living as the McCarthys in a house owned by one of Reader's associates on Winn Road in Grove Park, on the south-eastern fringe of London, close to the A20 road out into

Kent. Unlike other successful criminals, Reader never wanted to be a 'face' in London's pubs and clubs. Instead, he lived quietly with his family, perfecting an image of outward suburban respectability. But, although he had enjoyed a good payday the previous year, Reader never liked to be without work. A man of his abilities and connections was not going to be jobless for long. Reader met with Noye shortly after returning to Britain and, by the end of 1984, they had started working together, moving the stolen Brink's-Mat gold.

Looking at the photo of Brian Reader driving into Noye's grounds, the detectives were surprised and perhaps a little exhilarated. They knew Brian Reader was a major criminal but they had thought he was still on the run in Spain. Now, here he was in West Kingsdown. And, in the photo, he appeared to be wearing a wig. Something was clearly going on in Kent. A full-scale investigation into Noye and Reader's activities was ordered, with Brown in charge of a three-man intelligence cell. The Brink's-Mat inquiry had just received its first major lead in a year. And now it was about to get something else.

A new boss.

CHAPTER NINE

Surveillance

It is not easy to find Brian Boyce, and that is no accident. We are told by some that we will never find him, by others that he will not talk and by others that he is dead. None, thankfully, turn out to be true. Eventually a phone number is passed on. There is a tentative call and a summons to a small English village, which must remain anonymous. Boyce's caution is understandable. After a career spent, in part, convicting some of England's most dangerous criminals and working on terrorism cases around the world, he has a different retirement to many.

Boyce was the most significant commanding officer the Brink's-Mat investigation had, arriving late but injecting energy into a fading operation and supporting the widening of the scope beyond the robbers. Over many visits to his home, he will allow us access to closely guarded information and fill in the gaps in other accounts. He will make sandwiches and talk for hours at his kitchen table and in his garden, taking us deep into the most fascinating police investigation that Britain has ever seen. It will not always be an easy conversation. Boyce will share his insight, but he will also share his scars.

• • •

Detective Chief Superintendent Brian Boyce was promoted to become the operational head of the Flying Squad on 2 January 1985. By then, he had enjoyed a varied career, and a varied life.

Born into a poor Irish family, Boyce grew up in Fitzrovia, central London, close to the bustle of Tottenham Court Road. His father worked for a time as a market trader but was often unemployed. His mother took in needlework, once working on a dress destined for the royal family. His childhood coincided with the Second World War. As a young boy, Boyce played in the ruins left by Luftwaffe raids on the capital and, in December 1941, while sheltering under a table with his mother and father, felt and heard the houses on either side of his own being destroyed by German bombs. The family then moved into rented rooms near Hampstead Heath in north London.

It was a tough life, brightened by music, creativity and intellectual curiosity. As a boy, Boyce learned to play piano by ear and developed a lifelong love of jazz, appreciating the freedom it allowed for improvisation inside the clearly set structure of the twelve-bar blues. It was an approach he would later take into policing.

On leaving school, Boyce joined the army, continuing his family's proud history of military service. His grandfather served in the Boer War and First World War. Two uncles joined the Coldstream Guards during the First World War and during the Second World War, his father was a gunner in an anti-aircraft battery in Hyde Park. As a boy, Boyce had wanted to become an officer in the Royal Navy, but although he had the physical aptitude, as a grammar-school boy he was told he was not 'officer class'. Instead, he did National Service with the army, spending most of his time in Cyprus, actively engaged in the fight against EOKA guerrillas. He sympathised with the opposing forces, freedom fighters trying to rid themselves of colonial British rule.

Boyce hoped to continue in the army but was persuaded to return home to start a family by his young wife. He drifted at first, moving to Birmingham, where he worked as a book salesman during the day, earning extra money playing piano in pubs and clubs at night. Before long, he returned to London to visit family. Wandering down Tottenham Court Road, he passed the police station, then paused. Something sent him in and he never looked back.

He worked the beat in Brixton, then quickly progressed to CID. As a junior detective, he worked on the Krays investigation and was part of the team that arrested Reggie Kray. As his career as a detective progressed, he served in Scotland Yard's Criminal Intelligence and Anti-Terrorist branches, working on a series of major cases. He developed a reputation as a maverick with a willingness to bend the rules in pursuit of success. With his interest in poetry and tendency to quote the Prussian military commander Helmuth von Moltke's motto 'No plan survives first contact with the enemy' at the end of briefings, he stood out from other commanding officers. Boyce knew that leadership meant delegating individual tasks but never responsibility for the outcome. It was an approach that earned him the respect, admiration and affection of many of his colleagues.

Boyce did not forget his army experiences. Instead, he brought them to his police work. In Cyprus, he learned the value of constant intelligence gathering and developed what became a lifelong interest in military and covert surveillance techniques. In the early 1980s, while in Criminal Intelligence, he persuaded senior officers at Scotland Yard of the value of a dedicated elite surveillance unit. In 1981, he was given responsibility for setting up and recruiting a small group of officers to a Special Surveillance Unit, modelled on the Royal Ulster Constabulary's specialist surveillance squad in Northern Ireland. Before arriving at the Flying Squad, Boyce spent two years in counter-terrorism, working closely with the army and the RUC in the fight against the IRA.

He also developed a dislike and distrust of the Freemasons. He was approached to join as a young officer. Feeling it would contradict his oath of allegiance to the Crown to swear allegiance to the brotherhood, he refused. He was denied promotion the following day. Convinced the two were connected, he nurtured a career-long suspicion that hidden bonds influenced police activity and that in some cases, Freemason police officers put their allegiance to their fellow Masons above their duty to the public.

Having come from a similar London background to many of the criminals he pursued, Boyce felt he understood their motivations. He too had experienced hardship and he recognised the barriers that prevented working-class progress. He appreciated the codes of loyalty to which some still subscribed, but he was driven by a sense of moral purpose and a keen understanding of the wider social ramifications of crime.

However, Boyce had been disappointed to be given charge of the Flying Squad – four local offices and the central office at New Scotland Yard, about 120 officers in all. He distrusted it and was suspicious that it still contained officers who were there during the corruption crises of the 1970s. He wanted to continue his work in counter-terrorism, which he found more interesting than the armed robberies that were the Flying Squad's focus. He also concluded that the squad's detectives were not up to the job. Boyce proposed physical fitness tests, a move that brought immediate complaints from a squad that had long been associated with powerful motor cars.

He may not have wanted the job and had reservations about the officers who were about to become his command, but there was one glimmer of light for Boyce. In his briefing with Deputy Assistant

Commissioner Brian Worth, Boyce was told that the Brink's-Mat inquiry was still the most important investigation being handled by the Flying Squad. He was given the special brief of following up on the conviction of McAvoy and Robinson and tracing the stolen gold.

Now that, Boyce decided, was interesting.

• • •

By the time Boyce took up his new role in January 1985, Detective Chief Inspector Ken John and his men had established that Noye, Reader and Lloyd were moving what they thought was gold and money between Kent and London. Flying Squad surveillance teams had seen Reader arrive at Noye's house with briefcases thought to contain cash and then leave shortly after with a heavier-looking cases that they believed contained gold. After being briefed, Boyce decided to mount a major surveillance operation on Noye and Reader, eventually bringing together Flying Squad and Criminal Intelligence officers. It was under way within a week of him assuming command of the Flying Squad and, almost immediately, it began to bear results.

The operation began on the morning of Tuesday 8 January 1985. Flying Squad detectives took up positions outside Hollywood Cottage. At 9.05am, they watched Brian Reader leave in a green Vauxhall Cavalier and drive to his home in Grove Park. From there, Reader was tailed by four unmarked Flying Squad cars to Cowcross Street in central London, close to Hatton Garden. He parked outside Farringdon station and made two calls from a public telephone. A detective got into the next booth, close enough to see the number Reader dialled. It was for a local shop. Reader then left the station and looked up and down the street, before returning and dialling the number again. He walked out of the station again, looked up and down the street again, and wandered into the Cardinal Café. He was obviously keen to avoid surveillance. Two detectives followed and saw Reader take a seat at a table with two other men. Detectives later established that they were Christopher Weyman, a gold dealer who ran a business called Lustretone on Greville Street in Hatton Garden, and Thomas Adams, an up-and-coming member of the north London Adams crime family. The detectives saw Reader write something on a piece of paper and pass it to Weyman and Adams. All three left the café and walked to Reader's car. A heavy, oblong parcel about 30cm long was removed and transferred to the boot of a white Mercedes. It was 12.25pm when Weyman and Adams got into the Mercedes and drove away. At 1.10pm, the Mercedes was seen parked outside the premises of Pussy Galore at 9 Greville Street, a jewellery shop linked to the Adams family and Solly Nahome. To the watching detectives, it seemed highly suspicious.

The same day, other detectives who had been monitoring Hollywood Cottage saw Michael Lawson's Ford Granada being driven up to the house by another man. It drove away and was next seen outside Lloyd's house in Hever Avenue. That afternoon, they saw Noye and another man leave his house and drive to the Beaverwood Club, a nightclub set back behind trees on the A20. Noye sat in the car park for about five minutes and then drove off. Police later came to believe that he had waited there to meet Reader on his way back from London.

By the end of Tuesday, Boyce thought there was enough to warrant bringing in the experts from Criminal Intelligence. Undercover officers joined the operation and began three weeks of covert surveillance on Noye, Reader and everyone around them.

Wednesday 9 January 1985 saw more suspicious activity. Detectives watched Lawson in his black Ford Granada and Noye in his blue Range Rover leave Hollywood Cottage and drive to the Black Prince pub in Bexley, where they were met by Reader in his green Cavalier. The three cars then travelled towards central London. Lawson drove to Hatton Garden and parked briefly on Greville Street. Detectives later thought he was there to meet with jeweller Matteo Constantino. The Range Rover and the Cavalier turned off the main road and stopped on Ridgeway West, a street of suburban semis close to the A2 road in Sidcup. Detectives watched as the driver of the Range Rover, who they believed to be Noye, got out and handed a heavy black briefcase to Reader, who put it in his Cavalier and returned home. They thought the briefcase contained gold.

The surveillance continued the following day, Thursday 10 January 1985. At noon, Reader and Noye were seen again at the Beaverwood Club in Sidcup. From there, Reader drove to the Royal Hotel International in Russell Square, central London, where he was pursued by a female detective constable. Watching from a neighbouring table, she saw him meet again with Weyman and Adams. After abut ten minutes, the men left the hotel. Adams and Weyman then went to Paddington station – detectives there saw that Adams was carrying a heavy briefcase. He and Weyman bought first-class tickets to Swindon in the south-west of the country. The surveillance officers followed them onto the train.

At about 3pm, they arrived into Swindon station, from where Weyman made a series of calls from a payphone. At one point, Weyman and Adams shook hands, walked off and waved to each other as though they were parting. It was an act. They came together further down the street and went to a fish and chip shop opposite the station. At about 4.45pm, two more men pulled up outside the fish and chip shop in a Jaguar XJS. Adams placed the heavy briefcase in the boot of the Jaguar, which sped off. The two men in the car were later identified as Garth Chappell and Terence Patch. They were followed by detectives to Scadlynn, which to them was simply a scruffy precious metals dealer in Bedminster, a suburb of Bristol. At about 6.35pm, Adams and Weyman returned to the Mercedes they'd parked at Paddington station, Weyman carrying a briefcase this time. They drove back to the hotel at Russell Square, where, at about 7pm, they met with Reader and handed the briefcase to him.

The detectives were watching Noye and Palmer's Gold Chain in action. Gold was being moved from West Kingsdown to London and the south-west of the country; cash was making the return journey. The detectives knew they were watching a significant criminal operation. The men involved were for the most part familiar faces and, although the detectives could not be entirely sure, they were confident they had discovered some of the individuals who were handling the stolen Brink's-Mat gold.

After the trip to Swindon, there was a period during which nothing much seemed to happen, except for a few short meetings. Activity started up again on 22 January. Surveillance officers saw Reader drive his Cavalier from his home to the Cardinal Café on Cowcross Street. He arrived at around 5.55pm and took a table. Fifteen minutes later, Adams arrived in the white Mercedes, parked and joined Reader. At 6.38pm, a taxi pulled up outside. Weyman and another man got out, both carrying boxes. Adams came out of the café, spoke with them and allowed them to put the boxes in the boot of the Mercedes. Adams and Weyman then went into the café. After another fifteen minutes, Reader, Weyman, Adams and Derek Larkins – a jeweller and antiques dealer who the police had long suspected of being a major fence as well as a long-standing associate of Reader's – came out of the café and transferred the boxes from the boot of the Mercedes into the boot of Reader's Cavalier. Reader drove off and was followed by police to Hollywood Cottage, where he arrived at around 8.05pm.

The following afternoon, Reader again drove his Cavalier to the Cardinal Café, where at about 5.04pm he met with his friend Larkins. At 6.20pm, the Mercedes pulled up outside. It was being driven by Weyman, who joined Reader and Larkins in the café. Reader pulled a green Marks and Spencer carrier bag from his pocket and placed it on the table, keeping his hand resting on it. Weyman produced an envelope, which he passed to Reader, who then let go of the plastic bag so it could be taken by Weyman. The watching detectives thought the plastic bag contained gold and that the envelope contained cash. Reader then left the café and drove straight to Noye's home. After that, he went home, then into central London. At about 9pm he met Larkins at the Royal Hotel International at Russell Square, where he was again monitored by surveillance officers. Adams and Weyman arrived shortly after in the white Mercedes. Reader took a heavy package wrapped in brown paper from the Cavalier and handed it to Adams, who promptly placed it in the Mercedes. Adams then drove off with an unmarked police vehicle in pursuit. He was followed from Russell Square to the M4 and from there to the Plough pub on the A345, near Swindon. He arrived at about 10.40pm and parked next to the Jaguar XJS seen previously at the café. A detective walked past and saw the boots of both vehicles open and a group of men standing around them. A heavy package was taken from the Mercedes and put into the Jaguar, which had two men in it, and which was then driven west, in the direction of Bath and Bristol. Police followed but lost sight of the vehicle in the country lanes. They were left frustrated in the darkness, less than a mile from Palmer's home.

The next morning, Thursday 24 January, detectives saw the Jaguar XJS parked outside Scadlynn. The white Mercedes used by Adams and Weyman was also spotted and followed to Adams's home on Grantbridge Street, Islington, north London. Later that day, detectives watched Reader drive his Cavalier to the Royal Hotel International, where at about 6.45pm he again met with Larkins, Weyman and Adams. Weyman had with him a large leather briefcase. When he and Adams left the hotel half an hour later, Weyman no longer had the briefcase. Reader then drove to Noye's house, where he arrived at 8.20pm, and entered carrying a briefcase. The watching officers were increasingly convinced they were seeing the Brink's-Mat gold.

• • •

While the surveillance operation brought in valuable intelligence on the movements of Noye, Reader and their associates, Boyce gathered as much information as possible about Hollywood Cottage. Aerial photographs were taken and Boyce asked officers to make enquiries with the Land Registry. To his surprise, they came back saying the records were covered by the Official Secrets Act and could be viewed only by those with the highest level of security clearance. Luckily, Boyce had the necessary approval. The records showed that the original house and grounds had been used during the Second World War to brief British agents for the Special Operations Executive before they were flown into occupied Europe from the nearby Biggin Hill air base, and that three underground bomb-proof briefing cellars had been filled with rubble and sealed at the end of the war. Boyce was instantly intrigued. If someone was looking to hide stolen gold, a set of forgotten underground bunkers were about as good a hiding place imaginable.

After three weeks of surveillance, the detectives were convinced they were watching an illegal enterprise at work. Crime is a business. For money to be made, there needs to be an ongoing exchange. And that, the detectives decided, was what they had found. They had seen known and suspected criminals behaving in a highly suspicious manner, carefully moving packages across the country. Boyce and his team believed the heavy packages being taken to London and the south west were gold, and that the lighter ones coming the other way were cash. Noye appeared to be at the centre of the web, somehow coordinating the entire operation. Boyce was convinced a plot to dispose of the Brink's-Mat gold had been identified. He decided it was time to act.

On Thursday 24 January 1985, Boyce held a briefing with his heads of sections. He explained to them that he believed all or part of the gold was at Hollywood Cottage. The following day, Boyce obtained search warrants for thirty-six properties spread across Kent, London and Bristol. Details of what was planned were kept a closely guarded secret. Boyce was afraid that the police inquiry might collapse if information about it were leaked to Noye or any of the other suspects. His decision to move on the suspects was not universally welcomed. Several of the Flying Squad's prime suspects had not been identified during the surveillance operation and there were concerns that the stolen gold might be passing through far more hands than it seemed. As Tony Brightwell said much later, 'It caused a certain rift between officers of my rank and my team because we were firmly of the opinion that we wanted to run this for some weeks and get the whole gang, as opposed to one piece of it.'

Disenchantment among the team was not the only problem Boyce faced. Over the previous three weeks, officers had seen packages, envelopes, briefcases and heavy bags being exchanged in highly suspicious circumstances, but no one could say with complete certainty that they had witnessed gold being moved. For a successful prosecution, Boyce needed to catch some of the suspects with the stolen Brink's-Mat gold. Ideally, it would be in its original form, with all the identifying marks still present. But if the police moved against the suspects without knowing where the gold was, or without being confident that it would be found, then the operation could collapse if they were unsuccessful. And if they did not move against all the suspects at once, there was a risk that news would filter out to others involved and they – and the gold – would disappear permanently.

After all the activity of the previous weeks, Boyce believed that Noye had access to the gold, possibly having hidden it in the disused wartime bunkers at Hollywood Cottage. Before he triggered any raids, however, Boyce needed to see the gold.

And he knew who to turn to for that.

• • •

Boyce requested assistance from the experts in the Special Surveillance Unit, the small team he had nurtured while working in Criminal Intelligence. The entire unit comprised of around ten people. Its officers were a hand-picked elite, selected from the ranks of Criminal Intelligence for special training with the military. The only police unit of its type in mainland Britain, it was modelled on the undercover operations of the Royal Ulster Constabulary and 14 Intelligence Company, the British Army's secret special forces unit in Northern Ireland. Their specialities included living in outdoor dugouts for days at a time, concealing themselves in natural environments and remaining in the same position for hours on end while gathering information about their targets. Nicknamed 'rurals' by their colleagues at Scotland Yard, they had the skills and experience necessary to mount an operation in the Kent countryside.

The unit was a source of considerable pride to Boyce, as were those who served in it. And now, he turned to them for help. He gave instructions for a 72-hour intensive surveillance operation at Hollywood Cottage. On the afternoon of Friday 25 January 1985, he held a briefing in a south London police station with the twenty or so officers who would be involved, taken from the ranks of Flying Squad and Criminal Intelligence as well as the SSU. The unit's officers were to use their unique abilities to find the gold. A time limit was imposed because that was the longest a covert surveillance officer could be expected to maintain a position. It was also all Boyce's budget could afford. Because the operation would take place beyond the Metropolitan Police boundary inside the territory of the neighbouring Kent Constabulary, the chief constable of Kent police was informed, but due to the sensitivity around the case and fears that information about it might leak to Noye, the head of Kent CID was not.

The objective was to establish that the stolen gold was hidden at Hollywood Cottage and to watch it being passed from Noye to Reader. Close covert surveillance would pinpoint where the gold was hidden on Noye's property and see it being exchanged. Then, the gold would be followed along the chain seen previously to London and Bristol. After that, the search warrants would be executed and the various properties raided by sizable teams of Flying Squad and uniformed officers. It was a calculated gamble. There was no way of knowing if Reader would visit Noye while the surveillance teams were in place and no guarantee that gold would be exchanged during the time set for the operation. Boyce took the risk. Based on what had been seen in the preceding weeks, he had a hunch that gold would change hands. He knew it was a week since the last delivery to Scadlynn and not unreasonable to expect another to take place over the weekend.

The decision to strike had been made. But before that, the officers of the Special Surveillance Unit needed to see what Noye and Reader were up to at Hollywood Cottage. They had to do what they did best. Take up position. Observe. Stay hidden.

Stay safe.

CHAPTER TEN

A Cold Night in January

The visits to Brian Boyce's home fall into a pattern. He will talk about the case and the details he has recalled since our last meeting. He will talk of his time in the military and of his family's proud history of service. We will sit first in the kitchen and then in the garden. With persuasion, Boyce will play the piano, his fingers flickering expertly over the keys. And at some point, on every visit, we will visit a small room where Boyce has some mementoes from his career on display. On the wall in the room is a hand-drawn portrait of a handsome man, a former colleague of Boyce's in Northern Ireland, who would work with him again on the Brink's-Mat investigation. 'A wonderful man,' Boyce says as he shows us the portrait, 'and a brilliant detective.'

That man, that subject, was the first thing that Brian Boyce raised, the first time we sat at his kitchen table. And it would be raised again, on every visit after. It is not a topic of conversation that Boyce ever hides from. It is one he wants to address and knows he must.

'We should talk,' Boyce says on every visit to his home, 'about John Fordham.'

• • •

A few days before he ordered the Special Surveillance Unit into action, Boyce decided he needed more detail about the grounds of Hollywood Cottage than could be provided by aerial photographs. In a highly unusual move characteristic of the man, he chose to conduct a secret reconnaissance himself, reasoning that he could not ask an officer to do something he would not do himself. He asked Detective Constable John Fordham to join him. Fordham was one of the first men Boyce had recruited to the Special Surveillance Unit and was, as Scotland Yard said later, possibly 'the most experienced and best trained surveillance officer in the country'.

Fordham had worked in Criminal Intelligence for eleven years, taking part in numerous operations against dangerous professional criminals. He had received four commendations for bravery, two for work on murder inquiries. He was an expert in surveillance techniques, including how to deal with advanced electronic security systems. Fordham had repeatedly turned down offers of promotion, preferring instead to stay at the sharp end of police work, and was heavily involved in training other officers on the unit. His professional abilities were widely admired. He could, one officer said, 'crawl underneath the table you were sitting at in a restaurant and take a note of what you were saying to your wife and you wouldn't notice'.

Before joining the police in his late twenties, Fordham had worked a variety of jobs, including as a merchant seaman and a prison officer in New Zealand. His wife, Ann, was from New Zealand and the couple had three children. One of his colleagues described him as: 'One of the nicest guys you could ever wish to meet [...] a genuinely good copper who you could rely on, and who would do anything to help you. An all-round family guy, he was a smashing man.' Known in the police force for his professionalism and dedication to the job, he was sometimes called 'Gentleman John' for his old-fashioned manners.

Boyce was one of Fordham's greatest admirers. The two men had first met in the mid-1970s, when Boyce was in charge of CID at Bethnal Green in the East End of London. Fordham was posted to the station as a junior detective and helped Boyce to run incident rooms for murder inquiries. Boyce was impressed by the younger man's attention to detail. After Boyce was given the task of setting up and arranging training for the special surveillance Criminal Intelligence unit, Fordham was one of the first officers to join. He was also involved in training later recruits. Their close working relationship continued after Boyce's move to counter-terrorism and, in the two years before Boyce took over the Flying Squad, they worked together on a series of difficult and highly sensitive cases, including several in Northern Ireland. Fordham was Boyce's most trusted surveillance officer, the man he turned to in the most challenging situations. Although there was a difference in rank between them, Boyce felt there was a mutual respect and sense that as men they were equals.

On the cold winter evening of Wednesday 23 January 1985, Boyce and Fordham stood outside Hollywood Cottage. The lay of the land beyond the gates was clear but Boyce wanted to know more about the grounds inside. After exchanging a glance, the two men climbed over the perimeter fence and crawled on their bellies through the wooded grounds. They reached a position about thirty metres from the house. It was where Reader would probably pull up in his car. It provided a clear view of the house and drive, but was distant enough for surveillance officers to relay information over the radio without their voices being heard by someone at the door. It also had a clear view of the position of the three bunkers marked on the Land Registry map, where Boyce believed the gold was hidden. It would be an ideal spot for the surveillance officers to dig in once the operation began. This vantage point, and the ease of entry, satisfied Boyce that the operation could go ahead. The two men slipped away, knowing that they were operating on the edge of the law. By entering Noye's grounds they were technically guilty of trespass, but Boyce believed it could be justified in the pursuit of the gold.

The intense surveillance operation began shortly before sunrise on Saturday 26 January 1985. It was another bitterly cold day, with a thin dusting of snow lying on the ground. A command centre had been established inside Stacklands House, the Anglican retreat opposite Hollywood Cottage. The front parlour was used as a control room and a camouflaged hide made of branches and foliage was constructed in the bushes close to the retreat's gates. It was from here that the surveillance officers would keep an around-the-clock watch on Noye's home. The latest technology was also deployed, with a video camera disguised as a bird box placed in a tree directly opposite the gates to Hollywood Cottage. For some of the officers involved, the target came as a surprise. As Detective Constable Neil Murphy later remembered: 'All we did was follow major criminals, that's what my job was, nothing else, didn't do ordinary police work. And when it came to this job, everyone was like, "Who's Kenneth Noye?" No one knew who he was.' The team was told to dig in as close as possible to their mysterious target and stay there, relaying all movements to the control room by radio.

At 7.30am, Detective Constables Russell Sinton and Stephen Matthews of the Special Surveillance Unit took up positions in the hide. They were to keep watch for most of the day. In the trees above them, the video camera recorded activity at Noye's gates, and in the nearby lanes, Flying Squad officers lurked in unmarked police cars. In the warmth of the control room, Detective Inspector Roland

Hemming monitored radio contact with the two surveillance officers outside and kept a log of all transmissions. Robert Suckling of the Flying Squad, an acting detective inspector, was in charge of the surveillance operation in West Kingsdown. He sat in an unmarked police car near the entrance to Brands Hatch racetrack, a mile and a half from Hollywood Cottage.

More units were placed at key points along the route police believed the gold would travel. In Grove Park, Flying Squad officers Detective Sergeant Anthony Yeoman and Detective Constable Bruce Finlayson kept watch at Reader's address. In central London, a third team monitored Hatton Garden and Bloomsbury, while a fourth unit covered the M4 to the south-west. A smaller, fifth, mobile unit was on standby to cover any unexpected eventualities. The whole operation was coordinated from a control room at Scotland Yard by Boyce's deputy, Detective Chief Inspector Ken John. Other officers listened in during the day on the radio at Scotland Yard, expecting to crack a big case. Boyce was in London, wrapping up a series of terrorism cases. He reasoned that he was available to travel anywhere, should he be needed, but did not expect to be involved on the ground. He trusted his officers and waited to hear the results.

It was a dull, cold morning for almost everyone involved, with nothing of note happening at Hollywood Cottage until lunchtime. Sinton and Matthews' first sight of the Noye family came at 12.25pm. Brenda and the two children got into Noye's black Ford Granada, but the car would not start. Noye came out and brought his Range Rover alongside the Ford. He got a set of jump leads and used them to start the car. Brenda and the children got into the Range Rover and drove off. Noye followed in the Granada a few moments later. A police team went after him in an unmarked vehicle.

At 1pm, Noye reached the car park of the Beaverwood Club off the A20 road, a location where police had already seen what they believed to be gold exchanges taking place. He waited for about twenty minutes. Police assumed he was there to meet Reader, but no one else appeared. Instead he made a call from a nearby AA telephone box and left. The reluctant Granada had obviously unnerved him. It later transpired that while he was the subject of a major surveillance operation, Noye had taken the opportunity to join the AA.

At around the same time that Noye was seeking the reassurance of breakdown support, Yeoman and Finlayson saw Reader leave home in his Vauxhall Cavalier and drive towards West Kingsdown. They followed in their unmarked police car. Reader drove for four miles down the A20 and turned into the car park of the Beaverwood Club. Reader waited for four minutes, then drove off. If he was meant to be meeting Noye, he was too late. For the next half an hour, Reader drove back and forth along the same stretch of the A20, another deliberate tactic designed to shake off anyone following. It worked. Yeoman and Finlayson were forced to pull back. It did not matter. At 2.20pm, Reader pulled up outside the gates of Hollywood Cottage, where Sinton and Matthews were waiting. They watched from the bushes as he tried to gain entry, but finding the gates locked and no one at home, after five minutes, he drove off.

As the afternoon wore on, the surveillance officers caught glimpses of the everyday lives of their targets. Noye met a woman for a drink then returned with her to a friend's house. Reader took a walk in a road close to his home. At 5.05pm, Brenda Noye returned home in the Range Rover. Noye followed in the Ford Granada ten minutes later. He was home for barely any time; at 5.21pm he left the house again in the Granada. By this point, the officers from the Special Surveillance Unit had been in position for almost ten hours. It was time for a changeover. In Stacklands House, Detective Sergeant Robert Gurr relieved Hemming and took over as controller. Down in the hide, Sinton and Matthews were relieved by Detective Constables John Fordham and Neil Murphy. The three fresh officers always worked together.

Fordham and Murphy had arrived for duty around 2pm and had spent the afternoon inside Stacklands House, preparing for the night ahead. The two men shared a bond of close friendship forged through shared professional experience. Murphy had grown up in County Durham. After a brief stint in the army, he joined the Metropolitan Police in 1976. Four years later, he was recommended for a position in Criminal Intelligence and soon after was selected for the Special Surveillance Unit. His dedication to the job impressed Fordham, who became a mentor and friend to the younger man. A colleague would later recall, 'They were closer than brothers and had worked together on countless difficult undercover jobs.' Such were the experiences the two men had shared in their time working together, the operation at Hollywood Cottage seemed low-key. 'This one,' noted the colleague, 'presented no particular difficulties.'

January 1985 was notably cold, with a long spell of freezing temperatures and snowy weather in southern England. Fordham and Murphy expected to be in position all night and were dressed accordingly. Both had on camouflage suits and boots to enable them to hide in the bushes. Murphy had a thermal hood with him and civilian clothes underneath his camouflage kit. Fordham had with him a pair of night-sight binoculars, a webbing scarf, gloves, two balaclavas, a woollen helmet, a camouflage hood, a peaked camouflage forage cap and a green webbing harness to keep the radio in place. Neither man was armed. This was normal for surveillance officers, and they preferred not to be. Their job was to hide in the shadows, gathering information and passing it on to their colleagues.

There was another reason why neither Fordham nor Murphy, nor any of the other officers involved, were armed. Boyce was aware that if any of the officers involved in the operation carried weapons, police protocol meant he would have to inform Kent police. Boyce wanted to limit who knew about Scotland Yard's inquiries and had been warned about Noye's possible links to officers on the Kent force. He had been told Noye had a close relationship with a Kent detective and he knew that a few weeks before, he had attended a Christmas party at which Kent detectives were present. Noye had also been at another Christmas drinks party with local businessmen, an event Boyce suspected was a Masonic affair. In addition, there were rumours that Noye was close to another officer on the southeast crime squad. Before the operation began, Boyce outlined his security concerns to Deputy Assistant Commissioner Brian Worth and Assistant Commissioner John Dellow. They agreed with his assessment about the need for tight security, but Dellow insisted that at a minimum the chief constable in Kent be informed of the operation. In the days leading up to the operation, Dellow did so, and the plan remained secret from the wider Kent police.

The only weapon the two surveillance officers carried was a packet of yeast tablets. Fordham and Murphy had been warned that Noye had dogs. They had sought advice on how to keep them quiet if they came towards them and had been told that the best option was to feed them yeast tablets. As they prepared for their shift, the only issue they faced was that Murphy's radio would not work. When Matthews came back to control room Murphy hung back for fifteen minutes so he could take his working radio from him. Otherwise, everything was going to plan. By 5.56pm, Fordham and Murphy were in position. Fordham kept watch through binoculars from the hide, while Murphy found a spot from which to take the registration numbers of any cars arriving at the gates.

While the teams at West Kingsdown changed, Yeoman and Finlayson continued surveillance on Reader. At 5.45pm, they saw him again leaving his house in his Cavalier and followed him towards West Kingsdown. At 5.58pm, Fordham and Murphy saw Noye return home in the Granada. He checked the letterbox in the gate and then reversed the car down the drive. Fourteen minutes later, at 6.12pm, Reader arrived in his Cavalier. Yeoman and Finlayson, who were following Reader, drove past Hollywood Cottage and parked outside the nearby Portobello Inn. At 6.14pm, Fordham radioed that Reader had driven up the drive to the house, but that he was no longer in sight. The message was relayed to Suckling. It was the final piece he needed. Based on everything that had been seen over the previous weeks, it seemed as though gold was about to be exchanged between Noye and Reader. All the elements were in place. Suckling did two things. He started driving towards Hollywood Cottage. And he ordered Fordham and Murphy into the grounds.

In London, Brian Boyce had finished his business and was setting off for his home in Petts Wood, twelve miles from West Kingsdown. On the ground outside Hollywood Cottage, Gurr relayed the message to take up forward positions to Fordham and Murphy. In the hide, the two men briefly discussed their plan, then moved forward and climbed over Noye's perimeter wall.

Once inside the grounds, they crept forward along a fence, with Murphy around two metres behind Fordham, towards the house. They reached a further internal fence and trees. About a hundred meters into the grounds, they got to their target position, later described by Murphy as, 'quite close to the corner of the house so we could see two sides of the house, we could see the cars, the sort of place we'd be aiming for to stay the night and watch what happened'. The men had moved expertly through the grounds, using their skills and training to avoid detection. The evening was going as planned. Or so it seemed.

The dogs arrived without warning. Three Rottweilers, rushing through the darkness to encircle the two men, 'barking and jumping up at us, not biting us but making a real noise', Murphy said later. At 6.25pm, Murphy transmitted a message to Gurr: 'Dogs hostile.' He fumbled in his pockets and tossed out some of the yeast tablets, but they had no effect. Fearing their cover had been blown, Murphy decided it was better to retreat than to risk being found. The surveillance officers had a motto: it was better to blow out than to show out. If an operation was going awry, leaving in a controlled manner was always preferable to being detected. Murphy radioed, 'Neil out towards fence', and calmly began to make his way back through the bushes. In the darkness, he could see Fordham still in position, bent down on one knee. Murphy said later that he gave Fordham 'a nod to tell him that I'm going to leave here, and I assumed that he was coming with me'. When he reached the furthest end of the fence, Murphy used a tree to climb on top and was surprised on two fronts. The dogs had not followed him. And Fordham was not with him.

The dogs continued to bark in the shrubbery. Murphy looked along the fence and saw a torchlight. His radio crackled. It was a message from Fordham. It was logged inside Stacklands House at 6.27pm. Murphy heard his partner's voice: 'Someone out halfway down drive calling dogs.' But that was not the only thing Murphy heard. Coming from close to where he last saw Fordham, Murphy could now hear voices. 'That,' he would later recall, 'was the first time I was a little bit concerned.'

At 6.32pm, Murphy radioed, 'Man near John with torch. I will bang fence to draw him.' Afraid the man would find Fordham, Murphy tried to draw his attention away. He pretended to be a neighbour and, banging hard on the fence with his feet, shouted 'Keep those dogs quiet!' It seemed to work. The torchlight appeared to move towards him, so Murphy dropped quietly into the neighbouring garden. He could no longer see what was happening inside the grounds of Hollywood Cottage and made his way cautiously back towards the road.

Inside Stacklands House, Gurr decided Sinton and Matthews should go and help draw the dogs from Fordham. 'I think you had better go back,' he told them over the radio. Matthews had been preparing to go home and had taken off his equipment. He put it back on quickly. The two detectives made their way stealthily along the drive of the retreat back to School Lane. Battling their urgency to help Fordham with the need to stay hidden, they left the retreat, climbed over a fence, crossed a field and came out opposite the main gate where they made their way to an observation point.

Murphy continued walking back to the road. When he reached School Lane, he turned left and crept towards the gates of Hollywood Cottage. When he was within ten metres of them, he heard voices through the darkness: people shouting and a woman screaming. Murphy was filled with a building sense of horror. The high wall obstructed his view, so he moved into the bushes on the retreat side of the road and took up a hidden position. He could see two men and a woman standing just inside the entrance, with the woman standing slightly behind the two men. According to Murphy's later testimony, one of the men was pointing down at the ground with what he thought was a shotgun or a stick.

Murphy said that both men were shouting down at the ground: 'Show us your ID, then', 'I will blow your head off' and other phrases he could not make out. From their vantage point opposite the gates, Sinton and Matthews would recall a similar sight of three people standing looking down at something on the ground, one of them appearing to be holding a shotgun. Sinton heard the same phrases. Murphy said the man with nothing in his hands stepped forward and made a kicking motion at what he believed was Fordham's body on the ground. Despite his desperate and mounting concern for his partner, Murphy regained professional composure. At 6.37pm, he called out over the radio: 'Man compromising John. Stick. Shotgun.'

Suckling had by now reached the top of School Lane. It was obvious the operation had been badly compromised. Racing towards Hollywood Cottage, he ordered all police units in the area to converge on the house. At 6.40pm, Hemming ordered the cars into Hollywood Cottage. At 6.41pm, Detective Constables David Manning and John Childs, who had been in an unmarked police car in the drive of Stacklands House, were the first to arrive on the scene. Meanwhile, Sinton and Matthews moved down the side of Hollywood Cottage, into a small walkway. From there, they saw two people run off up the drive and the first police car arrive. When they entered the grounds moments later, after receiving the order to do so, they arrived at a crime scene.

A police officer lay wounded on the frozen ground.

• • •

What happened in the garden that night, after the police entered, would be debated fiercely in the trial to come. But inside Stacklands House, the radio transmissions continued to be noted. At 6.49pm, Sinton radioed, 'Ambulance. Urgent.' A minute later, the message, 'John stabbed. Lower stomach,' was received, followed by, 'Ambulance arriving. Neil to stay.' At 7pm, it was recorded that the shotgun was secure.

For Ken John, Ian Brown, Tony Brightwell and others monitoring events over the radio at Scotland Yard, it was clear that something had gone badly wrong. Brightwell remembered, 'All of a sudden all hell broke loose and it quickly became apparent, even in the control room [...] that the evening had turned into a total disaster.' At around 7pm, Ken John contacted Brian Boyce at home to tell him that Hollywood Cottage had been entered and that an officer was injured. Boyce set off on the drive to West Kingsdown, trying to hear what was going on over an inconsistent radio.

At 7.04pm, a radio message: 'Ambulance on scene. Two prisoners.' The ambulance rushed Fordham to Queen Mary's Hospital, Sidcup. Murphy and Hemming went with him. Murphy held an oxygen mask over Fordham's face while the paramedic, Bryan Moore, checked for signs of life, cut through Fordham's clothing and performed CPR. Seeing that Fordham's bare chest was moving up and down, Murphy was hopeful. 'At least he's alive, he's breathing, it's going well,' he said to Moore. The medic explained that the movement was from the oxygen being administered: 'It's blowing out his lungs,' he told Murphy, 'he's not breathing.'

Boyce later recalled arriving at Hollywood Cottage to find 'darkness and chaos'. The ambulance containing Fordham had left. Noye and his wife had been taken into police custody. Officers from the local Kent police force, completely unaware of the Metropolitan Police operation taking place on their territory, had arrived to take control of the crime scene and demand explanations from their London colleagues. The atmosphere was chaotic. Boyce battled his shock at hearing of Fordham's critical condition. He would later say he heard an inner voice telling him 'You're a soldier', as he tried to take control of the worsening situation.

John Fordham was pronounced dead at Queen Mary's Hospital at 8.02pm. The following morning, his body was examined by Dr Rufus Crompton, a pathologist at St George's Medical School in south-west London. He found ten stab wounds, all of them made with a single-edged blade about 1cm wide and 7cm long.

For the police, the loss was immense, and their grief for their colleague came with a sting. As Tony Brightwell later recalled, 'Not only did we lose a loyal and particularly well-liked police officer; I knew that was the end of any chance of recovering the gold. I thought that part of the Brink's-Mat robbery, or the investigation, died with John.'

CHAPTER ELEVEN

Aftermath

Because it occurred within their jurisdiction, the local Kent police constabulary took control of the inquiry into Fordham's death. Under normal circumstances, the head of Kent CID would have known about the operation and his officers would have participated. However, Boyce's hesitation in alerting the Kent constabulary to his team's interest in Noye meant that local police arrived at Hollywood Cottage entirely unaware of the major surveillance operation that had been conducted.

Noye was taken from Hollywood Cottage to the local Swanley police station. He is said to have had a 'commanding' air, demanding access to his solicitor, requesting that an eye injury be photographed by a doctor and repeatedly insisting that the matter should remain with the Kent police department and not be taken over by the Flying Squad. It looked like this last wish would be granted.

With an officer dead and his prime suspects in the custody of another police force, Boyce's inquiry was plunged into disarray. Kent detectives were understandably unhappy that a major operation had taken place on their territory without their knowledge. Boyce and three Flying Squad detectives were almost arrested and were instructed to provide the Kent police with statements. Boyce's request to question

Noye was rejected. With Kent police leading the investigation, Boyce had no grounds on which to speak with the suspect as he was not an investigating officer in the Kent constabulary. This alarmed Boyce, who believed there would be chaos if the murder and gold inquiries were separated and run by separate police forces. He reported his concerns to Kent Detective Chief Superintendent Duncan Gibbons and assistant commissioner at Scotland Yard, John Dellow.

For the time being, Boyce was forced to leave the search of Noye's house and grounds to Kent police. He told Duncan Gibbons of his suspicions about the three wartime cellars and hoped for the best, with a detailed search of the property starting on 27 January 1985.

Boyce was a man under pressure. Fordham's death was front-page news. 'Murder of top spy cop' screamed the *Sun*; 'Yard's "spy" is killed' said the *Daily Mail*. It was a shocking event that would later draw political outrage and public questions about the Brink's-Mat investigation as a whole. As well as the personal grief that Boyce and many others on the team were enduring, particularly Fordham's partner Neil Murphy, there was a building demand for them to respond to the tragic setback with signs of progress. There was one obvious step they could take. Armed with evidence gathered at Noye's house, intelligence from their surveillance operations and new information from another agency, the task force readied to pick off the rest of the Gold Chain.

It would not be as straightforward as they thought.

• • •

At dawn on Tuesday 29 January 1985, police mounted a series of coordinated raids at thirteen addresses in London, Bath and Bristol. They were carried out by members of the Flying Squad and regional crime squads. At one raid, police used a vehicle to smash through the gates to a mansion. Hundreds of officers were involved, many of them armed, and by the end of the day, ten men and two women had been detained, with the police warning that more raids were likely.

After the debacle at Hollywood Cottage, no risks were taken. Scadlynn director Garth Chappell lived in a luxury home known as Stonewalls in Litton, a village near Bristol. Early in the morning, fifty officers sealed off the entire village. Shortly before 8am, as Chappell was preparing to take his sons to school, his wife noticed a group of cars outside the house. Seconds later, the doorbell rang and a team of eight officers forced their way in. 'One second it was all quiet, the next there were sirens everywhere. It was real *Sweeney* stuff,' said one shocked neighbour. The detectives demanded to know if there was gold in the house. Chappell told them there was, upstairs in the bedroom. He showed it to the officers and pointed to a briefcase beside the bed. It contained nearly £15,000, including £12,500 in £50 notes. The case also contained a bag that contained a £5 Queen Victoria coin and a Krugerrand. Five more packages of Krugerrands were found.

When asked why he had so much cash, Chappell said he was a businessman who always dealt in cash. When shown the gold coins, he said they were the basis of some of his dealing, which could run to exchanges of half a million pounds a day. Searching the house, officers took a large amount of correspondence. They also found a pickaxe handle in the boot and a sheathed knife in the glovebox of Chappell's Jaguar XJS. When asked why he had them, Chappell explained that he had been robbed recently and that the items were for his protection. He was arrested and taken for questioning in London.

Terence Patch received similar treatment. At Bali-Hi, the luxury bungalow in Bishopsworth, Bristol, that he shared with his wife and two teenage sons, Patch was lying in bed when police burst in and arrested him. Police found six £50 notes and an accounts book that detailed some of Scadlynn's gold dealings during the previous December. Outside, in a blue Jaguar seen by police at Swindon railway station earlier that month, police found a pickaxe handle similar to the one in Chappell's car. Patch also claimed this was for protection. Later, police searched a nearby cottage used by Patch, where they claimed to have found the phone number of the shop in Hatton Garden that Reader had been seen dialling from Farringdon station. Police raided Scadlynn the same morning and seized a large quantity of paperwork. It included invoice books, telephone books, bank paying-in books, petty cash accounts and Christopher Weyman's phone number.

In London, police called at Thomas Adams's flat in Islington. There was no answer at the door but officers saw Adams peering out from a ground-floor window. The police shouted that they had a warrant and asked him to open up. Moments later, an officer at the rear of the house saw Adams trying to escape over his back wall into a neighbouring garden. Police found him hiding under a bush. 'Why did you run away?' he was asked. 'You've got to take the chance and run, haven't you?' he is said to have replied, before adding, 'I knew you were coming eventually.' A search of the flat turned up items including a 4.5-inch gold bar, nearly 200 rings, six watch chains, seven Krugerrands, a number of gold sovereigns and a set of scales. Adams was taken into custody.

At 6.30am, Matteo Constantino was woken at his home by officers from the Flying Squad. They seized cheques and paying-in books and took him to Greville Street, where they searched the offices of International Precious Metals. An account book was found. When he was asked why there were no transactions listed after October 1984, Constantino told officers, 'I haven't done any business much at all.' Like the others, he was arrested and taken for questioning.

A gold dealer told reporters, 'The police have been swarming all over Hatton Garden, and I've heard that two company directors have been taken away in handcuffs.'

Extensive searches were made at Noye's former home in Hever Avenue in West Kingsdown, but John Lloyd was nowhere to be found. Police also attempted to apprehend Christopher Weyman and Derek Larkins, but neither man could be located. But the police had a bigger target. With Noye in custody, they were looking forward to taking down the man they suspected of smelting the majority of the Brink's-Mat gold.

• • •

The raid at John Palmer's home, the Coach House, was witnessed by a local farmer, Fred Cullimore, and his twelve-year-old son, George. They had arranged to meet a friend near the gates to the house. It was around 7.30am and just getting light when a police car pulled across the road in front of their Land Rover, blocking the entrance to the house. Cullimore told reporters that a 'policeman came and said, "Lights off, engine off, and stay in your Land Rover and don't move."' Cullimore thought it might have been an accident. 'I did not realise what was happening,' he added, 'until I saw the guns.'

A bewildered Cullimore and his son watched two dozen police officers with rifles and handguns silently surround the house, creeping up using trees and bushes as cover. Cullimore's son remarked that it was like 'watching the telly'. 'Suddenly, I heard a thundering sound,' he said, describing turning to see 'a small army of men, dressed in black, running down the drive. The noise was from the heavy boots they were wearing. They had pistols in their hands, pointing at the Coach House. Only two weren't armed, one of whom was carrying an axe, the other a sledgehammer.' From their accents, he knew they weren't local.

When the police arrived at the door, a man, later revealed as Lee Groves, was seen holding a telephone. He dropped it and ran upstairs. As officers entered the building, they established that the ground floor was unoccupied and cautiously made their way to the first floor. At the top of the stairs, they were confronted by a locked door, with muffled voices heard beyond. Police shouted to open the door, then forced their way in.

The armed officers found three men, the eighteen-year-old Groves, John Thomas and James Harvey, and in the en-suite bathroom, a woman, twenty-five-year-old Carole Howe. Howe worked as a groom for the Palmers; Thomas was her boyfriend; Harvey was Palmer's partner in a building company; and Groves was an assistant at Palmer's jewellery shop in Bath. The men were spreadeagled on the floor and searched. All three were terrified. Harvey and Groves readily told the police what they were doing at Palmer's home. They were smelting gold.

After being given gold to smelt by Chappell, they had spent two days producing ingots in Palmer's garden smelter. However, a few hours before the police arrived, they had cause for concern. Driving in early morning darkness from the smelter to the main house, they had spotted two men parked in a strange car. Harvey explained that he had thought they were criminals. They were, in fact, police in an unmarked car preparing for the raid. Harvey told Groves to go inside with the gold, which Groves hid under a cushion on the sofa, while Harvey went to investigate. Inside, John Thomas, Howe's boyfriend and a greenkeeper at a local golf course, had also noticed the car and had noted its number. Harvey returned to the house and told Groves to phone the police. That was the phone call that Groves was making when the police burst in and, when they did so, Thomas had pressed a panic button that linked to the local police station.

With a police raid being reported to the police, the situation was threatening to grow farcical. And, for the Flying Squad, disastrous. A search of the ground backed up Groves and Harvey's story, with police finding a small amount of smelted gold, ingot moulds, bags of copper coins, £50 notes and some guns. Discussions with neighbours elicited reports of a 'roaring noise' from Palmer's grounds, which was the smelter. Police claimed to have found Kenneth Noye's telephone number handwritten on the front of a telephone directory, though that would later be disputed.

What was clear was that the police had not found a considerable amount of gold, and they could not prove what they had found had come from the Brink's-Mat robbery. Even worse, they had not found John Palmer. When they asked the inhabitants of Palmer's house where he was, they perhaps expected denials, lies or a suggestion of a cunning escape. Instead, the answer was another humiliating moment for the police, with their extensive intelligence operation, and their legions of armed men and thundering boots.

'John's on holiday,' they were told.

CHAPTER TWELVE

Goldfinger

As the taxi drives around the Spanish island of Tenerife, it passes the life that John Palmer would build in the 1980s and 1990s. We pass the timeshare villages that would one day place him on the *Sunday Times* Rich List. The water park he would own, and about which he would joke that its purpose was to clean his money. The office building where he is said to have installed armed guards and marble floors. The bars and nightclubs that he owned and frequented. The American Bar, with vintage cars outside, and the Flamingo Club, which would see extravagance and violence.

We are well into the tour when the erstwhile silent taxi driver guesses our purpose. 'Palmer?' he asks. We confirm and ask what he knows of Palmer. The driver shrugs and says, without judgement, 'mafioso'. The driver's opinion, and the tour itself, is a peek into what Palmer would become in Tenerife, and what Tenerife became to him. Over the following few days, we will talk to many about that. But for now, we're looking for where it began.

The Hotel Troya in Playa de las Americas is a nondescript hotel: five storeys and a pool, just off the main street that runs through the tourist area on the island's south-west coast. In 1985, it was a family hotel favoured by the British, which remains the case nearly forty years later.

We walk out by the pool, to a raised area near the bar. We check photos from 1985. It is hard to get the angles right, but then we work it out. We gather two chairs and sit, blinking, in the Spanish sun. Just like John Palmer and Kate Adie.

• • •

The line that police chiefs fed to the press was that they were 'delighted' with the raids of 29 January 1985. If that was spin, it didn't work. The media discovered Palmer's absence and revelled in it. Their coverage of Palmer slipping the net would be an increasing embarrassment for the police, pointing as it did to failed intelligence and a suggestion that the inquiry was still finding its feet after Fordham's death.

The press was naturally drawn to the story of the handsome, successful, young Bristol jeweller with a glamorous wife and a smelter in his back garden. When friends told the papers that Palmer was jokingly known as 'Goldfinger', the tabloids couldn't believe their luck. They dredged out an old photo that added a surreal touch to the coverage. Ten years before, Marnie Palmer had invited the *Bath Evening Chronicle* to cover the couple's wedding in the hope that it would generate publicity for her hairdressing salon. The photographs of the smiling young couple in their then-fashionable wedding outfits alongside their harlequin Great Danes were retrieved from the archives and the following day appeared in the national press. It was just the beginning of Palmer's new-found infamy – and just the beginning of the police's humiliation over their failure to catch them.

Reports that the Palmer family had flown from Bristol airport for a holiday in the Canary Islands began to circulate almost immediately. Within hours of the raid at the Coach House, the press had tracked the Palmers to Hotel Troya, on Playa de las Americas in Tenerife. The following day, reporters were on the island clamouring for an interview with the wanted man and Palmer was more than happy to oblige.

He relished the attention. On 31 January 1985, as the police search of his home intensified, Palmer spoke to Ted Oliver of the *Daily Mail*. 'Sipping a lager in his five-star hotel in Tenerife,' Oliver wrote, 'the shirt-sleeved businessman said: "I have nothing to hide. I am completely innocent."' Palmer declared through the pages of the *Daily Mail* that he was considering legal action against the police for 'blackening my name' and denied being involved in any criminal activity.

'Some people might think it odd that I am so rich at such a young age,' Palmer patiently explained, 'but there is nothing sinister. I started off as a marker trader with only a few quid. I bought a small house, converted it myself and sold it at a profit. I got into the property business that way and made a lot of money by taking chances. The fact that I have got a house worth a lot of money, a great deal of ground, three jewellery shops, three horses and other bits and pieces just shows how hard I have worked.' He admitted he had a smelter in his garden: 'But it's hidden only because of the valuable materials processed there. I have been involved in the gold bullion trade for some time. I buy scrap gold if the price is right and melt it down. I either hold it until the price is right to sell it or have it moulded into jewellery which I sell through my shops. I don't need to get involved in anything shady. I don't need to. If someone came to me with a lot of gold which they wanted me to melt down, I would inform the police at once.'

According to Oliver, Palmer was horrified at what the police had done at his home. 'At the very least, it is a gross invasion of privacy,' Palmer said. 'The police seem to have overreacted and I'm very concerned about the impression they may have created, but the people who know me in the area will know I am guilty of nothing. I just want to finish the holiday in peace. I understand that two officers from C11 are coming to talk to me. I will be happy to see them.'

Next up was Kieron Saunders of the *Sun*, who spoke to Palmer under a parasol beside his hotel pool. Palmer was surrounded by his brother, Mark, and 'four burly friends', who Palmer said he had met 'by coincidence' while he was on holiday. The trip, he said, was planned by his wife. 'She kept nagging me. It's just a simple holiday, a simple hotel, nothing elaborate.' He told the reporter of his surprise at hearing he was wanted by the police, and said, 'I am completely innocent of anything to do with the Brink's-Mat raid. No gold I have smelted came from that robbery that I know of.' Palmer went on, 'I was told the police had smashed their way into the house and had arrested the people looking after it for me. I was completely astonished, shocked and amazed. I just could not think of any reason for them doing that. Then my friend said it was connected with the Brink's-Mat bullion robbery and the murder of a policeman. I am still in a state of shock.'

Palmer said he had been bought out of his stake in Scadlynn's bullion-dealing business by Chappell. 'Garth, as far as I'm aware, has always run a very legitimate and prosperous business. We parted company purely for business and financial reasons. I was more interested in the retail jewellery trade.' The *Sun* had talked to one of Palmer's neighbours in Bristol, who had spoken of the smelter 'roaring' in the middle of the night and strange people 'delivering objects shaped like cannon balls'. Palmer explained that this was all very innocent. 'In my line of business security is important,' he told the reporter. 'You don't advertise what you're up to.' One of Palmer's friends, a balding man with arms covered in tattoos, gravely told the reporter, 'John is very, very frightened that the police will fit him up in some way.'

As Palmer sat in the sun in Tenerife, the police search at the Coach House continued. On the afternoon of the raid, a crane was used to remove the smelter and in the days that followed, earth-movers and excavators were used to dig up some of the grounds and surrounding woodland. Part of the swimming pool was dug up with pneumatic drills and inside the house floorboards were removed. As soon as he heard about the police raids, Marnie would later recall, Palmer got on the phone to his associates in Britain. 'Get rid of everything,' Marnie says Palmer told them. 'The police want to take me to the cleaners.'

In Spain, Palmer offered a running commentary to the press. He said he was amazed to hear of the 'SAS-type raid', over which he was 'planning to take some legal action'. When the press uncovered stories that he had been convicted of fraud in 1980 and given two suspended six-month sentences and ordered to pay £40,000 compensation, Palmer calmly batted it away. 'Problems arose with a furniture business I had,' he said. 'A warehouse burned down and we couldn't get compensation. I was left with the bills. But I pleaded guilty and paid back every penny.' He claimed the charges against him were part of a smear campaign: 'I have been in trouble before, but then, as now, I was innocent. A lot of people are jealous that I have made so much money for someone so young.'

For the press, the story provided some welcome sunshine in the middle of a bleak winter. Palmer and Marnie were persuaded to pose for photographs under the palm trees. Looking tanned and healthy, she stood in a striped bathing costume, while he was shirtless with casual trousers and Velcro trainers. Marnie also spoke to reporters, telling them, 'I wish the police would fly out here and get it all cleared up. I know nothing about the robbery. But I do know John had nothing to do with it.' She worried for her home. 'John and I put a lot of work and money into making our house beautiful and I am dreading what I might find when I go back. We have been told that police have dug up our lounge and our swimming pool using pneumatic drills.' 'I stand by my man', Marnie reportedly told the *Sun*. She worried that 'people are bound to think there is no smoke without fire'.

Palmer was a man attuned to the spirit of the age. His was a rags-to-riches story, he emphasised, of a poor Birmingham boy who moved to Bristol, a canny entrepreneur willing to work hard and take the risks that brought the big rewards. As a self-made businessman, he was an emblem of the Thatcherite 1980s. His visible enjoyment of his success – the grand home, flash cars and winter holidays – were true to the times. This was 1985, when Del Boy and *Only Fools and Horses* were finding their stride. It was hardly surprising the press lapped it up. For the police, the newspapers' embrace of Palmer was a hard process to endure. And then came Kate Adie.

The celebrated journalist was at the time a young news reporter for the BBC, who had been despatched to Tenerife to try to secure a television interview with Palmer for the nightly news. The segment, that went out on the main BBC news, began with Adie presenting an introductory piece to camera, the arid Tenerife landscape behind her. 'John Palmer is a jeweller and bullion dealer,' said Adie. 'With his name very much in the news, his home raided by police, its grounds searched and several of his friends and colleagues being questioned, it might be thought that he would, in a way, have "gone to ground" in Tenerife. Not at all. Among all the holiday-makers, he was to be found with his family and several friends, intent on pursuing his holiday and giving his views on the events of the past few days.'

The report then cut to Adie interviewing Palmer at an outside table near the hotel bar, his friends close to hand. This was a new challenge for Palmer. It wasn't having a beer with a journalist, it was sitting in front of a camera and presenting himself as an innocent man to the nation. It was a challenge he readily accepted.

In his lilting Birmingham accent, Palmer described to Adie how he learned of the raid on his home: 'I simply had a message, an urgent message, to ring home. I rang home and I was simply told the police had smashed into my house and arrested the people who were looking after the house, that was the message I had. I was completely astonished and amazed.' He told Adie that he had no idea why he had been targeted. 'At first, I couldn't think of any reason. I was amazed, and then they told me it was connected with some bullion robbery and the murder of a policeman and I was just amazed.' As Adie prodded him, Palmer calmly denied any knowledge of the robbery and insisted that he had nothing to do with the stolen gold, making a verbal slip it is hard not to consider might have been mischievous: 'I'm completely innocent of anything to do with this so-called Mat's-Brink bullion raid. I know nothing of it.'

The Palmers' holiday had been booked to end on 15 February 1985. When the day came, Palmer told journalists that he had decided to stay on the island. Sipping a brandy in the foyer of his hotel, he refused to say why that was: 'I'm not going to say why I am not going home. But for the moment I'm staying here. My wife and the children are also staying.' He told the assembled press that he had spoken with police by phone and that he had simply decided to extend his holiday: 'The first two weeks' holiday were ruined by the press, and we just plan to take another couple of weeks now. Whatever is going to happen to me when I get back to Britain will happen in two weeks' time as well as it would today. I have nothing to fear.'

The *Telegraph* reported a rumour that Palmer had slipped out of his hotel and gone into hiding on the island. The rumour was correct. The night before the holiday ended, Palmer's friend Jonny

Groves flew out to Tenerife and smuggled the Palmers out of the hotel at 2am. They went first to Groves' holiday apartment, then on to a villa belonging to a British expat.

The *Guardian* noted that as part of Spain, Tenerife did not have an extradition treaty with Britain. The sanctuary offered by the island would certainly be the main appeal of the island to Palmer over the years ahead. But he had already sensed something else in Tenerife.

Opportunity.

CHAPTER THIRTEEN

Silence

As Palmer charmed Adie and enjoyed the sunshine, the police continued to search the grounds of Hollywood Cottage. The search would last a total of six weeks and at one point even involved a police helicopter equipped with an infra-red device to find hidden or buried metal. The result was an eclectic list of discoveries that came with varying degrees of danger for Noye. It included: large quantities of copper coins, a child's drawing of a gold bar, a copy of *The Guinness Book of Records 1985* with the entry for the Brink's-Mat robbery as the largest ever robbery circled and two flick knives. More potentially damaging for Noye was the discovery at the back of the house near the swimming pool of what the police later believed to be the weapon that killed Fordham – a white-handled kitchen knife, stabbed into the ground near a tree.

In the house, police found a safe that contained a large quantity of jewellery and £2,500 in brand-new £50 notes. The banknotes had consecutive serial numbers that began with the prefix A24, a detail that would mean much more to the police later (similar notes were also found at Reader's home, while £50,000 of A24 £50 notes were found hidden in the woods behind Noye's parents' home). In the barn of Hollywood Cottage, police found an instruction leaflet for an Alcosa GF080/2 smelter like the one supplied to Michael Lawson in December 1983. Secret compartments behind wood panelling contained antique Meissen porcelain worth £3,000 that had been stolen from a stately home two years earlier. Police also found Masonic regalia that confirmed their suspicions that Noye was a Freemason. Perhaps, most promisingly of all, however, the police finally found some gold.

Initially, the search had been disappointing. The wartime cellars were finally located but were filled with stones and bricks. As the sky began to darken on Sunday 27 January, Sergeant Peter Holloway, a Kent officer drafted in to help, was searching the area between the garage and the swimming pool when he noticed that one of the slabs on the terrace looked to be slightly raised. He lifted the slab, expecting to find a drain, and found a paint tin. Beneath the tin was a folded red and white cloth. 'As I opened it up, I remember the brightness of the gold,' he said later. 'It was quite amazing. I think my jaw must have hit the floor.'

Wrapped up in the cloth were eleven bars of roughly cast gold, later analysed and found to be either 9999 or 999 purity. Elsewhere, forensic tests revealed gold fragments and globules produced during smelting on the boot mat of Noye's Granada and in Reader's Cavalier. More gold particles were discovered on a leather apron and gloves found in the barn, in the back of a Ford Transit at Noye's house, on a pair of driving gloves taken from the Granada and on a pair of gloves taken from Noye at Swanley police station.

It was not quite the haul that Boyce had hoped for but it did suggest to the police that Noye was handling the Brink's-Mat gold. Boyce pressed his case that the two inquiries, Fordham's death and the gold-handling case, should be looked at together. Boyce's immediate senior officer, Commander Corbett, assured him that he and

Assistant Commissioner John Dellow were to meet with the Home Office and press for the cases to be led by Scotland Yard. On Sunday 27 January, Scotland Yard was granted full control of the case. The following day, Boyce was formally placed in charge of the inquiries into Fordham's death and the Brink's-Mat robbery and its aftermath. Noye was moved from Dartford police station to Bromley, within the borders of the Metropolitan Police area.

Now Boyce and his team could speak to the suspects. Not that it would do them much good.

• • •

Ultimately, the police interviews with Noye, Brenda Noye and Reader would be ineffective. They did not elicit confessions or guilty pleas and their content was later furiously debated in Noye and Reader's murder trials. Boyce denied access to solicitors for the suspects, a decision he would later have to defend in court, while Noye fought to keep the inquiry under the auspices of Kent police. It was not an atmosphere conducive to cooperation.

Noye was interviewed several times by the Brink's-Mat detectives. Detective Inspector Tony Brightwell claimed that Noye began their interview by offering a Masonic handshake and telling him, 'You have got to believe one thing, I didn't know he was a policeman,' before declaring, 'I will give my story to a judge and jury.' Over further interviews, including with Boyce, the police claimed Noye offered more damning statements, all of which Noye would later deny at trial.

Brian Reader offered little more. His chief concerns were being prosecuted for murder and the health of his wife, who suffered with diabetes and was due to go into hospital the next day for treatment. He was interviewed a number of times, usually refusing to leave his cell and making the police come to him, only to offer an array of 'no comments' and vague responses. Brenda Noye claimed to know nothing about the killing, insisted her husband was not capable of it and remained immune to the pressures of being handcuffed and held in custody. 'I'm not frightened of anyone,' she is noted as saying by the police who claimed that she then refused to sign the interview notes. Brenda Noye later denied having said everything attributed to her, except her admission that she left the house, and said no notes were taken when the police spoke with her.

In the evening of Tuesday 29 January 1985, Kenneth Noye and Brian Reader appeared before Dartford magistrate charged with murdering John Fordham. When the charges against them were read out, Noye cried out, 'No!' Reader simply said, 'I'm innocent of that charge.' They were remanded in custody again.

Once Noye and Reader had been charged with murder, the rules around interviewing prisoners meant police could not question them any further about Fordham's death. But Noye and Reader had not been charged with any offences related to the gold found at Hollywood Cottage, meaning both men could still be questioned about their connection to the Brink's-Mat robbery. During the morning of Wednesday 30 January, after police raids on others thought to be involved in the smelting and laundering ring, Noye was interviewed again, this time at Bromley police station. 'Tell me,' Noye asked the detectives, 'What happens when you go out of here? Do you write all this down?' Yes, the detectives told him. 'I can't say anything then, can I?' he replied. The detectives asked what he meant. 'That Black's a dead man, isn't he?' said Noye, referring to Tony Black, the Brink's-Mat security guard who had colluded with the original robbers. 'You lot wrote down what he had to say. He's a dead man when he comes out. You don't think I'm going to get myself killed because you've told people I helped you.'

This set the tone. Noye occasionally drifted close to talking about some form of deal, while trying to discover more about what information the police had on him; at the same time, the police pressed him on some of the evidence they had unearthed in the surveillance operation. It was cat and mouse, and unsatisfactory for both parties, and led to a murky conclusion when Noye asked to speak to Boyce alone at Bromley police station. What was discussed between them would make front-page news at the forthcoming trial.

Reader was also interviewed about the gold, in a set of interviews he would later dispute. For example, he later denied the police suggestion that when asked if the gold he had been involved came from the Brink's-Mat robbery, Reader replied, 'Of course it does.' The police would claim that Reader discussed in general terms the disguising of gold in order to sell it back into the market before deciding the police's questioning was growing overly intrusive and declaring, 'You're stitching me up. I'm not saying any more.' At the conclusion of the interviews, Noye and Reader were charged with handling stolen gold, charges they would face after their charges over Fordham's murder, and remanded in custody.

Police had a similarly frustrating time in their interviews with those arrested for being part of the Gold Chain in Hatton Garden and Bristol. Matteo Constantino, who had been arrested in Hatton Garden after information was given to the Brink's-Mat team by another agency was asked if he had any idea what the police inquiry was about. Constantino was said to have admitted, 'Well, I've been doing a lot of fiddling.' He explained that, after being approached by Garth Chappell, he had allowed Scadlynn to use the name of his companies as cover for the large amount of gold coming in to Scadlynn. In exchange for several thousand pounds a week, Constantino would be shown on Scadlynn's records as having supplied them with gold. Scadlynn created a paper trail by paying Constantino for the gold by bank transfer, but made him withdraw the money in cash and pay it back to them. Scadlynn's records showed it had bought between £9 and £10 million worth of gold from Constantino's companies. But Constantino did not give the police the crucial confirmation that Scadlynn was actually dealing in Brink's-Mat gold. He maintained he had no idea where Chappell's gold came from, but that he thought it might have been smuggled in and was possibly melted-down Krugerrands.

Chappell's story was different. Constantino was not a stooge, according to Chappell, he was a tycoon. He told detectives that Scadlynn's recent boom was because of the astonishing custom that the aged Constantino had suddenly rustled up from his humble Hatton Garden office. Constantino, insisted Chappell, was 'a businessman of substance'. The only reason, Chappell said, that he, John Palmer and others had picked up gold in London and motorway service stations was that Constantino did not know his way around Bristol. Detectives were incredulous that Constantino, who was in his seventies and in poor health, could carry 22kg of gold. 'He's a very powerful man,' claimed Chappell. Police records show that Constantino was later told of Chappell's versions of events and replied, 'That's stupid, ain't it?'

Terence Patch stuck to the story that Scadlynn had received the gold from Constantino and had thought nothing of his occasional role picking up gold deliveries at service stations, for which he insisted his only payment was the odd bit of jewellery and being allowed to use the Scadlynn office phone. Adams refused to leave his cell for interviews and, according to the police, said, 'We all know the score. I'll either walk from here or walk from a court after a six-month lay-down. You've got nothing on me.'

The police had also picked up Michael Lawson again, the driver of the car carrying the smelter that they had lost in pursuit near West Kingsdown, only for him to stick to his story of two mysterious characters – 'a man called Benny' and 'a Turk' – asking him to purchase the smelter. Chappell, Patch, Constantino, Adams and Lawson were all charged with dishonestly handling gold stolen in the Brink's-Mat robbery.

The police gleaned little on the absent Palmer from his colleagues' interviews. They learned that a call had been made to Adams's flat from Palmer's car phone. Chappell admitted that Palmer smelted metals for Scadlynn, sometimes with the help of Lee Groves and James Harvey, who had been in Palmer's house when it was raided, but he denied the company had ever handled the Brink's-Mat gold.

For Boyce and his team, Palmer's absence was only one part of their frustration. They had identified and arrested a large number of those they were sure were involved in the Gold Chain, but now faced the enormous challenge of achieving guilty verdicts against Noye for Fordham's murder, and against Noye and the rest for their gold-handling activities. Particularly with regards to the handling charges, the Flying Squad needed insight that they had simply failed to gather using traditional police techniques.

Salvation would arrive unexpectedly. What the Flying Squad detectives did not realise was that, while they had been watching the Gold Chain, others had been watching them too.

CHAPTER FOURTEEN

Her Majesty's Customs and Excise

In the aftermath of Fordham's death and with the inquiry into the whereabouts of the Brink's-Mat gold seemingly in tatters, Brian Boyce was approached by Mike Newscombe and Jim McGregor, two lead officers from HM Customs and Excise Investigations Division. What they told him was to be crucial in putting the faltering inquiry back on its feet and would later assist in several key Brink's-Mat convictions.

Initially, Customs provided information that would help in the arrests of the Bristol branch of the Gold Chain operation as well as Matteo Constantino. As time passed and the police and Customs grew to trust and value each other more, the information became a steady stream of invaluable expert insight that would transform the police operation and both widen and deepen the Brink's-Mat investigation. The officers' revelations also came with a sizeable shock for the police. Customs had been watching Scadlynn. And they had been watching Kenny Noye.

For some time, Customs and Excise had suspected Noye was engaged in gold smuggling and VAT fraud using gold. It was Customs officers who had picked up on his visit to Jersey in May 1984, and they now suspected a connection of some kind between the eleven gold bars Noye had bought in Jersey at Charterhouse Japhet and the eleven found by the police at Hollywood Cottage. This led police to conclude that Noye had purchased the gold to provide cover for the small consignments of stolen gold being moved from Kent to Bristol. At trial, Noye would later deny this and argue it was coincidence that eleven bars were found at this home.

In addition to their suspicions regarding Noye, Customs and Excise had been conducting an in-depth investigation into Scadlynn for some time. It had started when the Investigations Division received a tip-off from an underworld source that Scadlynn employee Roger Feltham, using the name Peter James and giving a false address, was trying to sell South African Krugerrands in the City of London. This was not in itself illegal but Feltham was using a false VAT number, which suggested that the coins had been smuggled into Britain and that Feltham was pocketing the 15 per cent VAT a London dealer would have to pay on top of the fixed gold price. Feltham was followed by undercover Customs officers from the dealer's shop through the Underground to Farringdon station, where he collected a car from a nearby car park. It was obvious from his behaviour that Feltham was wary of being followed. With a Customs car in pursuit, he drove west along the M4 and eventually pulled off outside Swindon. He drove on to the Plough pub, where a blue Jaguar was waiting for him. The Jaguar was subsequently traced to Garth Chappell. Later that evening, Customs officers followed Feltham to Terence Patch's house. Scadlynn was now in the Customs' crosshairs.

The Customs officers knew Chappell ran Scadlynn, and that the company had been less than forthcoming in the past in declaring VAT and allowing VAT inspectors to check its books. Its name had come up in several fraud cases and, although it had never been the subject of a specific inquiry, Customs investigators suspected it was involved in illegal activities. Feltham's behaviour suggested it was time to take a closer look. The Customs investigation began in autumn 1984, with Jim McGregor leading the team. The first step was for investigators to check the computerised national VAT records in Southend. These showed that over the preceding months, Scadlynn's fortunes had improved dramatically. Before spring 1984, the company had a turnover of less than £100,000 a year. After that, turnover shot up into the millions. It was an unlikely transformation for a scruffy business in a down-at-heel Bristol suburb.

Over the following months, Customs officers made a series of apparently routine visits to the company to inspect its VAT accounts and gather further information. Unlike the police, Customs had the power to require a company under investigation to submit documents and provide explanations. They were also able to search premises while hunting for smuggled goods without a warrant. The Scadlynn paperwork showed it was buying large amounts of scrap gold, which was being smelted, assayed and then sold back to gold dealers. Customs investigators established that the principal seller, on paper, was Matteo Constantino in London and that the main buyer was Dynasty Metals in Leeds. Customs established an operation they called Operation Law Degree, a reference to the LLB degree, which matched the initials of the cities involved: London, Leeds and Bristol. The name also hinted at the more academic backgrounds of the recruits who went into the Customs service than those who went into policing.

Scadlynn was selling the gold for only marginally more than the price at which it had been bought. Given the levels of activity involved in smelting and transporting the gold, it did not make sense, unless the gold was being acquired at a lower price or the company was pocketing the VAT paid by the buyer. Chappell claimed that the scrap gold was made up of old jewellery and bric-a-brac that had been bought at county fairs and from other informal sources. The Customs team thought the amounts involved were too large for this to be plausible and doubted that Constantino and the other companies involved would be able to supply gold in such large quantities. There was clearly something amiss.

Customs investigators' suspicions were shared by staff at the Assay Office. Scadlynn had been using the Sheffield office for some time, but before 1984, the amounts involved had always been relatively small. The office's metallurgists now found that the ingots being supplied were very crudely smelted, often with traces of copper still visibly mixed within the gold. They all had to be resmelted to properly analyse their purity. Staff wondered why Scadlynn had bothered to smelt it in the first place, given that they offered a melting service, but when they tried to persuade them to let them do it for them, Scadlynn refused. Staff began to wonder where the gold might have come from. They also knew that in the past, Scadlynn had submitted gold sovereigns and Kruggerands as scrap gold, even though they would have fetched a higher price if they had been sold as coins. But their doubts amounted to little and confidentiality rules meant they were not revealed until the Customs officers came asking.

By late 1984, the Customs investigators were in an extraordinary position, well ahead of the police. They had essentially discovered the handling operation that was processing a significant proportion of the Brink's-Mat gold. The problem was that they didn't know it. They certainly believed that Scadlynn was trading in illegal bullion but could not establish whether it was smuggled or stolen and didn't have a clear theory on where exactly the gold was coming from.

However, the Customs investigators were sufficiently concerned about the company's activities that a covert observation post was set up in an office opposite Scadlynn. Close surveillance of Chappell and his associates revealed that couriers appeared to be transferring gold between sites and that Feltham often collected consignments from Patch's house as early as 4am. But they weren't the only names on the growing list of suspects and Customs officers soon added another: John Palmer.

The Customs officers knew that Palmer and Chappell had been in a business partnership together and that he had been a director of Scadlynn until early 1984, just before large profits started arriving. They also knew of his garden smelter. Delving further into Scadlynn's activities, they discovered that Krugerrands were being smuggled into the country in the fuel tanks of cheap cars imported from the Channel Islands by associates of Chappell and Palmer, called John Groves (father of Lee Groves) and James Harvey.

At the end of 1984, Customs investigators shared details of their investigation with Scotland Yard. They told two officers that they were keeping Scadlynn under surveillance and that they believed the company was dealing in smuggled gold that, they had now concluded, could include some of the stolen Brink's-Mat gold. Scotland Yard officers showed little interest and continued to pursue their own lines of inquiry, which by then had begun to focus on Noye's end of the gold operation. This was a little over a month before the death of John Fordham. When Brian Boyce took over the Brink's-Mat investigation in January 1985, he was not made aware of the Customs investigation.

Without knowing it, two branches of law enforcement had discovered the Brink's-Mat gold-handling operation. In both cases, they had a partial view of events. If they had pooled knowledge and resources earlier, the result might have been very different. Instead, they were brought together through crisis and the publicity over Fordham's death. The result was a remarkable situation: dual investigations working their way to separate conclusions, both tightening nooses around their targets, both planning their final moves, and entirely unaware of each other's activities.

While the Scotland Yard surveillance on Noye intensified, Customs continued to probe Scadlynn. On 16 January 1985, ten days before Fordham was killed, Customs officers visited its offices and asked to see the company's accounts. Chappell told them, 'I am a dealer. I don't understand books. Books are all Chinese to me.' Two days later, the customs officer returned to tell him he owed nearly £80,000 in unpaid VAT. A visit to Constantino was planned for the near future.

When Boyce and the men from Customs spoke after Fordham's death, they realised that they had separately investigated two sides of the same plot. Through the surveillance mounted in January 1985, Scotland Yard had pieced together much of the Kent and London operation centred around Noye, but they knew very little about the Bristol end centred around Scadlynn. It was information from Customs, in the initial period of cooperation between the investigations, that increased police understanding of Scadlynn and Palmer's actions and led to Constantino being arrested.

It would have been mutually beneficial if the police and Customs had realised the value of each other earlier but, once they did, it offered Boyce what he saw as the final piece of the puzzle. He, along with many of his team, had reached a conclusion. The Brink's-Mat robbery and what came next was moving into areas that existed beyond traditional British crime and beyond traditional detective work. It was now about crimes including gold handling, money laundering, fraud and corruption. It was time for the investigation to show similar innovation. A new type of policing for a new type of crime.

The Brink's-Mat robbery, and what it had become, had outgrown the Flying Squad.

CHAPTER FIFTEEN

Task Force

Still reeling from the death of a close colleague, Boyce met with Deputy Assistant Commissioner Brian Worth's principal aide, Detective Chief Inspector Roy Ramm, and told him what he thought the inquiry needed. To carry out a complex commercial and financial investigation, the police would need to dismantle the fencing and money-laundering networks that had grown from the gold and doing this would require skills, knowledge and experience not common among Flying Squad detectives. For the investigation to have any chance of success, officers from the Fraud Squad would need to be brought in to work closely with Customs. Boyce suggested that he should lead a special task force of around eighty officers, similar to the task forces set up to investigate the Great Train Robbery, the Krays and the Richardson Gang in the 1960s. The request was granted. Boyce was relieved of the Flying Squad and placed in command of the newly formed Brink's-Mat special task force. Now he had to fill it.

The Flying Squad team who had been investigating the robbery since the beginning, including Detective Chief Inspector Ken John, Detective Sergeant Tony Curtis, Detective Inspector Tony Brightwell and Detective Sergeant Bill Miller, and Detective Inspector Ian

Brown from Criminal Intelligence, went with Boyce to the task force. They were joined by a team of officers from the Fraud Squad led by Detective Inspector Ron Smith, divisional CID officers and liaison officers from the City of London, Avon and Somerset, Wiltshire and Kent police forces. HM Customs and Excise agreed to attach a senior investigator and five investigators to the new team. By the end of the process, Boyce had close to eighty officers under his command. They were supported by a secretary, two typists and an administrator, rare women in an almost exclusively male environment.

In Boyce's estimation, it was a mixed bunch. Boyce knew some already and was pleased that a group of excellent detective inspectors had been attached to the inquiry, but many of the new team were an unknown quantity, something that would become more significant as its inquiries progressed. Furthermore, many of the officers on the task force had grown up in the same London areas as the robbery gang or had served their police careers there. This proved useful when the task force was gathering intelligence but also left them open to corruption or an inappropriate closeness to the criminals they were investigating. Again, this fear from Boyce would not be entirely unwarranted.

In choosing a home for the task force, for Boyce there was only one option. Tintagel House, a building across the river from Scotland Yard in Vauxhall, was named from Arthurian legend and had housed some of the most sensitive criminal investigations in the Metropolitan Police's history. The building had been used in the 1960s by the teams investigating the Kray and Richardson gangs to keep a distance from Scotland Yard and prevent any information getting back to criminals via corrupt officers. Boyce had similar concerns, remaining in constant fear that criminals might infiltrate the Brink's-Mat investigations and wanted to maintain a discreet distance from Scotland Yard. He also ensured that the task force was operationally placed within the Serious Crime Department and not the Flying Squad.

Boyce organised the task force and set it to work. Different sections of the inquiry were allocated to different groups led by a detective inspector or senior detective sergeant. Their daily enquiries were coordinated by Detective Chief Inspector Ken John, who reported back each day to Boyce. At the end of each week, there was a meeting of the whole team. The size of the team increased the risk of leaks but the complexity of the inquiry meant it was a necessity. The inquiries into Fordham's death and the complex gold-handling operation were the immediate focus. Gathering evidence in both cases meant the workload was immense. Senior management at Scotland Yard decided that Boyce needed a deputy, and that a detective superintendent should be brought in to handle all the fresh leads being thrown up by the inquiry. When that deputy was identified, Boyce was surprised. He wasn't alone. The man Corbett and Worth suggested as Boyce's new number two was one of the most controversial figures in the Metropolitan Police force.

• • •

There weren't many detectives at Scotland Yard with a record like Tony Lundy's, which is not entirely a compliment. He was widely regarded as one of the best thief-catchers in the building, but he was also viewed in some quarters with suspicion.

A blunt northerner with a thick Lancashire accent, Lundy had always stood out from many of his colleagues. Working his way through the ranks in the early 1970s, he developed a reputation as an excellent detective. This continued after 1977, when he led a team of Flying Squad detectives against the rise of armed robberies in the capital and was said to have solved more crimes and put more major criminals in jail than any other officer in the history of the Metropolitan Police force. During the 1970s, he was closely associated with the rise of the supergrass system. Lundy was an enthusiastic exponent of the approach and successfully 'turned' a number of suspects, which resulted in the conviction of several major criminals. In one case, sixty-nine people were charged as a result of confessions that Lundy extracted. Lundy claimed his success earned him the enmity of some of London's top criminals and that they had decided to use their own contacts within the Met to exact revenge.

In March 1980, a gang of armed robbers hijacked a lorry at Tilbury Docks and stole £3.5 million of East German silver bullion. Lundy provided information to the investigation that led to the recovery of most of the stolen bullion and the conviction of the key criminals. Twelve silver ingots worth £127,000, however, were never found. It was alleged by a criminal supergrass called Billy Young that Lundy had personally benefited from the missing ingots. It was also alleged that he had improperly secured a reward for one of his informants. Around the same time, journalists began to explore rumours that Lundy had a corrupt relationship with one of his informants, a major north London criminal and drug trafficker called Roy Garner. Lundy was moved from Scotland Yard to a Metropolitan Police division while an inquiry was made into his actions. When the internal investigation concluded in August 1983, the senior investigating officer wrote, 'I feel bound to express a personal opinion and regrettably there is a dearth of evidence to support it, but it is my belief that Lundy is a corrupt officer who has long exploited his association with Garner.' The report was passed to the director of public prosecutions but the lack of credible evidence meant no action was taken. Lundy was given a minor admonishment by Scotland Yard for failings in his paperwork and his transfer to a Metropolitan Police division was made permanent. By January 1985, however, Lundy said he had been fully exonerated by the investigation.

Senior management at Scotland Yard was split between those who thought Lundy was the best detective the Yard had ever had and a victim of a conspiracy to bring him down, and those who thought he lacked integrity and was guilty of corruption. It was testament to those divisions that Lundy, by now a detective superintendent, was appointed as Boyce's deputy by Corbett and Worth.

Commander Corbett had been Lundy's superintendent on the Flying Squad. By posting him to Scotland Yard's biggest, most sensitive and high-profile ongoing inquiry, the four assistant commissioners gave a powerful rebuttal to Lundy's detractors.

Lundy was a workaholic with an ascetic demeanour and an obsession with physical fitness and long-distance running. Many of Lundy's colleagues found his single-minded commitment to the job difficult to handle, such as when he alienated some of his Flying Squad colleagues by banning drinking on the job. His personal manner was abrupt and abrasive. As one senior officer said, 'He did not take to either "time servers" or those who, for one reason or another, were unsuccessful. His record as a murder investigator was excellent. His manner was of a man who got results, but he did not care who knew it.'

And yet, some of those qualities were what made the relationship between Boyce and Lundy more nuanced than expected. Boyce was a zealous anti-corruption voice in the police, but he also appreciated fine detective work and respected those who shared his heightened work ethic. Although he and Lundy were very different, they shared more characteristics than they expected. Both were highly suspicious of the Masonic culture that prevailed in much of the Metropolitan Police at the time. They had both remained beyond the brotherhood's reach; Boyce by choice, Lundy by committing the Masonic sin of being a Catholic. Both Boyce and Lundy were working-class, former grammar-school boys, and both were thought to have a maverick streak. The two men shared an in-depth knowledge and lack of respect for the criminals of south-east London.

Boyce and Lundy came together warily. They were not friends and never would be. But a mutual respect was quickly formed. They could work together.

Tony Lundy was on the team.

• • •

The task force was now set up to widen its investigation, with its remit eventually expanding all the way through to international money laundering and the movement of criminal assets overseas. The criminal money generated by the Brink's-Mat robbery was now of equal interest to the robbery itself. The team got to work and Lundy began poring over the files, looking for missed clues.

But one issue still lingered. The police might have realised that there was a wave of crimes that travelled ever further from the Brink's-Mat depot on the Heathrow trading estate, but the media weren't aware of any of that. In the wake of Fordham's death, some quarters of the media returned doggedly to a central question. It had been fourteen months since the robbery. Other than eleven bars of disguised gold found at Noye's house, which couldn't be accurately identified, the police had come up short on the media's recurring refrain: where was the gold?

As much as Boyce's task force wanted to launch themselves into the brave new world of policing that the Brink's-Mat investigation would create, the original sin still needed investigating. What helped was that the original sinner had had a change of heart.

Micky McAvoy wanted to talk.

CHAPTER SIXTEEN

It's Been Traded

After Tony Lundy joined the task force in March 1985, he meticulously worked through the files and met with the officers who had been on the inquiry since the robbery in November 1983. He found a lot of frustration with how the inquiry had been handled before Brian Boyce took charge. Lundy later told the crime journalist Martin Short that the detectives were 'keen as mustard, bursting to nick the other robbers and recover the gold. They knew who the robbers were but had received no backing to get them. They had put forward proposals on to what to do but were getting nowhere. They'd had a very frustrating year.'

Lundy was particularly surprised that no pressure had been put on the men who had been convicted to glean information on the missing gold. Lundy suggested to Boyce an approach that had served him well in the past: speak with the criminals and persuade them to provide information in exchange for a reduction in their sentences. Tony Black had already given police everything he knew, at considerable risk to his own safety, but Robinson and McAvoy had said very little. Lundy asked if any efforts had been made to get them to talk and tell all. None, he was told.

Lundy knew both men were going to the Appeal Court and thought they would welcome a reduction in their twenty-five-year sentences. Lundy arranged for an officer who had dealt with McAvoy in the past to visit Leicester prison, where McAvoy and Robinson were being held in a secure wing. Lundy later told Short what happened next: 'I asked this detective superintendent, "Go in and have a general chat, and see if they're interested in talking about their appeal and any ways we might be able to help each other." Lo and behold! They agreed to talk.'

Lundy had timed the approach well. The death of John Fordham and subsequent arrests of Noye and others connected to the gold-smelting operation had alerted McAvoy to the possibility that what was said to be the £7 million share of the gold he thought was being kept safe for his return was being converted into cash. As he read press reports that connected the surveillance officer's death to the hunt for the gold that he had stolen, he became concerned that he was losing control of his £7 million share and that he might have nothing left at the end of his sentence. Now, he reasoned, might be the time to talk. While McAvoy showed no intention of sharing any information that would incriminate others, he began to consider the possibility of trading his share of the gold for a reduction in his sentence.

In spring 1985, Boyce and Lundy visited Leicester jail to speak with the only people so far convicted of the robbery. Boyce was reluctant, thinking negotiations with criminals were a waste of time, but felt it was an exercise that needed to be undertaken. When the men eventually sat down together, there was a moment of shared understanding, as McAvoy and Boyce recognised that they both lived their lives by codes of honour. 'You and I are the same,' Boyce recalls the convicted robber telling him. 'You don't take money and I don't grass.'

Lundy asked McAvoy what he thought they would get on appeal, then pitched two possibilities: 'Either he could name everybody else and get a big reduction, or he could help us recover what was left of the gold and still get a big slice off his twenty-five years.' Lundy thought the first was unlikely. As he recounted later to Short, 'I never really thought that McAvoy – or Robinson – would grass the others because they were in the same jail. This was unfortunate because you can't really talk to two robbers together, as neither wants the other to see he's harming their mates.' If they had been held in separate prisons, Lundy felt, perhaps optimistically, that he might have had more luck.

Lundy and Boyce spoke with McAvoy and Robinson together. As expected, the two convicted Brink's-Mat robbers refused to entertain the idea of naming anybody. However, they were interested in what they might get in return if they gave back all the gold that had not been smelted. The police had information that suggested the remaining £13 million worth of stolen gold was buried somewhere. Increases in the gold price meant it was now worth £18 million. Lundy regarded the recovery of the gold as even more important than jailing the remaining robbers because if it was converted into cash then it could go on to fund other criminal activities, including drugs. Information about the whereabouts of that gold was therefore worth a significant reduction in criminal sentencing.

With the possibility of a deal on the table, Boyce and Lundy met the convicted robbers on a couple of subsequent occasions in summer 1985. It seemed like a deal was imminent. By Lundy's recollection, at one point, 'McAvoy said point blank, "I've got control of half the bullion. Nobody else can touch it unless I give the instruction."' With that admission, Lundy remembered, they had him over a barrel. McAvoy's paranoia came to the fore. 'First he's saying he wants to do it, then he doesn't; then he rants and raves about how could he be sure, if he gives it back, that we're not going to arrest everybody in sight for handling. We say that won't happen but I'm also saying, "Look, you've told us point blank that you control half this gold, so what's going to happen now when you go to appeal? We'll have to tell prosecuting counsel and the DPP what you've said so no judge is going to cut your sentence when you're saying, 'I've got the gold but I'm not giving it back!'"'

McAvoy was incensed, flying into a rage when he realised that he now had to return the gold. Robinson agreed with that conclusion. McAvoy's response was to try to dictate terms. As Lundy remembered, he eventually made a suggestion: 'There's no way I'm going to tell you where you can just go and get it because then you'll have to nick the people looking after it … but if you get a call one day to go to a certain street where there's a lorry parked and nobody with it, that way you can't nick anybody because you won't know who's put it there. So that's what we're going to do. It's just going to be left somewhere, you'll be told immediately and you go and get it.'

Boyce and Lundy put the plan down on paper and passed it to Deputy Assistant Commissioner Brian Worth via Commander Corbett. Lundy was hopeful but, before any further steps could be taken, he was sent abroad in connection with the Brink's-Mat inquiries. Boyce was also preoccupied with other matters on the sprawling inquiry and, unlike Lundy, remained sceptical of what could be gained by talking to criminals. Deputy Assistant Commissioner Worth took personal charge of the negotiations with McAvoy and Robinson, travelling up to Leicester jail with his staff officer, Roy Ramm, for discussions with the two convicted robbers, sensing that a major victory for Scotland Yard was close.

Worth and Ramm began negotiating with McAvoy and Robinson in September 1985. They met regularly. Ramm and McAvoy were of a similar age and had both grown up in inner London. Sitting across from someone who had a completely different outlook on life, and who would return to a cell where he might spend the next twenty-five years, was for Ramm an unnerving experience. 'We had some very strange conversations,' he recalled to an interviewer later, 'we would ask them to tell us who else had been involved in the robbery, drop a few likely names, say we'd seen so-and-so out on the town flashing a wedge of fifties, having a good time with a couple of dolly birds.' Their teasing got them nowhere. McAvoy was never comfortable with talking to the police, Ramm remembered, and 'they would not even hint at the identities of the other gang members'. The problem, as Ramm saw it, was that McAvoy and Robinson 'had nothing to do all day but to think about the possibility of a deal, and so they came to each meeting with a prepared set of demands'.

Two or three weeks passed between each visit, giving the two prisoners time to prepare what they would say in advance and to establish a game plan for each meeting. Eventually, McAvoy told Worth that he knew where at least half of the gold had gone. As one of the architects of the raid, he had received a large share of the proceeds, as well as some of that allocated for Tony Black. He had entrusted associates to look after his share and he knew some of the gold had already been fenced. McAvoy now suggested that he ask another associate to arrange the return of the money and all of the gold that was left. In return for the gold, he would receive a letter from the police that could be lodged as part of his appeal. Worth was not optimistic, fearing that once the middleman knew the whereabouts of the cash and the gold he would vanish along with it, but McAvoy was insistent.

The negotiations continued but were almost derailed by McAvoy's paranoia. He now became fixated on the idea that the police would simply keep the gold for themselves. Worth and Ramm assured him this was an outrageous suggestion and tried to reach a solution. As Ramm remembered, 'We suggested the gold should be put in a van by their own agents and associates – people they could trust. These intermediaries would then tell us when and where to collect the bullion and the whole thing could be overseen by independent observers, the media, lawyers or whoever. At a certain time, we would find a van in a certain street. The observers would verify the exchange, they would get their letter and that would be the end of it.'

As the meetings progressed, the deal became increasingly complex. To Lundy's horror, 'Everything had turned cripplingly formal. The next thing, defence solicitors were demanding written guarantees. There were even meetings with the director of public prosecutions.' It was reported later that McAvoy had asked for a year off his sentence for every £1 million he returned. The offer was referred to Sir Thomas Hetherington, the director of public prosecutions, but he refused to negotiate. McAvoy and Robinson initially offered to return half the stolen gold. That was said to eventually reduce to 15 hundredweight, worth £6.5 million, if their help was recognised in future Appeal Court and parole board hearings. As more people became involved, news filtered out to the underworld. Lundy described what happened next: 'Other villains started jumping around saying: "Bollocks to them! They've got their bird and they'll just have to do it. If we'd been nicked, we'd have had to put up with it, so that's it: we ain't giving it back!"' Police surveillance suggested that others involved with the robbery, including the Arif family, were opposed to McAvoy's plan to return the gold.

To Ramm, McAvoy appeared desperate for a deal to advance his appeal and get a reduction in his sentence. He clearly did not like being in Leicester jail, where he had been placed in a special high-security wing alongside IRA prisoners. McAvoy eventually asked acquitted robber Tony White to be an intermediary, acting as a go-between between him and the police.

For someone required to handle an increasingly complex and sensitive negotiation, White was an unlikely choice. He was an intimidating figure in an armed robbery but those talents were not hugely transferable to this new task. White met with Robinson and McAvoy in jail, then met with the police to discuss the parameters of the possible deal. The meetings between White and the police were not overly successful. It was obvious to Worth and Ramm that White was uncomfortable in his role. He would fail to turn up for meetings or arrive drunk and struggling to put together a sentence. Rather than negotiating, he tried to obfuscate. Whenever he referred to the gold, he dropped hints that it had gone away, that the deal was not possible. The police had White under surveillance while he was acting for McAvoy and thought other people involved in the robbery were putting a halt to any deal. McAvoy may have believed that he controlled half the gold but it was becoming increasingly clear that he had little actual control of what happened outside Leicester jail. There was a risk that the others involved may simply step in and take what he thought was his, leaving him with nothing and unable to do the deal he so desperately wanted to reduce his long sentence.

By January 1986, McAvoy was becoming increasingly worried that he had been betrayed. He asked his girlfriend, Kathleen Meacock, to try to find out what was happening. In a letter beginning 'Hello mate', believed to have been intended for Brian Perry and thought to have been passed to Meacock in a parting kiss, an increasingly paranoid McAvoy wrote: 'I know it sounds unbelievable that one of our own was thinking of a private trade to get the reward money and the licence off the police to walk about.' McAvoy said that it would be signing his own 'deaf' warrant. He went on: 'If he believes we are away too long to worry about – well, that will already be done for me! It is our share we are talking about here and really you and Fatty out there, he should not even think about holding us up here.' He then closed the letter with: 'I was told you had so much under control […] If that is right, why delay now? Or if you don't have it, why did Fatty say you did? […] I won't have anyone else keeping my share for their own needs. It seems someone's getting a lot of interest – well, not from mine he fucking won't! All I want is for you to make sure we are not fucked and the game is played here – otherwise it's another 14 years of this.'

In March 1986, Worth and Ramm received a call from White requesting another meeting. This time, he would be joined by an associate. Worth and Ramm were growing sceptical that a deal would ever materialise and demanded assurances that the meeting would bring some progress. They arranged to meet at the National Theatre on London's South Bank on 25 March 1986, a location that might appear incongruous but was just a few miles from the south-east London criminal heartlands. When the day arrived, Worth and Ramm sat at a café table drinking coffee, waiting for White and his associate to turn up. When they did, they immediately recognised Brian Perry from police surveillance photographs in the Operation Kate files.

The police knew Perry as a major south London criminal fixer who had been behind the attempt to free McAvoy from jail as well as threats against Robin Riseley during the robbery trial. The men began to talk, Perry puffing on a cigar, with the conversation taped by a police wire. White told them that the gold had been 'dealt for'. Ramm asked him what he meant. 'Well, as I said, it's been dealt for, you know?' he repeated. 'It's been traded.' Worth and Ramm were surprised and asked for clarification. Had all the gold gone, had it been converted into cash? 'It's been dealt for. I mean, Micky thinks he's in control of it, but he ain't.' Worth and Ramm sat for a few moments, taking in what this meant.

Perry took over. Where White had been vague, he was direct and to the point. 'Listen, it's no good being in there and trying to keep everything for yourself, right? Once that cell door's closed, what's he got to trade with? Micky's out of touch, he's not in control. He might think he is, but he's not. They're away. They're out of the loop.' He made a gesture that suggested McAvoy was not in his right mind. Perry's confident assertion confirmed what Worth and Ramm had begun to fear: McAvoy no longer controlled the gold.

As theatre-goers chatted over coffee, the detectives probed Perry further, keen to establish as much as they could. Perry was clear: 'Micky's not in control, things have moved on out here, the deal can't be done.' Worth and Ramm tried to get him to say more but he dodged and hedged. Perry rose to their suggestions just once: 'Suppose it could come back but it wasn't as it was when it got nicked?' The detectives asked him what he meant. 'Well, just suppose it wasn't in the same form.' The detectives had been pursuing the stolen gold, not the proceeds, but they were willing to change tack if it meant they could stop the vast amount of money getting into criminals' hands. 'Providing we can be sure that we are getting the proceeds of the Brink's-Mat robbery, then we're relaxed,' said Worth. 'What we're not about doing is copping £12 or £13 million from someone that might be the proceeds of a separate crime.' When they tried to nudge this suggestion further, Perry dodged some more, saying any such deal would have to be much later.

Ramm returned to the fact that McAvoy himself was no longer in control of the Brink's-Mat gold. 'If he hasn't got possession,' said

Ramm, 'then he is in trouble.' White grunted in affirmation and with that, the meeting ended. 'Well, this is it,' White said. 'Have a nice day.' Perry and White stood up and walked off. Following the meeting, Perry was placed under much closer police surveillance.

Confirmation of McAvoy's slipping control over the gold came from a further, surprising source. When the police visited Kathleen Meacock, they claim that she told them, 'Micky can't get it back – he's lost control.' According to the police, Meacock also said the gold had been hidden under the floorboards of a house in Dalston, east London, owned by an elderly couple. The only additional information the police had was that the husband was dying of cancer. It was a tantalising clue but the house – and the gold – was never traced.

In the weeks after the National Theatre meeting, Worth and Ramm made a final visit to McAvoy and Robinson in Leicester jail. McAvoy was subdued and angry. Ramm came quickly to the point: the deal was off. He told them what had been said by White and Perry. McAvoy was enraged. He asked why Perry had been present. Ramm told him they did not know and suggested that McAvoy tell them instead. Ramm relayed Perry's words to him. McAvoy asked the detectives, 'Where is the gold, what has Perry done with it?' The detectives could tell him nothing, they knew as little as he did. They rose from the table, the meeting over. As McAvoy was led away, the police claimed that McAvoy shouted back at them, 'Tell Brian Perry to mind his own fucking business and stop having affairs.' Since McAvoy's arrest, his marriage had ended and Perry had set up home with McAvoy's ex-wife, Jacqueline.

Having admitted that he controlled half the gold, McAvoy knew that his appeal was now doomed. He and Robinson dropped their appeals and the two men settled into the rest of their long sentences. It has been suggested that McAvoy did not take his setbacks lightly, including reports that he spoke to IRA inmates in Leicester prison about commissioning revenge attacks on those who had wronged him. What actions he might have taken as a result are a matter of debate, with possible repercussions extending far into the future.

For Brian Boyce and his team, the talks with McAvoy were ultimately another dead end and a new entry in an ongoing series of disappointments. By then, it was not the first or even the most painful setback the Brink's-Mat inquiry had encountered. Elsewhere, however, the police had the chance they had been waiting for. An opportunity to reverse their fortune. And, in their eyes, an opportunity for justice.

CHAPTER SEVENTEEN

A Murder Trial

In late November 1985, the Brink's-Mat robbery returned to the Old Bailey for Kenneth Noye and Brian Reader's trial for the murder of Detective Constable John Fordham. Security was intense. When Noye and Reader came and went from the court, the surrounding streets were closed with armed police posted at vantage points. The jury received twenty-four-hour police guards and intercepts on their telephones. The trial played out to full press benches and a packed gallery, which included several well-known criminal faces, and would last for sixteen days.

The lead barrister for the prosecution was Nicholas Purnell QC, who had only recently become a QC. Noye's defence team were familiar from the robbery trial twelve months previously. He had instructed Henry Milner as his solicitor and in court was represented by John Mathew QC and Ronald Thwaites QC, the same barristers who had defended White successfully in the robbery trial.

The murder charge against Brenda Noye did not survive the committal hearing. While dismissing the charge, the magistrate, George Bathurst Norman, said, 'The only evidence against her is her presence at the time Fordham was on the ground. It is not surprising that she was at the scene. If someone comes into your

premises, it is not surprising that you go to see who that person is.'
For the prosecution, it was a hint of the difficulties that were to come.
For Boyce and his team, there was another, separate, concern. That
Noye might have other defences, and other connections, available
other than those made in court.

While Noye was waiting on remand for the trial to begin, officers from Scotland Yard spoke with him again in a series of secret
meetings about the gold. What exactly happened has never been
made clear. One suggestion is that Detective Inspector Ray Adams
from the Flying Squad approached Deputy Assistant Commissioner
Brian Worth and asked that he be allowed to speak with Noye, as he
had him as a registered informant. At the time, Adams had not been
publicly linked with Noye. Officers thought it would not be a bad
idea to see if Noye was willing to talk about the gold, especially as he
had a murder charge hanging over him. It was agreed that Detective
Inspector Ian Brown would be given the job of escorting Noye from
Brixton prison to a remand hearing at Lambeth magistrates court
and that he would surreptitiously approach Noye to establish if he
would speak with Adams. Brown later said he 'felt at that stage that
it might be a major breakthrough'. Brown spoke with Noye in early
March and the meeting with Adams was set up.

Although he was in charge of the inquiry, Boyce was not told
until a decision to allow the meeting had already been taken. He was
aware of the dangers involved but hoped it might result in information that would lead to the recovery of the stolen gold. Adams and
Brown had two meetings with Noye in the cells at Lambeth magistrates court on 21 and 28 March 1985. What was discussed at those
meetings is unclear.

After the second meeting, Adams spoke with Boyce and told him
Noye would say nothing. Later, it was alleged that Noye had offered

Adams a large payment if he helped corrupt the Brink's-Mat inquiry from the inside, though this was never substantiated. Boyce later felt that the decision to allow Adams to meet with Noye was a mistake and it only added to his concerns going into the trial.

One of Boyce's other worries was the charges themselves. Behind the scenes, there had been debate about whether Noye and Reader should face a murder or manslaughter charge. A decision was taken to proceed with the murder charge; the ten stab wounds on Fordham's body were thought sufficient to show an intent to kill. There was also a feeling that a judge would want the prosecution to be clear about the crimes the defendants were accused of committing. Perhaps confident that no jury would acquit a man of murdering a police office, the prosecution opted for murder or nothing, with no option for manslaughter as an alternative verdict. The defence team thought it was a mistake. They weren't alone. Privately, Boyce had concerns that a murder charge would almost inevitably lead to Noye claiming self-defence and felt that, given the circumstances in which Fordham was killed, with no eyewitnesses, a manslaughter charge might be easier to prosecute. Murder, Boyce felt, would be hard to prove beyond all reasonable doubt in a highly contested criminal trial.

He was right.

• • •

The trial began on 21 November 1985. The two defendants sat in the dock flanked by four wardens. Noye wore a grey suit and maroon paisley tie, clutched ring binders under his arm and was said to watch proceedings looking arrogant and slightly amused. Reader was said to sit with a worried frown, smiling only occasionally. As the jury were sworn in, Noye turned to look at each one as they answered their name.

A MURDER TRIAL

The prosecution set out the reasons that police suspicion had fallen on Noye, which led to the surveillance operation on his home. They argued that, alerted by his barking dogs, Noye had discovered Fordham and had assaulted him with a knife, stabbing him ten times. The number and severity of the wounds, they said, showed Noye intended to kill and that he was willing to do so to protect himself and the Brink's-Mat gold he was sheltering. They argued that when police had apprehended him, Noye had said, 'I took the knife from him and did him. Old Bill or no, he had no fucking business being here.'

This straightforward beginning to the trial took an unusual turn when the defence raised an objection to the prosecution's use of a video and photographs of the grounds of Hollywood Cottage that had been taken in daylight. With Fordham's death having occurred in darkness, the defence claimed the materials were misleading. To the prosecution's surprise, the judge ordered that the court should be taken to Hollywood Cottage that evening at dusk.

That evening, the jury were driven in three limousines from central London to West Kingsdown, where they were met by a group of newspaper and television reporters, causing the jurors to hide their faces in their coats. A convoy of police vehicles arrived, escorting a green prison van containing Noye.

The scene was surreal. On a dark and cold winter night, in the middle of a heavy rainstorm, the Old Bailey was formally reconvened on the driveway of Hollywood Cottage. The entire court was present: the judge, wearing a bowler hat; the clerk; counsel for both sides; solicitors; and the official court shorthand writer, who sheltered beneath an umbrella as he noted everything that was said. Noye stood handcuffed to one of four prison guards and was permanently escorted by four police officers. At the house, Brenda Noye, her two sons and another woman waved forlornly from a window.

The large group of reporters were warned not to take pictures of the jury and were instructed by the judge to follow at a discreet distance as the court and jury were shown the grounds of the property. Before they set off, Brenda provided a coat and a pair of wellington boots for Noye, which he put on after they had been checked by police. The procession proceeded through the driving rain by torchlight. 'Some of the women jurors were ill-equipped for the tramp through the rain,' one report read. 'Two were wearing high heels and another had only a cardigan over a thin summer dress.'

In preparation for the trial, Milner had visited Noye's home to take photographs of a friend of Noye's standing in the shrubbery wearing a balaclava and camouflage clothing similar to those worn by Fordham. It was agreed that he would be present at Hollywood Cottage during the jury's visit and that the jury would see him dressed in the same way in the same location with a torch shining in his face. 'Even though everyone knew it was coming,' Milner recalled, 'it was still quite terrifying.' When the man appeared 'with the wind howling and the moon flitting through the trees, it put the fear of God into everybody,' Mathew remembered.

For Noye's defence, it had been a worthwhile exercise.

• • •

The prosecution called Neil Murphy. With no counselling and little psychological or emotional support available from the Metropolitan Police, two months after his close colleague had been killed, Murphy had suffered a breakdown. A colleague told the press, 'Neil had tremendous guilt feelings that he had left John to die. What we didn't recognise was that, being a single man, he had no one to go home to and talk it through with. He had just four bare walls. He bottled it all up and it all got on top of him and he cracked up. It has taken a lot of courage for him to turn up at court and relive it all and be cross-questioned about it.'

On the stand, Murphy recounted that he had seen Fordham on the ground being threatened by a man with a shotgun. A succession of police colleagues gave the same account. The defence did not dispute that Noye had killed Fordham but, as expected, argued that he did so in self-defence. From the outset, their wider strategy was clear. They argued that police statements were not truthful and that Noye was the victim of wholesale and coordinated police verballing. In addition, Mathew was relentless in picking out inconsistencies and contradictions in police officers' statements, and in challenging their version of events. Finally, they challenged what police claimed was the operational plan in place that evening.

While the prosecution argued that Murphy and Fordham had entered Noye's property to execute a warrant, the defence inferred that it was an illegal surveillance operation that had gone wrong. As the succession of police officers gave evidence, Mathew combed through their statements, suggesting inaccuracies and distortions at every turn. He cast doubt on Detective Constable David Manning's claim that Fordham had told him, 'He's done me. He stabbed me.' He grilled Detective Sergeant Anthony Yeoman, who claimed Noye had said, 'I took the knife from him and did him,' forcing Yeoman to admit that he was 'very distressed' when it happened. A balaclava was shown by the prosecution that had a large, single opening for the eyes. It was torn and frayed. Noye had said that he had seen only Fordham's eyes, and that the balaclava had two smaller openings for the eyes. The defence later got a scientist who had examined Fordham's clothing to admit that when she had first handled it, the balaclava had looked different to how it did in court. Over and over, Mathew picked holes in the police statements, casting a pall of doubt over everything they said.

The evidence provided by the pathologist, Dr Rufus Crompton, was crucial. Under questioning by Purnell for the prosecution, Crompton explained the wounds found on Fordham's body. It was powerful, detailed evidence. One wound in the armpit could only have been made if Fordham's arm had been held aloft. There were no obvious signs of grappling and no defence wounds on Fordham's hands. When photographs of Fordham's injuries were shown to the jury, one of the female jurors became visibly distressed. But when he was cross-examined by Mathew, Crompton seemed to suggest that if Noye had been hit in the eye by Fordham, it was likely to have happened before he received the first stab wound. Crompton later told the journalist Andrew Hogg that Mathew misrepresented his answer, but the damage had been done. The defence could say that Fordham had struck first. It was a huge blow for the prosecution. One of their key witnesses had effectively been turned into a defence witness.

Brian Boyce took the stand on 28 November. He explained the police operation and described his interview with Noye on Wednesday 30 January 1985. He told the court that he had spoken with Noye alone and outlined what happened: 'He began by asking me if I thought he was a cold-blooded killer. I told him that I didn't know but that as far as I knew there was nothing in his record of that nature.' Then Boyce made the claim that would grab the court's attention. He said that Noye alluded to his wealth and asked how long Boyce had until retiring, before making an offer. 'He said,' Boyce told the court, 'he would put a million pounds in a bank anywhere in the world.' On that revelation, the court was adjourned for lunch. The reporter from the *Evening Standard* rushed to file copy and that afternoon, with Boyce still on the stand, the headline 'I was offered a £1m bribe' landed on the capital's newsstands.

Mathew's cross-examination of Boyce was as challenging as expected. He attacked Boyce for his decision not to let suspects see solicitors, dismissing Boyce's reasoning that solicitors would pass information about the inquiry to others involved in moving the gold. With regards to Boyce's interview with Noye, Mathew poked a hole in Boyce's statement. He suggested that Boyce had talked of his police work in Egypt, which Boyce confirmed, only for Mathew to point out that it was not mentioned in the notes of the interview. When challenged by Mathew over the truthfulness of his account of the attempted bribe, Boyce stated, 'I couldn't be mistaken about being offered a million pounds.'

Mathew had successfully cast doubt on the police's version of events and pushed the impression that the police had established a line in the aftermath of an operation gone disastrously and tragically wrong, and were sticking to it. The defence's strategy played into the popular concept, developed over years of corruption cases, allegations of police verballing and planted evidence, that the Met was closing ranks to protect itself from criticism, and that the officers of the Flying Squad were disregarding the rules in their pursuit of criminals.

The defence put their case. Noye took the stand and began by arguing that he was not 'a top-class violent villain', as Mathew put it. Noye admitted he 'has not been a saint all of his life', and had been involved with illegal gold dealing, but denied that the gold found at his house had anything to do with the Brink's-Mat robbery. He turned his charm on the jury. A female reporter who followed the Brink's-Mat trials for the *Sun* later said, 'He has one of the most luminous smiles I have ever seen. In a second, it turns him from a stony-faced hard man into a charismatic charmer.'

Noye had a narrative ready to present. The knife that killed Fordham had been used earlier that day to clean his car's battery terminals. When he had gone to investigate his barking dogs, he had retrieved a torch from the car and picked up the knife at the same time, only to ensure his wife did not see it in the car and castigate him for using it for such a purpose. This both explained why he had a knife when he came face to face with Fordham and tied into the defence's picture of Noye as a family man concerned about his wife and children, and not the violent criminal alleged by the prosecution. From a legal perspective, the defence was trying to prove that Noye did not leave the house intending to commit murder, and merely picked up the knife when he went to get the torch from the car. If he did not intend to kill Fordham, he could not be guilty of murder.

Noye said he believed his dogs might have found a group of glue-sniffers who had broken into his grounds or a trapped animal. Instead, his torch beam caught a masked figure standing in the bushes. Noye said he 'froze with horror' and that he thought he was 'going to be a dead man'. He claimed the figure struck him first and he then began to fight for his life, resulting in the injuries suffered by Fordham. His brandishing of the shotgun was to protect his family if the man or others returned.

Noye denied the statements attributed to him by the police officers and claimed that it was only because he was repeatedly denied access to a solicitor that he had not given his version of events. When it came to the allegations of bribery put by Boyce, he was dismissive. He did not even know Boyce's name, he claimed, thinking that he was called 'Mr Walsh'. It had been Boyce, Noye claimed, who had made an offer, not the other way round. Boyce had said he would speak with the Home Secretary to get the charge reduced to manslaughter. Noye was outraged; he was an innocent man, so why would he entertain a charge of manslaughter? It was a memorable point on which to end the defence's questioning of the witness.

By the time Purnell came to question Noye, the jury had been presented with an image of a family man, a bit of a rogue in business, not a stranger to breaking the law, but someone who had acted with justifiable self-defence after finding a masked attacker in his darkened garden. In order to change that perception, Purnell began by questioning Noye on his business dealings. Noye admitted to dealing in gold that was smuggled to avoid tax but denied having anything to do with the stolen Brink's-Mat gold. His gold dealings, he admitted, were conducted in secrecy. At this point, the judge made a joke about Noye not wanting to advertise such activity 'in the Yellow Pages'. A judge joking with the accused is hardly a positive sign for a prosecution, and both they and the watching police realised with alarm that Noye's studied charm was steadily spreading through the court.

Noye explained that he used offshore accounts and shell companies to store his wealth and to reduce his tax liabilities. The jury were not told, however, about the unusual circumstances in which some of these accounts had been opened or of the vast amounts of cash that had been paid into them in the preceding months, or evidence that suggested that Noye knew the Brink's-Mat robber Brian Robinson. Noye denied everything the police claimed he had said. When asked about Manning's statement, where he was reputed to have used the phrase 'Old Bill or no,' Noye calmly told the jury, 'I don't call police officers "Old Bill". I call them cozzers.'

Noye's performance on the stand was exceptional and his natural, confident answers stood in contrast to the stiffness of those given – or read out – by the police officers who appeared for the prosecution. Whereas the police appeared to be guarding their words, carefully managing what they did and did not say, Noye appeared as an ordinary family man caught up in strange and tragic events. There were revelations that suggested otherwise – for instance, most family men don't keep shotguns in the bedroom and cartridges in a bedside cabinet – but these did not detract from the overall impression. By the end of the trial, the prosecution may have been doubting the wisdom of the murder charge. Ultimately, there were no eyewitnesses to the events that led to Fordham's death other than Kenny Noye. As a result, there was no other narrative to offer that had anything like the immediacy of Noye's.

On Friday 6 December 1985, the judge summed up the case for the jury. He told them to put any prejudice from their minds and that it should not count against Noye or Reader that both had admitted to dealing in illegal gold. He told them they could not find Noye guilty of manslaughter as an alternative to murder. He recalled the jury's visit to Hollywood Cottage at the start of the trial: 'Were those beautiful grounds desecrated by the vicious murder of a man,' he asked, 'or was the man killed lawfully because he was an aggressor who had petrified the owner, and the owner – almost paralysed with fear – killed him and, in his terror, stabbed him not once, twice or thrice, but ten times, not only in the front, but also in the back, not only in the torso but also in the scalp?' It was a matter for the jury to decide if Noye was a truthful witness, he told them, but he urged them to 'remember the mask'.

The jury was sent to consider its verdict at a secret London hotel. When, after five hours, the foreman said they could not reach a verdict, the judge told them that they were under no pressure to reach one. Amid the tension, proceedings briefly grew farcical when a female juror said she had toothache. In what was thought to be a legal precedent, court administrators arranged for her to have treatment. Two court ushers were sworn to prevent her from talking about the case with the dentist and the other eleven jurors were forbidden from discussing it while she was away.

On Thursday 12 December, after twelve hours and thirty-seven minutes' deliberation, the jury told the judge that they had reached verdicts on both men. The court was packed as the foreman delivered the verdicts. Reader was not guilty. That was not an enormous surprise. Then came the verdict on Noye. By a ten-to-two majority, the jury found Noye not guilty.

There were screams of joy from Brenda Noye and Lyn Reader in the public gallery. Noye smiled, then said to the jury: 'Thank you, ten of you. May God bless ten of you forever for that is what I am, not guilty.' Reader turned to the jury and said, 'Thank you for proving my innocence.' Noye turned to the Flying Squad officers assembled in the court and mouthed, 'Fuck the lot of you.' He grinned as he left the dock.

In a statement read out by her solicitor, Brenda Noye said she felt 'great sympathy' for John Fordham's family but that 'the responsibility for Mr Fordham's death is on the shoulders of others, and not my husband'. In a press conference later, while Noye's family celebrated the verdict at a nearby wine bar, Ann Fordham responded to Brenda Noye's sympathy. 'Not accepted,' she said.

For the police, it was a devastating blow. They had various concerns over aspects of the trial, centring largely on the jury, but none of their suspicions were ever proven. Later that afternoon, Assistant Commissioner John Dellow held a press conference at which he praised Fordham and defended the decisions taken on the night. He was, he said, 'satisfied that the operation was as properly and professionally conducted as it could have been'. Despite this, the press who had followed the trial were highly critical of the police and raised questions about the operation. As the *Observer* put it, 'The collapse of the court case exposed a catalogue of errors in one of its major operations this year and, more seriously, disclosed publicly for the first time the fragile legal basis of its secret work.' More subtly, the case raised questions about the conduct of police prosecutions and the questioning of suspects and collection of evidence, while also highlighting how police-surveillance operations often operated at the very edge of the law.

For Boyce, it seemed as though many at Scotland Yard were keen to distance themselves from him. The criticism of the operation was hard to bear. That evening, he spoke with all the officers involved with the inquiry. There was no possibility of an appeal, so he outlined his plans for the future. Starting the next day, they would focus on getting convictions in the gold-handling case. He offered any officer who wished to transfer off the case the opportunity to do so without any criticism. No one left.

The police had lost a battle but were doubly determined to eventually win the war. Noye remained in custody, with his handling charge still to come. As the police attention moved to the charges against the Gold Chain, it was hard to ignore the missing link.

It was time to bring Goldfinger home.

CHAPTER EIGHTEEN

Desperado

By May 1985, John Palmer's exile in Tenerife had become both lucrative and lonely. Marnie and their two young children had returned to England, with Marnie's solicitor, Philip Albery, telling the ever-attentive press that Palmer was staying in Tenerife to pursue his business interests and because he knew he would be arrested if he returned. Through Albery, Marnie explained that Palmer was staying on the island 'to earn enough money to keep us'.

Palmer's business ambitions in Tenerife were on a grander scale than a simple attempt to meet his domestic demands. He had become entranced with the concept of holiday timeshares, the building of cheap holiday accommodation that could then be sold on a weekly basis, fifty-two times over the year, to generate huge profits. He began to make plans and contacts on the island, his entrepreneurial zeal undimmed by being one of Britain's most wanted men. His activity was reported by the press, with articles suggesting that Palmer hoped to make £80 million within four years with his new venture. Left unsaid was that the operation would likely be funded with part of the proceeds of the Brink's-Mat robbery.

As he plotted in the sunshine, however, Palmer was unaware that Tenerife's sanctuary was not as secure as he thought.

• • •

By the mid-1980s, the absence of an extradition treaty between Britain and Spain was becoming a problem for both governments. The issue dated back to 1978, when the Spanish government failed to ratify a revised extradition treaty with Britain, accusing the British of not doing enough to present those wanted by the Spanish authorities. Estimates in the 1980s suggested that up to a hundred Britons suspected of involvement in major crimes were living openly on a stretch of the Costa del Sol that had become known as the 'Costa del Crime', often in lavish villas and safe in the knowledge that they could not be sent home to face justice. This stretch of the Spanish coast had become a home from home for British criminals, where they ate English food, drank English beer and watched English television beamed in from Gibraltar. It had also been dubbed 'Bethnal Green-on-Sea.'

Neither government was happy with the situation and by spring 1985, when Palmer decided to stay in Tenerife, they were close to agreement on new arrangements. In July 1985, a new treaty was signed to come into effect in the autumn of that year. Under Spanish law, the treaty could not be retrospectively applied to anyone who had settled in Spain before it came into force. To address this loophole, the Spanish government passed a tough aliens' law that made it easier to exclude 'undesirable foreigners'. In part, the law was designed to rid the country of suspected British criminals who could not be touched by the new extradition treaty.

The chief of the Policia Nacional's Foreigners' Department in Marbella, where many Brits lived, told a British newspaper, 'No one wants them here. Their lives will be made insupportable. In two years, the idea of the Costa del Sol being a haven for crooks will be just a memory.' The new regulations were introduced on 31 January 1986. Spain asked the British Home Office to draw up a list of their twenty most wanted men who were sheltering in Spain. On the list, likely near the top, was John Palmer.

Palmer's problems began with his passport. Among the new regulations brought in at the end of January 1986 by the Spanish aliens' law was a requirement that foreigners who wanted to stay in Spain had to have a valid passport. Palmer's passport expired two days before Christmas 1985. He tried to renew it at the British Consulate in Las Palmas but was refused on the grounds that police in Britain wanted to question him. Palmer was told that an emergency travel document could be issued but would only be valid for a trip to Britain. For obvious reasons, Palmer refused that offer.

From then on, Palmer was a target for the Spanish authorities, yet his chutzpah remained intact. Despite having an expulsion order hanging over him, Palmer was said to be convinced he was safe and continued to live in Tenerife for another six months as he set about creating his embryonic timeshare business.

His luck ran out on Saturday 28 June 1986, when Palmer became the first Briton ordered to leave by the Spanish authorities under the new law. The Spanish news agency EFE reported that police escorted Palmer to the airport and told him to go. Palmer was not a man to take defeat lightly. When given a choice of destination, Palmer saw one last opportunity to escape British justice. He would follow the example of another British criminal that the tabloids had taken to their heart, the Great Train Robber Ronnie Biggs, who had lived in untroubled exile in Rio de Janeiro since 1970. Palmer told the Spanish authorities that he wanted to fly to Brazil.

Palmer boarded a flight to Madrid that would connect to a Varig Brazilian Airlines flight to Rio de Janeiro. With Brazil not having an extradition treaty in place with Britain, Palmer had reason to be confident in this latest dodging of the British police. However, the reach of Scotland Yard is long and often hidden, with senior Met officers often maintaining contacts within the intelligence services. Brian Boyce, with his history of counter-terrorism work, was one of them.

The Brazilian authorities received word that Palmer was on his way and swooped into action. Palmer might have legally been allowed to stay in Brazil but he had to get in first. When his plane arrived in Rio de Janeiro, Palmer was refused entry into the country and held by Brazilian police at the federal police headquarters while his case was investigated. He was told that he would not be allowed to enter Brazil and would have to leave. The Brazilian authorities maintained that he was being refused entry to the country simply because his passport had expired. They denied there was any pressure from their British counterparts. It was hard to believe. The press described Palmer as 'the centrepiece in a huge international police operation in which diplomats tried to ensure his return to Britain. Scotland Yard detectives had been working closely with the Spanish police monitoring his movements.'

On 1 July 1986, Palmer bought a ticket for Varig Brazilian Airlines flight 706 from Rio de Janeiro to London Heathrow. By now, the media had caught up with events. A Brazilian police spokesman, Giovanni Azevedo, told reporters that he had spoken with Palmer before he left. Palmer had said that a 'small problem' awaited him, and that, 'I think I may have some trouble in London.' When asked if it was to do with the Brink's-Mat robbery, he reportedly said, 'Yes, the press has tried to accuse me of that, but I had nothing to do with it.' Palmer signed a declaration to say that he was leaving for London voluntarily. Brazilian police escorted Palmer to the airport and he remained under police guard until shortly before the plane took off.

The DC-10 carrying Palmer arrived at Heathrow at 12.35pm on Wednesday 2 July 1986. After the plane had landed, an announcement was made over the internal speakers asking Palmer to identify himself. Minutes later, two airport security men boarded the plane and asked Palmer to accompany them. As Palmer walked onto the gangway, he found a group of detectives waiting. The Brink's-Mat task force's Detective Chief Inspector Ken John formally arrested Palmer, who was then driven in an unmarked car to Kennington police station, close to the task force's headquarters at Tintagel House, for questioning. A stewardess told the press that Palmer had sat in an economy seat, had appeared preoccupied during the flight and had greatly enjoyed the inflight move, a Western called *The Desperado*.

Palmer's capture received major coverage in the British newspapers but he had competition for the front pages. As Palmer sat in Kennington police station in south London, a few miles across the city, his former associate was once again earning media attention.

Kenny Noye was back at the Old Bailey.

CHAPTER NINETEEN

Confessions of
a Smuggler

In early May 1986, the Brink's-Mat case returned to the Old Bailey
for the gold-handling trials. After spending five months on remand in
prison, Noye was charged jointly with Brian Reader, Garth Chappell,
Terence Patch, Thomas Adams, Matteo Constantino and Michael
Lawson of conspiracy to handle the stolen Brink's-Mat gold. All but
Lawson faced a second charge of conspiracy to evade VAT payments
on the gold. The absent Christopher Weyman, Derek Larkins and
John Palmer were not charged but referred to as having been co-conspirators. Brenda Noye was listed as a co-conspirator on just the
handling charge. As in the murder trial, Noye was the principal defendant. He was accused of coordinating the gold-smelting operation,
and if the jury could not agree that he was guilty of the charge then it
could not convict the others. For the embattled Brink's-Mat task force
the challenge was clear. They had to get Noye or get nothing.

As with the previous Brink's-Mat trials, significant security
measures were put in place. The members of the predominantly
young jury were given police protection, guarded by court bailiffs
throughout the trial and asked by Judge Richard Lowry QC to be

'fair, decisive and courageous'. The prosecution case was led by the experienced Michael Corkery QC, while Noye had once again retained Henry Milner and John Mathew QC.

Noye and his team were confident. The defence saw the evidence connecting Noye to the stolen Brink's-Mat gold as circumstantial at best. Noye and the other defendants had clearly been involved in substantial illegal gold dealings, but that crime and the relatively short prison sentences it would attract was not being disputed.

The prosecution got to work on proving the far more serious crime that the illegal gold was part of the Brink's-Mat haul. Corkery told the court that the Brink's-Mat gold had been disguised by Noye and others, then taken on a 'gold run' to Bristol to be sold back into the gold trade by Scadlynn, with the proceeds withdrawn from Scadlynn's bank account in cash, totalling £10 million in a matter of weeks. Corkery outlined the roles within the Gold Chain. From his house at West Kingsdown, Noye would release small parcels of gold to Reader, who would take it to London and pass it on to Adams, Weyman and Larkins, who couriered it to Chappell and Palmer in Bristol. They smelted the gold at Scadlynn and Palmer's home so it could be sold into the legitimate gold market. Constantino was accused of providing bogus documentation to give the gold 'an honest history' and Lawson was accused of providing smelting equipment.

The prosecution detailed how, during 1984 and early 1985, Noye had deposited substantial sums of money in cash into various bank accounts, and how that money had been funnelled into accounts held abroad, sometimes under false names. He paid in over £1.5 million into the Bank of Ireland in Croydon between September 1984 and January 1985. Staff at the bank remembered him because he brought the money in suitcases, and because he was wearing 'a spectacular gold watch with diamonds set in it'. Noye had been wearing a gold Rolex with diamonds set around the face when he was arrested following the death of John Fordham. He had also deposited large sums in cash at the Royal Bank of Canada in the City of London and at Barclays Bank, Dartford, and had travelled to Zurich and dealt with a bank there. The prosecution alleged that the money was generated by the sale of the stolen gold.

It was a confident opening from the prosecution but they soon hit problems. Although a police forensic scientist, John Williams, gave evidence that the gold bars found at Hollywood Cottage were of a suitable purity to have been part of the Brink's-Mat gold, a second expert disagreed. John Williams, a bullion instruction manager at Johnson Matthey, testified that due to purity and composition issues, those particular gold bars could not have come from Johnson Matthey and therefore could not have been those stolen from the Heathrow depot.

It got worse for the prosecution when Martin Coomber, a director of Charterhouse Japhet in Jersey, took to the stand. A significant part of the prosecution's case was that Noye had used the receipt for the gold he bought in Jersey as cover for moving the disguised Brink's-Mat gold back in England and, to allow him to do so, Noye had specifically asked that the Jersey receipt not show the bars' serial numbers. According to Coomber, Noye had in fact asked that the serial numbers be shown on the receipt, to protect his investment if the bars turned out not to be fine gold. Mathew went on to point out that Noye had left the receipt in Jersey, in the safe-deposit box with the gold.

Mathew was equally dismissive about the smelter instruction manual found at Noye's house, grilling the police officer who found it about apparent discrepancies in his account of the discovery, and batting away the suggestion that the smelter Michael Lawson was transporting was intended for Noye – a fact that the police had never been able to prove. Watching proceedings in the courtroom, Boyce and his colleagues felt a familiar, creeping concern that their case against Noye was being steadily weakened by Mathew. Not for the last time in the Brink's-Mat investigation, it was their new-found friends in HM Customs and Excise who would come to the rescue.

The Brink's-Mat detectives had invited Customs to examine the paperwork seized from the defendants. Just five days before the end of the prosecution case, the cooperation paid off, with Customs investigators providing Corkery with new evidence about how the gold-smelting operation worked. Their comprehensive analysis appeared to show a pattern of gold dealing that could be tied to the stolen gold, while they also highlighted the significance of financial documents that the Scotland Yard detectives had overlooked. It was a crucial intervention, with one defence lawyer telling a reporter that the Customs investigators 'pulled it out of the fire for the police'.

Noye's defence team deployed the same tactics that had been so successful in previous trials, with Mathew swiftly explaining away circumstantial evidence and proving ruthless in questioning the veracity of any police statement. His fiercest attacks were on the accounts of police interviews with Noye. Mathew said Noye had been denied access to a solicitor, that no notes had been taken during lengthy interviews, and yet later, detailed, incriminating notes had been produced by the police on 'a verbatim conversation of over fifty minutes' which Mathew suggested was 'born of incredible feats of memory or the fertile and practised imagination' of the police. Mathew pointed out factual errors, such as the police assertion that Noye took a private jet to Jersey when he was recorded as flying on a chartered airline, and concluded that this was all yet another example of police verballing. Noye, Mathew summarised, was being stitched up by the police who had planted evidence and invented confessions.

Bolstered by his acquittal in the murder trial and the apparently positive direction the handling trial was taking, Noye opted to appear as a witness for his own defence. It was at this point in the case that many observers believed the tide began to turn. Noye's unshakeable confidence had brought him great wealth and opportunity but, on the witness stand at the Old Bailey, it would lead in part to his undoing. Boyce would later recall that 'Noye destroyed himself in the witness box'.

• • •

In the austere surroundings of the courtroom, Noye told a colourful story. He briskly admitted that he had been illegally dealing in gold since 1976 but insisted none of the gold in his possession had come from the Brink's-Mat robbery. His obvious wealth, Noye explained, came from a sizeable, and somewhat complicated, smuggling operation that had been in operation for several years.

Noye told the court that it all began when he met a man called Lorenzo in Barcelona, who had gold contacts in Rwanda. Noye did a deal with a company in Kuwait to receive and refine the gold from Rwanda. Using the alias Sidney Harris, Noye then sold it through an office in Eindhoven where he had installed a West German smelter in the basement. When two Americans, who Noye met on holiday and developed a business relationship with, heard about the Dutch gold operation, they told Noye that they had contacts with a Brazilian company who were smuggling gold into Belgium with the knowledge of the Brazilian military government. Noye incorporated the Brazilians into his existing operation, leading to an arrangement where gold was bought from Brazil and Kuwait to evade tax, then smuggled to the Netherlands, then sold to other dealers, usually Orthodox Jews, in Britain and Europe, who would then add tax when they sold it on the legitimate market and pocket the tax as their profit.

In Noye's view, this impressively convoluted story explained all the evidence that pointed to him being a major dealer in illegal gold. The first problem for Noye was that he refused to provide any corroborating evidence, name his partners or produce any records of the transactions. The second issue was the money.

Noye needed to explain his wealth to the court in order to assure the jury that it was not a result of the Brink's-Mat robbery. He did so with trademark gusto. He told the court that in 1982, the combined total of the smuggled gold from Brazil and Kuwait was £20 million and that he made a profit of £1.3 million. The following year, the year of the Brink's-Mat robbery, Noye said that he made £1.6 million profit on trade of £32 million and, in 1984, the year of John Fordham's death, he made £1.5 million.

Noye also admitted that over this period, he had been dealing with Reader on large-scale gold handling. Noye told the court that he supplied Reader with £3.6 million worth of gold during January 1985, which he claimed was smuggled into Britain from the Netherlands in lorry drivers' Tupperware lunch boxes. 'There was no difficulty at all in smuggling 20 or 30kg of gold from Holland,' Noye insisted. 'The quantity was no problem at all.' Noye refused to provide the names of the lorry drivers who were driving around Europe with what must have been particularly heavy lunch boxes.

The other defendants either backed up Noye's story or said nothing at all. Reader told the court that the gold was being smuggled into Britain from 'an Arab country'. Chappell maintained he had purchased the gold from Matteo Constantino. Patch said he knew nothing about any shady dealings. Adams did not take the stand at all, with his barrister saying he had no idea of the contents of the packages he handled. Nor did Lawson give evidence, with his barrister telling the court an alleged admission that the smelter had been bought for Noye was a police fabrication. Constantino denied all the charges against him.

In short, Noye's defence was that in the years after the Brink's-Mat robbery, he handled a huge amount of gold as the leader of a handling network and made a vast amount of money as a result, but that none of the gold involved had come from Unit 7 of the Brink's-Mat depot at the Heathrow Trading Estate.

The prosecution rested on a simple summary. They had shown a swathe of supporting evidence that pushed Noye's position into the realms of impossibility, while Noye had not produced 'one shred of independent evidence' to support his explanations. Now it was in the hands of the jury.

In keeping with the occasionally absurdist touches of the court proceedings, the jury's deliberations were marked by an unlikely backdrop of lurid rumours. The largely youthful jury were booked into an £80-a-night London hotel, but on the Sunday were given a day out in a country hotel to assist with their complicated deliberations. It was suggested that they found some time around their duties for recreation, with rumours of sexual relationships and drunkenness. It was also said that one juror was himself on the run from the police. These stories reached the judge who ordered an inquiry, which concluded that the reports were unsubstantiated rumours.

After five days and thirty-six hours of deliberation, the jury returned to court with a verdict on Wednesday 23 July 1986. By a ten-to-two majority, the jurors found Noye guilty on both counts. Reader and Chappell were found guilty of both counts. Constantino was found guilty of conspiracy to evade VAT, while Lawson, Patch and Adams were found not guilty.

A jury may have been prepared to believe that Noye was an innocent homeowner confronted by a mysterious, threatening and masked figure in the gloom of his garden, but they had taken less kindly to an international gold smuggler who readily admitted large-scale criminal activity. Some of those present in court thought that Noye's brashness had been a key factor. Andrew Hogg of the *Sunday Times* wrote, 'Veering between candid roguishness and injured innocence, Noye's performance was to fall entirely flat on the listening court – a fact that the prisoner didn't discern until it was all over.'

As the verdicts were read out, there was furore in the court room. Scuffles broke out in the gallery between members of the public and the police, and the judge struggled to be heard. Lyn Reader and Brenda Noye burst into tears, with Brenda shouting from the public gallery, 'Never has such an injustice been done. There is no fucking justice in this trial!' Brian Reader wagged his finger menacingly at the jury and said, 'You have made one terrible mistake. You have got to live with that for the rest of your lives.' His son Paul, later arrested and charged with contempt of court, fought with police officers in the public gallery and shouted, 'You have been fucking fixed up!' Some of the jury were visibly distressed, a situation that will not have been eased when Noye turned to the jurors and shouted, 'I hope you all die of cancer!' Years later, Noye's own QC, John Mathew, would recall his shock at his client's reaction. 'I'd never seen that side of Noye before. His face used to change in a flash. This tough mask would come down and you could see him killing somebody, and the next moment he's an absolute charmer.' At the time, an enraged Mathew told Noye that his behaviour would hardly help when the judge decided the sentence. In the cells afterward, Noye was served with a writ by Customs officers for the £1 million of VAT he had evaded. A six-page writ from Inland Revenue was also served on him, claiming almost £1 million in back tax.

The next day, Noye, Reader, Chappell and Constantino returned to court for sentencing. Noye apologised to the judge for his outburst the previous day 'in the heat of the moment'. The unmoved judge sentenced Noye to a total of sixteen years, Reader nine years, Chappell ten years and Constantino one year, suspended. After the sentencing, Brenda Noye called from the gallery, 'I love you, darling!' Noye blew her a kiss and shouted, 'I love you too.'

Outside the court, there were chaotic, violent scenes as relatives of the convicted men left the court. Brenda Noye was surrounded by burly minders. A photographer working for *The Times* was knocked to the floor and kicked when he attempted to take photographs. The following day, Corkery told the court that the Crown was dropping the charge of conspiracy to handle stolen bullion that had been hanging over Brenda Noye.

For the police, it was a moment of vindication and some small consolation for the failure to convict Noye seven months earlier. It also seeded some of the Brink's-Mat task force's challenges ahead, with Scotland Yard publicly demanding massive changes to the banking system as a result of the evidence shown in court of how easily the proceeds of the Brink's-Mat robbery were being laundered. The revelation that almost £10.5 million had been paid out in cash by the Barclays branch in Bedminster to Scadlynn associates over a five-month period had caused shock and consternation. Brian Boyce had wanted to charge the Barclays manager in Bedminster but was dissuaded after consulting with legal counsel. Prime Minister Margaret Thatcher had been briefed personally on Scotland Yard's concerns, with the expectation that legal changes would be introduced. Chasing the money, Boyce and his team had realised, might be their greatest challenge.

But first they had another task. As the verdict was read out, members of the task force rushed forward to shake Boyce by the hand and tell him, 'Well done, guv'nor.' But Boyce and his senior officers were already focusing on what was to come. Two and a half years after the robbery, they had successfully convicted two of the robbers and four of the smelting gang. There was a long way to go. They needed more results, and that started with John Palmer.

CHAPTER TWENTY

A Little Goldmine

While the trial of Noye and others continued at the Old Bailey, police began questioning their suspected co-conspirator, John Palmer. The interviews began the morning after Palmer returned to Britain. He was defiant from the start. He explained that he was no longer a director of Scadlynn, though could not remember when he resigned. He said he knew nothing of Matteo Constantino and that he used his garden smelter to smelt bullion for legitimate reasons. He was, Palmer explained, essentially a freelance smelter for hire. He admitted smelting gold for Scadlynn but had no idea where it came from. The police continued to struggle, with Palmer denying any knowledge of various pieces of circumstantial evidence. When Customs investigators questioned Palmer about VAT and his connections to Scadlynn, they were similarly frustrated, with Palmer refusing to answer any questions and offering 'no comment' whenever shown a document.

The police interviews were cordial, with Palmer apologising for not being able to offer any significant help. When police showed Palmer a photocopy of a telephone address book from his house on which they claimed to have found a written record of Noye's telephone number, the atmosphere changed. When the police asked why Palmer had Noye's number, Palmer replied, 'This is the last question I will answer. I do not know Kenneth Noye. This is not my handwriting and I do not know how it got there.' With that, Palmer was told that he would be charged with conspiring with Noye, Chappell, Patch, Reader, Adams, Lawson and Constantino to dishonestly handle stolen gold bullion between November 1983 and February 1985.

Between interviews, Palmer and Marnie were reunited for the first time in several months with the couple spending an hour together and Palmer offering words of comfort as they hugged. Marnie, who had been in hiding since news of her husband's return broke, was smuggled out of the police station to avoid press photographers and driven away sobbing on the back seat of a police car. On the way out, she passed a note to a reporter: 'My husband is exhausted. I hope to see him again soon.'

A week later, at Horseferry Road magistrates court, Palmer offered £1.6 million in bail sureties but it wasn't enough to satisfy the judge that Palmer wasn't a flight risk. He was remanded in custody, waving to Marnie as he left the dock for Brixton prison. Because he was on remand and therefore allowed luxuries denied to convicted prisoners, Palmer's time in Brixton prison differed considerably from other inmates. Marnie brought him roast dinners, snacks, magazines, money for phone cards, batteries for his radio and clean clothes. Palmer appointed a new legal team in the form of Henry Milner's firm. Michael Lawson, recently acquitted of the same charges brought against Palmer, acted as an intermediary in attaching Milner to the case. Milner once again turned to John Mathew QC, this time to put Palmer's defence against the charges that he conspired with Noye, Reader and others to dishonestly handle stolen bullion, with a second charge of plotting with the same men to evade VAT on the gold.

Palmer's trial began at the Old Bailey in early March 1987. Christopher Weyman, who had recently returned to the UK and handed himself in, stood alongside Palmer as a co-defendant. Many of the protagonists were familiar from previous Brink's-Mat trials. The judge was Richard Lowry, who had presided over Noye's handling charge. The case for the prosecution was put again by Nicholas Purnell QC. Palmer's defence was the 'A Team' of Milner, Mathew and Thwaites, that had been successful for White in the robbery trial and in Noye's murder trial.

That was not the only note of familiarity. When Purnell set out the case for the prosecution on 9 March 1986, he reached for established themes. Purnell explained once more that the Brink's-Mat robbers did not anticipate that 'their haul was going to bring them £26 million. In order to turn that amount into money, an extremely sophisticated arrangement came into being.'

Noye and Palmer, Purnell said, were at the centre of this arrangement with 'crucial roles to play' while 'great efforts were made to keep [them] in the background'. He walked the jury through the Gold Chain operations with Palmer's role, Purnell said, being to get up every day at 4am, go to his smelter and work long hours to disguise the pure gold by mixing it with other metals. Purnell said that Palmer was one of the 'most shadowy figures' in the sophisticated operation set up to fence the gold, which, 'Ultimately ... achieved the sale back to Johnson Matthey of the stolen gold – so the very losers were deceived into buying back the gold, believing it was genuine gold for sale on the legitimate market.' The re-smelted gold, Purnell explained, was sold in 'lumps' on the open market, leading to vast profits for Scadlynn, protected by false invoices provided by Matteo Constantino, who was by now dead. The telephone-code book that police claimed to have found in Palmer's house with Noye's number written on it was proof, the prosecution alleged, that Palmer knew Noye. And then there was Palmer's smelter, that was hidden 'down by a horse box in the back bushes of his home'. 'What better place,' asked Purnell of the courtroom, 'for the melting of the Brink's-Mat gold?'

Palmer's defence stuck rigidly to his opening position in the police-interview rooms. He had taken on smelting work for Scadlynn but had no idea where the gold came from and did not know that it was stolen. He claimed not to have known Noye nor any of the robbers. On the stand, Palmer was calm and consistent. Looking each juror in the eye, he told them, 'I may have touched the gold, melted it down even … But I didn't know where it was from.' He told the jury about his new life in Tenerife, detailing his timeshare scheme that was the fastest-growing development on the island, which he called 'a little gold mine'. The jury warmed to the straight-talking, open persona that Palmer was projecting. Marnie wrote later, 'The jury clearly thought he was a nicer bloke than they did the officers giving evidence against him. [He] cast a spell on them with his charm.'

The defence built on this promotion of Palmer as an everyday family man with an eye for opportunity, but who operated a long way from the world of serious crime. They referred to his media interviews in Tenerife and his referral to the robbery as the 'so-called Mat's-Brink' job, while Marnie testified about Palmer's honesty and legitimate business dealings, telling the jury he worked seven days a week to provide for his family. She denied angrily that her lifestyle, horses and the £19,000 Porsche 944 that had been delivered to her in January 1986 were paid for with money from the Brink's-Mat gold. The defence produced a handwriting expert and Marnie's mother to say that the writing found on the telephone book giving Noye's phone number was not Palmer's, which was a repeat of the accusations of evidence-planting that had characterised Noye's defence.

Towards the end of the trial, it was revealed that a female juror had been at the centre of a nobbling scare. Counsel alerted the judge to the fact that members of the public had been spotted pointing out the woman juror and confided in the judge that a nobbling attempt might be being considered, although they admitted that it could also be nothing of the sort. For the final two days of the trial, the judge ordered round-the-clock armed-police guards for the jury of seven men and five women. A police officer subsequently reported that he had seen Brenda Noye, who had been present at the trial, speaking with a woman the officer thought might be a jury member. Brenda Noye denied it and issued a statement through her solicitor, Ray Burroughs, saying 'these rumours are totally without foundation.' She said, 'I went to court to hear Palmer's evidence. My husband and I have never met Palmer. On the occasions I was at court, I never spoke to any person having any involvement in the case.'

After eighteen days, the trial came to an end, on 1 April 1987. The jury deliberations lasted just two hours and twenty-five minutes. When they returned to court, the jury returned verdicts of not guilty on both the charges levelled against Palmer and Weyman. Marnie shouted for joy as the verdicts were read out and then burst into tears. Weyman's relatives applauded. Palmer blew a kiss to both Marnie and the jury. Weyman and Palmer shook hands and smiled before they were discharged by the judge. Palmer and Marnie drove away from the court in a silver-blue Mercedes.

After the verdict, Milner told reporters that Palmer's family 'were over the moon. His wife always believed in his innocence.' He explained that the only reason Palmer had been hesitant to return from Tenerife was 'because he did not want to remain in custody for over a year waiting trial, which happened to various defendants who stood trial last year.'

The following morning, Palmer spoke with reporters outside his house. With his Range Rover and Marnie's brand-new Porsche 944 in the background, and their Rottweiler guard dogs chained up beside them, he told the waiting press that the verdict had 'restored my faith in British justice. I was never in any doubt that I would be acquitted.' Palmer noted that, 'the judge was terrific', and suggested the police had wanted to frame him for involvement with the robbery. 'I was absolutely innocent of any crime. The police knew it, the jury knew it, everybody knew it,' he declared.

Palmer denied knowing any of those accused of being involved in the Brink's-Mat robbery and its aftermath, claiming he was a victim of police persecution. 'Kenneth Noye is a man I have never met. But if I had stood in the dock with him, I'm sure I wouldn't be free today. I wouldn't have got a fair trial.' When asked why Noye's phone number had been in his contacts book, he told them, 'When the police were searching my house they must have done it themselves. I've never met the man and it wasn't my handwriting.'

Standing outside his house, Palmer lamented that 'the past two years have been torture but I've pulled through. When I was in Tenerife, I wasn't running away, I was just waiting for the right time. I was waiting for the big conspiracy trial involving Noye to finish.' He dismissed the rumours of jury nobbling: 'As far as the so-called jury nobbling is concerned, it's complete nonsense. I have been persecuted by the police and when they realised they were losing the case they put stories like this about. They knew all along I was innocent.'

Palmer told reporters, 'Maybe I'll write a book about all this, there's a lot to tell,' before joking, 'Don't call me Goldfinger any more because I'm finished with jewellery – I'm in the construction business now.' Stories had emerged during the trial that he had begun an affair in Tenerife with a woman called Christina Ketley, but Palmer dismissed them as 'complete nonsense'. A reporter handed Marnie a Terry's All Gold chocolate Easter egg, which she clutched grimly as she and her husband posed for the gathered photographers.

The following day, John Palmer slipped out of Britain and returned to Tenerife, alone.

• • •

Palmer's acquittal gave the Brink's-Mat task force a further dose of what had become an overly familiar combination of disappointment and embarrassment. What eased their frustration was that it came during a period of growing enlightenment.

Tony Lundy's forensic re-examination of the Brink's-Mat investigation's files, along with the now continual cooperation of Customs and other government agencies, was lifting the horizons of the enquiry. What the task force were beginning to appreciate was both exhilarating and intimidating. In Noye, Palmer and the Gold Chain, they had only ever had a partial view of what had happened to the Brink's-Mat gold and the vast criminal proceeds it was generating.

They had seen half the picture. As the other half came steadily into view, it brought new revelations, new worlds and new names.

CHAPTER TWENTY-ONE

The Launderers

The most significant money-laundering operation of the Brink's-Mat criminal proceeds all began with Brian Perry. An old friend of Micky McAvoy, Perry was thought by some to have provided logistics, and maybe transport, for the robbery. Perry found himself in a powerful position after McAvoy's arrest and incarceration. It is believed that Perry passed some of the Brink's-Mat gold to Noye so that it could be smelted and sold back into the market, which might have included McAvoy's share. When the money came back to Perry, it had to be laundered to avoid detection. As often happened in the story of the Brink's-Mat robbery and its aftermath, new criminal alliances needed to be formed, and Perry didn't have far to look. His daughter was in a relationship with the son of a south London businessman called Gordon John Parry. Perry needed someone who had the knowledge, contacts and criminal ambition to launder an enormous amount of money. Some of that he would find with Parry, the rest would be found in the unlikely form of a respected London solicitor.

Born in 1945, Gordon Parry was the son of a south London bookmaker. As a young man, he established a market garden business and worked as a warehouseman at Heathrow Airport. When his father died, Parry took over the chain of betting shops but also became involved in drug smuggling. In 1972, Parry was charged for his role in a major cannabis-smuggling ring that brought over 250kg of hashish with a street value of over £1 million through Heathrow. Using his experience of Heathrow's freight clearance systems, Parry devised a method of evading Customs control where crates containing cannabis were substituted for other crates brought into the airport with the labels switched. The case was heard at Middlesex Crown Court, where Parry pleaded guilty and was sentenced to three years in jail. More significantly, the case had inadvertently created an unusual pairing, who would play a unique role in the London criminal underworld over the next decade.

Parry's solicitor in the drug-smuggling case was Michael Relton, a man whose background could not have been more different. Born in 1938, Relton was the son of a solicitor and as a boy attended Westminster School, the ancient and exclusive public school set in the precincts of Westminster Abbey. He went on to study law and in 1961 qualified as a solicitor. A dapper, well-spoken presence, Relton took pride in being a connoisseur of fine food and wine. By the 1970s, he had built a thriving legal practice, Lynn Relton & Co., and had developed a reputation as a top criminal defence lawyer. Relton cut a flamboyant and controversial path through the legal world as he built up his practice and was said to be obsessed with money and status. His financial drive meant that Relton supplemented his income from legal practice by dabbling in property development in Britain and Florida, making substantial profits. He and Parry had bonded during their time together, sharing an entrepreneurial zeal and an eye for opportunity. When Parry was released, they began working together.

In 1976, with the help of a £17,000 loan from Relton, Parry bought a hotel on the Isle of Wight for £80,000 and sold it three years later for £150,000. He spent around £200,000 converting a grocery shop in New Cross, south-east London, into a recording studio that was used by the musicians Jeff Beck and Manfred Mann. In 1981, Parry turned the studio into a disco. Relton joined as a partner in the venture and would later say that nightly takings soon amounted to £40,000. They were, Relton would recall, 'coining it'.

In 1978, Relton and Parry bought Brief's, a wine bar on Newington Causeway, near Elephant and Castle in south London and opposite the Inner London Crown Court. The wine bar would soon become a microcosm of the Relton and Parry story, a shady mix of solicitors, police and criminality. Relton entertained criminal clients and journalists in the wine bar, which was also frequented by off-duty police officers, to the extent that three of them bought it. In 1980, Relton and Parry sold Brief's to brothers Michael and John Ross and their fellow officer Paul Rexstrew. According to one detective, the Ross brothers 'were not well regarded, and they were seen as dangerous, and destined for the sack'. The three ran Brief's as a sideline, employing as one of their staff a former armed robber and police supergrass called Maurice 'Mo' O'Mahoney, who also supplied information to leading figures within the criminal under-world. Brief's clientele included armed robbers and members of the Flying Squad, who would drink together in the bar.

In 1982, Relton defended the Ross brothers and Rexstrew when they were prosecuted at the Old Bailey on charges of demanding money with menaces and fitting up armed robbers. Relton's defence was successful, yet the Ross brothers were subsequently sacked from the police force by a disciplinary board. Relton maintained contact with the Rosses and later employed Rexstrew as a clerk at his law firm. This was not Relton's only business link to the police. After selling Brief's, Relton bought several other drinking clubs and wine bars in south London, including Docks Diner, a restaurant behind

Guy's Hospital on the southern bank of the Thames. His partner was Martin King, an ex-Metropolitan Police detective turned private eye, who was also suspected of – and later prosecuted for – corrupt practices.

Relton's police connections were also evident in his day job. The location of his office at 120 Horseferry Road, near Scotland Yard, brought him into routine contact with police officers. He counted the Police Federation among his clients, as well as several major criminals, and defended thirty-six officers accused of misconduct, famously achieving success in all but one case. He developed friendships with serving officers and was invited to police social events. One detective said later that Relton 'was always very polite and pleasant and liked to buy a round of drinks ... but it was hard to get to know him'. Another former detective recalled, 'Relton was extremely well known among the police. At every Wembley soccer international, he'd hire a hotel suite nearby where drink would flow all day. Scores of police enjoyed his hospitality.' Many of those he represented were accused of corruption and misconduct as part of the clean-up of the Metropolitan Police in the 1970s and early 1980s. In 1980, when he was living in a plush flat in central London and driving a Rolls-Royce, Relton represented four detectives caught up in Operation Countryman, the Metropolitan Police's anti-corruption sweep.

Relton operated in the shady middle ground between criminality and law enforcement, where boundaries and loyalties were frequently blurred and compromised. In 1970, he had been suspended by the Law Society for unprofessional conduct after he was found to have misused money in a client's account and had to sell a house to make up the deficit. By the 1980s, while outwardly a respectable, successful solicitor with a family, he was suspected by some at Scotland Yard of passing information gleaned from police contacts to help criminals and of having cultivated a coterie of corrupt officers around him. Senior officers at Scotland Yard were said to despise him.

In 1982, Relton's life began to show signs of seismic change. He divorced his first wife and married his second, Helena 'Terri' Luff, a barrister's clerk. More tellingly, he abandoned his legal career and became a full-time property developer. London, after all, was full of possibility. Particularly down by the river.

• • •

By the early 1980s, Gordon Parry, like many other property developers, sensed huge opportunities in the decaying heart of the imperial city. For centuries, ships had brought goods up the River Thames into London, Britain's principal port. The banks of the river east of the city were lined with wharves and docks that dated back to before the Elizabethan period, and which had reached a peak of development in the early twentieth century, when London was at the heart of a trading network that stretched around the globe. Thousands of warehouses stored goods and materials, and for generations, the neighbourhoods that bordered the river were shaped and defined by their connection to the shipping industry. But the invention of the standardised shipping container in the 1950s had dealt a death blow to this centuries-old industry. The Thames could not accommodate the larger ships that came with containerisation, and shipping moved to deep-water ports like Tilbury and Felixstowe.

London's collapse as a port was catastrophic. Between 1960 and 1980, all of London's docks closed. Thousands of buildings were vacated. What had once been a thriving part of the city became an eight-square-mile wasteland of derelict docks, wharves and warehouses, stretching east from Tower Bridge on both banks of the river. For the communities involved, it was a disaster, but for the developers, it was a potential goldmine.

Efforts to redevelop the area commenced almost as soon as the shipping began to depart, with the first warehouses converted into housing in the early 1970s. In 1981, the London Docklands Development Corporation was established by Michael Heseltine, the secretary of state for the environment, and redevelopment started to take off. A democratically unaccountable body, the LDDC served as the planning authority for the area and was given powers to acquire and sell land. The government designated the area as an enterprise zone, offering businesses property-tax exemptions, simplified planning rules and other incentives. It made investing in the newly rebranded Docklands a significantly more attractive proposition and helped kick-start a property boom.

As investors rushed in, so too did criminals and fraudsters. Parry, like many others involved with the Brink's-Mat robbery, had grown up in south-east London and knew the streets that bordered the docks at Rotherhithe intimately. The London of the past was vanishing, being replaced by something new. Parry was keen to get involved, he just needed the funds to do so. Meanwhile, Brian Perry had a large amount of criminal money and was seeking places to launder it.

It is thought that over a series of meetings in late 1983 and early 1984, Parry persuaded Perry to invest some of the Brink's-Mat money into property development. It wasn't as easy as it sounded. Perry effectively had a huge amount of cash, but the process of how that money was spent had to be one that could avoid detection. Parry turned to his business partner for help. At some point early in 1984, Michael Relton entered the conspiracy.

The most significant money-laundering operation of the criminal proceeds of the Brink's-Mat robbery was in place. It would play a part in London's 1980s property boom and change both British crime and policing forever.

• • •

The laundering operation began in spring 1984. As the torrent of cash began to pour out of Scadlynn, Relton, Parry and Perry implemented a series of complex measures to conceal its origins. Relton's first suggestion was to set up companies in the Channel Islands with local people as nominee directors to disguise the identity of the real beneficiaries. On 12 March 1984, Parry and Perry flew to Jersey, where they visited Samuel Montague Bank and met with a banker to discuss setting up a company. Soon after, Relton and Parry created several new companies in places where the true owners could be easily obscured. Principal among them were Selective Estates, incorporated in Jersey on 22 May 1984, and Melchester Holdings, incorporated in Panama on 4 July 1984. Both would later be used to make significant property purchases.

The money started to flow. On 7 March 1984, Parry made a cash deposit of £260,000 at the Bank of Ireland branch in Balham, south London. The money was transferred to an account at the Investment Bank of Ireland on the Isle of Man, with £10,000 transferred on to a gold credit card. Between March and July 1984, Parry paid another £461,000 in cash into the same account. As with Noye's smelting operation, several people were involved in moving the money and paying it into banks. In summer 1984, Parry asked John Elcombe, his common-law wife's cousin, to deposit cash into banks on his behalf and to courier cash by car to Europe, where it could be paid into secret accounts in Switzerland and Liechtenstein. Elcombe had an antiques business, Van Gray Antiques, that provided ideal cover for frequent trips abroad. At the beginning of August 1984, Elcombe and his wife Ann drove from England to Zurich with what Elcombe later said he thought was £500,000 in £50 notes. When they reached their destination, they met Parry at the Hotel Zurich and handed over the cash. Parry then went to Hong Kong and Shanghai Bank with Ted Wein, the managing clerk of Relton's legal practice and a former police officer, to meet with the manager. Relton had provided a letter of introduction, which was handed over, and Parry was allowed to open an account with Relton given power of attorney. He named the account 'Burton', after the actor Richard Burton, who had recently died in Switzerland, and made an opening deposit of £850,435 cash, probably the true amount brought by Elcombe. The bank was instructed to keep all documentation related to the account in Switzerland.

Two weeks later, on 15 August 1984, a man walked into the Bishopsgate branch of Hong Kong and Shanghai Bank in the City of London, handed over a suitcase containing £500,000 in cash, asked that it be sent to the Burton account care of the Hong Kong and Shanghai Bank in Zurich, then left without giving a name. It took the cashiers eight hours to count the cash and they charged £500 for doing so. At the end of August, Parry was in Zurich again, along with Perry and Relton. They stayed in three of the world's most expensive hotels: the Dolder Grand Hotel, the Savoy and the Ermitage. Another £490,000 was deposited into the Burton account, and on the night of 29 August 1984 they were joined by the Elcombes, who brought with them another massive consignment of cash, thought to be over a million pounds. The following day, Parry and Perry travelled to Liechtenstein, where they opened accounts codenamed 'Glad' and 'Como', after Perry's mother and her favourite singer. They paid £45,000 in cash into each and returned to Zurich, where Parry paid £999,701 in cash into the Burton account.

September 1984 was a busy month for Elcombe. He visited the Bank of Ireland in Balham and arranged to open an account in his name, paying in £250,000 then another £250,050 in cash less than a week later. He was back behind the wheel on 19 September, driving another massive shipment of cash to the Alps. He stayed again at the Dolder Grand in Zurich. Parry joined him and drove with him to Vaduz in Liechtenstein. The following day, they opened an account at the Bank of Liechtenstein in Elcombe's name, again giving Parry power of attorney. Elcombe told a bank official that the money came from his antiques business; he would later tell another it came from betting shops. In the days that followed, more trips were made and on one, it's thought that Elcombe carried a million pounds across Europe. Further trips were made at the beginning of December 1984 and January 1985, by which point over £2.5 million had been paid into the secret accounts in Switzerland and Liechtenstein, and was then funnelled through offshore companies and ready for property investment.

Relton and Parry went on an eclectic buying spree. In June 1984, Relton bought a number of buildings for £470,000 from Cheltenham Ladies' College, the exclusive girls' public school. Further purchases would be made in Kent and Surrey but the greatest investment was made in the London Docklands. For the Brink's-Mat cash, the docklands investment completed a circle. Many of the old wharves and warehouses that the money bought were just a short walk from the south-east London neighbourhoods where Black, McAvoy, Robinson, White and the other robbers had grown up, and were being redeveloped into housing targeted at the young professionals coming to work in the financial services industry in the City. The investments were shrewd and highly profitable. They included New Caledonian Wharf, which was bought for £750,000 in February 1985 and sold a year later for £1.75 million; Cyclops Wharf, bought for £2.7 million and later sold for £4.5 million; and Globe Wharf, bought for £1.6 million and sold for £8 million.

At South Quay, Parry and Relton organised a racket in which they would pay the area's remaining council tenants £1,000 for their rent books. This then allowed them to buy the properties from the council. In back-to-back cash deals, the old council flats were then sold for three times as much to private buyers keen to get a toehold in the booming area. Local residents were able to buy the new flats going up along the riverside at a big discount. Other investments made with the laundered Brink's-Mat money included houses, flats and even a newly built shopping centre. All of them were sold on quickly or redeveloped and sold, generating about £7 million. This profit was paid back to the gang members, successfully cleaned of its origins.

So successful were Relton and Parry's investments, and so plentiful the opportunities in London at the time, that they persuaded others to invest in their schemes. Relton and Parry were said to have funded wild parties at Docks Diner, characterised by some as orgies, to persuade businessmen to invest. 'One girl had champagne poured over her body and clients licked it,' recalled one, perhaps bewildered, estate agent who attended a Docks Diner investment event. It was a time of excess. Relton and Parry were said to have worked out deals over champagne and cigars, while regulars at the Elephant Club, another of Relton's bars, remembered him turning up at the time with his car boot full of cash.

Parry was so successful at posing as a legitimate businessman that at least two police officers asked him to back their own business ventures. Detective Chief Inspector David Eager urged Parry to invest £50,000 in a security company he set up when he left the police force in the early 1980s, while another detective is said to have asked Parry to back a plan to establish an indoor tennis complex designed to appeal to the young professionals moving into the new Docklands developments.

These were good times for one set of Brink's-Mat money launderers. And they weren't the only ones.

CHAPTER TWENTY-TWO

John Fleming

In the Brink's-Mat files, the name John Fleming had caught Tony Lundy's eye. Fleming was a heavily built south Londoner with a reputation as a professional criminal and armed robber, and a record of ten convictions reaching back to 1960. He had been identified as a possible suspect in the Brink's-Mat robbery soon after the event. Police knew he was an associate of Brian Robinson, and a surveillance photographer had captured him meeting with Robinson, Micky McAvoy, Tony White, John Lloyd and another unidentified man shortly before the raid took place. Robinson had introduced Fleming to his brother-in-law, Tony Black, some years before. Black felt he was 'a mean-looking person', while Black's sister, Jennifer, described him as 'a nasty type who flew off the handle easily'. The Flying Squad detectives would have arrested Fleming in December 1983 at the same time as Robinson, McAvoy and White, but he could not be found. But then, as with much of the original enquiry, impetus was lost. Lundy was surprised that Fleming wasn't still being actively sought and instigated a manhunt. He arranged for phone taps on known south London criminals with links to Fleming and it wasn't long until these provided valuable intelligence.

By May 1985, the task force had an address. Fleming had abandoned south London for the Costa Blanca, purchasing a luxurious villa built into the hillside in Mascarat, a new marina complex near Altea, just north of Benidorm. He had become a popular figure in the local bars and discos, where he was known to like a drink. He was a particularly celebrated presence in the Penelope disco in Benidorm, where he put up prize money for the 'Miss Topless' and 'Miss Big Boobs' competitions, often inviting the winners back to his villa for a private party. No one knew where Fleming's money came from, but he certainly didn't hide it. Along with the £130,000 villa he also had a £50,000 cabin cruiser and interests in a Barcelona company dealing in furniture, boats and cars.

With the approval of Commander Corbett and working with connections he had in the Spanish police, Lundy put together a plan for a major surveillance operation in the country. For this to happen, a formal request had to be made in person to police chiefs in Madrid. Scotland Yard at first refused to allow Lundy and Corbett to go, but behind-the-scenes lobbying eventually overturned the decision and the two officers flew to the Spanish capital. There, they were told that their Spanish counterparts already had files on Fleming and suspected he was involved in local criminal activity.

It wouldn't be the first time. In 1970, a Spanish court had sentenced Fleming to twelve years in jail for trafficking forged currency. He served five, becoming fluent in Spanish and making connections with high-level figures in the Spanish underworld and Marseille's Corsican mafia. On his release, Fleming was expelled from Spain and made subject to an exclusion order. When Lundy and Corbett told the head of Spain's International Squad about Fleming's alleged links to the Brink's-Mat robbery and possible involvement in drug trafficking and money laundering, the

Spaniards agreed to provide support. The local force did not have the manpower or expertise for such a sensitive surveillance operation and, perhaps more importantly, lacked the language skills needed to understand the Cockney slang spoken by Fleming and his associates. The Spanish agreed to let Scotland Yard use their own surveillance teams, the first time such international cooperation had been allowed.

Lundy arranged for intercepts to be placed on Fleming's telephone and for bugs to be inserted at various strategic locations, including one in his home. Undercover surveillance experts crept into the villa late one night while Fleming was out drinking in a Benidorm nightclub. With the devices in place, Lundy began rotating teams of officers in and out of Spain every month to monitor Lundy's calls and activities. At one point, Lundy had eight detectives monitoring recorded conversations in an improvised operations room above a butcher's shop. Detective Inspector Ian Brown was among those who went to Spain to work on the operation, which expanded to target other East End villains who were living in Benidorm and were suspected of links to the Brink's-Mat raid.

Before long, Lundy and his men realised they were listening to a multinational conspiracy. In among conversations recounting Fleming's sexual escapades, the officers listened to an intriguing call between Fleming and a company formation agent in the Isle of Man named Patrick Diamond. For Lundy, it was an exhilarating moment. Lundy knew Patrick Diamond; if John Fleming knew him too, then that was very interesting indeed.

• • •

In February 1984, Patrick Diamond had been arrested in London with Bobby Dixey, a convicted armed robber and cocaine smuggler with connections in Florida. Three months later, Dixey was jailed for four years, with Diamond receiving a short sentence for cocaine possession.

In March 1985, one of Lundy's informers told him that Diamond had visited Dixey in jail. Lundy took a routine look at Diamond and discovered that Scotland Yard's Special Intelligence Section had amassed a wealth of intelligence on his activities. Lundy was amazed at what he read and told Corbett that he thought Diamond should be targeted for his likely money-laundering activity. And now, Patrick Diamond was on the phone talking to John Fleming.

Lundy thought they had possibly identified a link in the laundering of some of the proceeds of the Brink's-Mat robbery. Diamond was a money launderer, Fleming was a suspected Brink's-Mat robber and the professional criminal Dixey was a likely candidate to have made the introduction. Further research added weight to Lundy's guesswork. The police discovered that Dixey and Diamond had met in a drinking club in July 1983. Shortly afterwards, Dixey had introduced Diamond to Fleming at the A&R Club on Charing Cross Road, which Dixey and Fleming co-owned at the time. On 1 December 1983, just five days after the robbery, Fleming and Dixey flew to the Isle of Man to meet with Diamond. There, they discussed the formation of offshore companies with nominee directors, which could be used to conceal the identities of the true beneficial owners. On 7 December 1983, Fleming and Diamond flew to Miami. Diamond was stopped by Customs and was found to be carrying a banker's draft for $185,000. He could give no reason for having it, just that he was going to the United States for business and pleasure. To Lundy, it appeared as though that was an early instalment of the Brink's-Mat money. And there was more to come, as Diamond and Fleming found they had much to offer each other.

Diamond, an Irishman who had arrived in the Isle of Man in 1976, had a law degree from Queen's University Belfast. He owned a business called Comprehensive Company Management, which offered advice on how to exploit the Isle of Man's highly protective company laws and set up shell or front companies for clients. These would have nominee directors and could be used to conceal the source of the money flowing in and out of them. Dozens of companies were registered to his office in Douglas, the Isle of Man capital.

In February 1984, Fleming bought a ready-made company called Marblemay from Diamond. He immediately gave Diamond £100,000, which he transferred to an account in Florida. In June 1984, Fleming bought another company from Diamond, this time named Seapath Investments, and began transferring large amounts of cash into it for transfer to Spain, where Fleming had another company, also called Seapath. The money was used to buy six apartments in Barcelona and two villas near Benidorm. Whenever Fleming needed money moving, he asked Diamond to do it. Police later established that between February and July 1984, he received £370,000 in cash.

When Lundy's attention focused on Diamond as a result of the Fleming phone taps, Diamond was placed under police surveillance. As Lundy would later recall, it was a lively assignment. Standing at six foot four inches, Diamond was known in the Isle of Man social circles as a charming divorcé with a way with women. His urbane manner and social charm concealed his involvement in some questionable business activities, and erratic behaviour when drunk. Lundy later told the journalist Martin Short, 'Diamond is very posh-spoken and very intelligent. He really thinks he's God's gift to the underworld, that he's brilliant and way above us mortal plods. He's also a headcase. He was always getting barred from the Palace Casino for being drunk or drugged and shouting his mouth off.' On one occasion, the surveillance officers saw an inebriated Diamond in a Douglas casino with several female companions. 'Suddenly he goes to the airport,' recalled Lundy, 'gets on a plane with these girls and ends up in Blackpool.' Lundy said Diamond and his companions were tailed to a bank then a hotel, 'where he's either shacked up with the birds or having a cocaine party. The next thing, they're seen driving along in a taxi and he's throwing handfuls of bank notes out of the window!'

Lundy decided that the task force's international operations needed to expand from Spain to the Isle of Man. A request was made for an intercept on Diamond's telephone, the first time such a request had been made on the island for financial matters, and a full-scale surveillance operation was mounted. Lundy was only able to secure it by asking the Home Office to authorise an application and taking it directly to the governor of the Isle of Man. He was keen to involve as few people as possible, fearing that Diamond could learn of any action taken against him from his many friends in the island's social and business circles. Lundy found the local force was keen to help, having fielded numerous requests from forces all over the world for information on Comprehensive Company Management. For years, Diamond had blocked all inquiries by claiming confidentiality over any of his business activities.

Lundy's re-examination of the suspected Brink's-Mat robber John Fleming had now created an unfolding international investigation that was only going to grow more complicated, exotic and dangerous.

• • •

After Lundy's team began monitoring Patrick Diamond's telephone in the summer of 1985, they soon picked up on a strange series of calls. A man named Stephen Marzovilla was phoning Diamond from various European countries, each time asking that Diamond send him thousands of pounds. All the detectives knew about Marzovilla was that he had an American accent. They checked American criminal files, but there were none for that name. At the end of August

1985, Marzovilla called to say he was coming to London and that Diamond should meet him. With detectives monitoring their movements, the two men enjoyed London clubs and met with known criminals. Marzovilla was seen visiting three safe-deposit-box centres. After a couple of days, Diamond returned to the Isle of Man. On the phone intercepts, he was heard telling Fleming that Marzovilla would be flying out to Spain the next day to meet him.

Lundy decided it was time to act. He arranged for Marzovilla to be stopped and searched at Heathrow. Security guards found he was carrying flick-knives concealed in a vanity case. This enabled police to arrest him for carrying offensive weapons onto a plane. He told the arresting officers he was a businessman on his way to Spain. When they found $18,000 on him, Marzovilla said he was from a rich family and that he travelled the world. Warrants had been obtained that allowed detectives to open the safe-deposit boxes he had been seen visiting. Two contained $80,000 in $100 bills. One had everything needed for a complete new identity: passport, driving licence, birth certificate. It was all in the name of Craig Jacobs, with a photograph of the man who identified himself as Stephen Marzovilla. Detectives contacted the American embassy and asked them to check on Craig Jacobs. A short while later, the FBI came back with the news that Craig Jacobs was an alias used by Scott Errico. And Errico, now an associate of both Diamond and Fleming, was one of America's most wanted criminals.

• • •

Scott Errico was an enforcer within a major Florida drug-smuggling gang overseen by the well-known Floridian crime figure Ray Thompson. Errico had been convicted of possessing marijuana in May 1981 and sentenced to five years but skipped bail and disappeared when his appeal was dismissed in 1982. In 1985, he had been re-indicted on more drug-smuggling charges and for murders committed on Thompson's behalf. Errico was accused of having killed three men who were kidnapped, taken out to sea in a yacht, weighted down with anchors and dumped overboard. Florida police had cracked two accomplices involved in the murders who later testified against Thompson and Errico. By 1985 Thompson had been convicted but Errico was on the run and being urgently sought by the American Drug Enforcement Agency. Lundy and his team were overjoyed to have captured him, not least because his high criminal status cast a long shadow of suspicion over Diamond and Fleming.

Scotland Yard chiefs were impressed by Lundy's arrest of Errico but wanted to bring the focus closer to home and secure results for the Brink's-Mat inquiry. Lundy decided there was enough to act against Diamond. Working with the Isle of Man police, he applied for a search warrant then assembled a twelve-man team that he took to the Isle of Man, where they were sworn in by the governor as special constables and established themselves in a Douglas hotel. At 8am on 12 March 1986, Detective Inspector Tony Brightwell served the warrant on Diamond and cautioned him before the task force squad searched his offices and seized a mass of paperwork.

In initial questioning, Diamond made a gesture of cooperation, offering to name Errico's companies, but refused to say anything about his own operation, including the laundering of the Brink's-Mat money. Lundy set about interrogating Diamond. Like many others involved with the Brink's-Mat operation, Diamond was not a professional criminal in the traditional sense and it wasn't long before he cracked under intense questioning. As Lundy said later, 'He tells us about Fleming taking cash up there to him, giving him hundreds of thousands of pounds, and how he also collected money directly from Fleming's house.'

Lundy and Diamond struck up an unexpected rapport. It turned out that both had run the London Marathon on 13 May 1984. Diamond said he had stayed with Fleming at his house in Denmark Hill, south London, and that Fleming had even sponsored him at £4 a mile, contributing over £100 to the charity. That weekend, Diamond said, Fleming had also given him £200,000 in cash. Diamond paid £145,000 of it into the City branch of the Bank of Ireland, into the account held in the joke name of G. Reedy, a company he had registered in the Turks and Caicos Islands. The money was later used to buy two working oil wells on Fleming's behalf in Kansas. It would later emerge that the oil wells were themselves a scam and Fleming was duped out of the Brink's-Mat money he paid for them.

Among the paperwork seized at Diamond's offices were records that linked him to Michael Levine, a lawyer in Miami who acted on behalf of Florida-based drug gangs. Diamond had set up dozens of offshore companies for Levine to launder the criminal profits generated by his clients. It was through Levine that Errico had become aware of Diamond's services. Millions of dollars derived from the drugs trade moved through accounts and companies managed by Diamond, who would transfer money to wherever his clients wanted it. Levine also used Diamond's companies to buy land and property in Florida on behalf of clients like Errico, and possibly Fleming, whose names would never appear on the company documents. Land, houses and shopping malls were all purchased through companies Diamond had set up. The information was shared with American law enforcement agencies and was taken up by the Drug Enforcement Agency (DEA), who had been working on the Florida drug gangs for years. They sent two agents to the Isle of Man to assist with Lundy's team.

While he was waiting on remand, Diamond was talked into helping the DEA with the investigation into Levine. Lundy told him that cooperating with the American investigation would help persuade the director of public prosecutions that his case should be heard in the Isle of Man system and that he should not be prosecuted in Britain. He agreed to make a monitored phone call to Levine, during which Levine made remarks that placed him at the heart of the Errico money-laundering conspiracy. Later, Diamond travelled to the United States and met with Levine while wearing a wire.

It was an intriguing situation: the Brink's-Mat money, that the police believed Fleming had provided to Diamond, was moving through the same company formation agent as the proceeds of American drug trafficking. Whether the money had entwined at all was unclear. For now, Lundy acted on what he had. In September 1985, Diamond was charged on the Isle of Man with handling £100,000 derived from the Brink's-Mat gold. It was a highly symbolic moment, the first prosecution of an individual who was purely involved with laundering the Brink's-Mat proceeds and not also, at some level, with the gold. The Brink's-Mat hunt had moved beyond the gold; the police were chasing the money too. And they soon had somewhere even more exotic to chase it. It came from a throwaway comment that Diamond had made while explaining how his money-laundering operation worked. 'If you think I've been busy,' Diamond told the police in March 1986, 'you wait till you get into a bloke called Shaun Murphy, down in the British Virgin Islands.'

CHAPTER TWENTY-THREE

Aachen

On 30 January 1985, West German border police at Aachen, a small city on the border between West Germany and Belgium, flagged down a Mercedes with British number plates. It was a routine stop. Inside, they found the Elcombes and £710,000 in new £50 and £20 notes hidden in the boot and under the back seat. John Elcombe told the *Bundesgrenzschutz* (Federal Border Guard) officers that he had saved the money from his business as an antique dealer and was going to invest it in an antiques shop in Switzerland.

The police were not convinced. The attention of Peter Foerster, one of the *Bundesgrenzschutz* officers, was drawn to Elcombe's tattooed arms. 'I had the impression something was wrong,' Foerster later told an interviewer. Checks were run on the vehicle registration and on the Elcombes, and the police sent a telex to West German Interpol at Wiesbaden with the vehicle registration, the Elcombes' passport details and details of the cash, including serial numbers, asking that anything known or suspected about the Elcombes be forwarded on to them at once. The request was passed to British Interpol, who sent it to Scotland Yard. An answer came back quickly. There had been no recent big cash robberies in London and there was no warrant out on Elcombe. The car was owned by Gordon

Parry, a south London businessman with past criminal convictions, but it had not been reported stolen. The Elcombes appeared to have done nothing wrong. 'We had no reason to hold them any longer,' said Hans Schmidt, one of Foerster's colleagues, 'so sadly we had to let them go.' The Elcombes continued on their way to Zurich where they stayed a few nights, then travelled into Liechtenstein and paid £100,000 into an account there and another £608,000 into a numbered account that had just been opened by Parry.

Back in London, news of the incident at the border caused alarm. It could not have come at a worst time, just a few days after the arrest of Noye following John Fordham's death, and around the time of the police raids in Bristol and London, all of which can't have failed to spook Relton, Parry and Perry. It was clear from news reports that police were making moves against Noye's gold-smelting operation. It was possible that the police might have picked up intelligence on the laundering ring.

With the police moving on Noye and the others, Relton, Parry and Perry knew there would be no new money for them to launder and profit from, so they concentrated on distancing themselves from the money that had already passed through. Fearing that the secret accounts might be discovered, Perry decided some should be closed and the money withdrawn and transferred elsewhere. On 22 April 1985, Perry travelled to Zurich and stayed at the Dolder Grand Hotel. The following day, he met Parry and Relton at the airport in a chauffeur-driven Mercedes. The men were driven to Vaduz in Liechtenstein where Parry set up the Moyet Foundation, a Liechtenstein trust company that, like those they set up in the Isle of Man and Jersey, was under no obligation to disclose its beneficiaries. The name was a reference to Moët, the champagne. Whether the clerk opening the account misheard or whether Parry misspelled it is unclear. Two local men were installed as directors, but the paperwork gave Parry, Perry and Relton power to direct its affairs. The numbered account that had been opened in early February was closed and the funds in it – over £3 million – were transferred to the Moyet Foundation. It was used, like the Burton account, to fund a series of property purchases in Britain.

From this point, when money was brought back to Britain to fund property purchases, Relton would instruct the Liechtenstein agents to issue a credit transfer to Credit Suisse in Zurich. A banker's draft would be issued for one of the front companies in Jersey or Panama, which would then acquire the property. Anyone trying to trace the money would come to an end at Credit Suisse, where no account was held by Relton, Parry or Perry. This extra protection likely relaxed the three men to some degree. Nothing further happened after the Aachen border incident and, over the next three months, another £2.5 million was paid into the Moyet account. Meanwhile, the three men got back to doing what they did best. Spending money. It was time to buy some houses.

At the end of 1985, Perry moved from south-east London to Meadowcroft, a large house at Biggin Hill in Kent, bought for £275,000 with funds from the Moyet Foundation, but he had barely moved in when he bought a nearby four-acre plot and had an architect get to work designing a vast £700,000 home. In summer 1985, Relton helped Parry purchase Crockham House in Westerham, Kent, through Feberion, a front company registered in Panama, from the former local MP, Gerald Williams. Costing £400,000, Parry's new home was a five-bedroom fifteenth-century country cottage set in twenty acres of grounds, with gardens designed by Octavia Hill, the founder of the National Trust. It had once been owned by a relative of the Queen Mother, who was said to have played in the gardens as a child. Parry spent thousands on alterations and refurbishments, including gold-plated taps for the bathrooms. He also spent heavily on security, began work on a swimming pool and tennis court, and filled the cellars with vintage Louis Roederer pink champagne. It was quite a leap from the small terraced house in Royal Hill, Greenwich, in which he'd lived before the robbery. Parry had been refused a car loan in 1983 – now, two years later, he had a red Bentley Turbo Mulsanne, bought for £87,000 and nicknamed 'the fire engine', parked in the drive.

Relton, who was already wealthy and had a flat in Carlisle Place in Westminster, acquired Chase Farm in Haslemere, Surrey, and land in Torremar, Spain. In December 1984, he transferred $3 million from the Burton account to one held in his second wife's name in Florida for the purchase of a condominium. Relton also indulged his passion for luxury cars, touring his London restaurants in Rolls-Royces, Cadillacs and Mercedes.

It wasn't these houses, however, that would be the problem. What Relton, Parry and Perry could never escape was that the source of their wealth was the Brink's-Mat robbery, which meant they would always have a complicated debt to the Brink's-Mat robbers. So when Micky McAvoy decided that he wanted two houses, one for his estranged wife Jacqueline and one for his new partner Kathleen Meacock, the money launderers had to comply.

In May 1985, Michael Osborn, a car dealer from Maidstone in Kent and long-standing associate of McAvoy, contacted an estate agent and asked if she had any properties for sale around £150,000, but where the seller would be open to a transaction in which the official sale price was listed as less than the amount actually paid. The estate agent sent him details of 45 Bird-in-Hand Lane, a house in Bickley, Kent. On 25 June 1985, Brian Perry and Jacqueline McAvoy (who, to add a further layer of complication, were now said to be in a relationship) viewed the property and agreed to buy it. The house was purchased, with a sizeable side payment to the vendor, using money sent by Relton from the Moyet Account in Liechtenstein and a £50,000 mortgage from the Bradford and Bingley Building Society arranged by Joseph Medayil, a north London accountant who had worked with Parry and Relton. The mortgage application gave her name as Jacqueline Sheffield and falsely stated she was employed as a fashion model earning £18,000 a year, when she had actually been claiming social security benefits since McAvoy's arrest. With the sale complete, McAvoy moved with the couple's two children from their small flat in Herne Hill, south London, to her new home in Kent, where she would have a surprising nearby neighbour.

Kathleen Meacock was browsing *Country Life* magazine when she spotted an advertisement for Turpington Farm, a six-bedroom Grade II-listed farmhouse available for £258,000. It was, like Jacqueline McAvoy's new house, also in Bickley in Kent. Meacock viewed the house, then wrote to McAvoy to tell him she wanted it and that it was going to be bought for her. The purchase was overseen by Relton, using funds from the Burton account in Switzerland, funnelled through a new offshore company in the Cayman Islands, and using a property dealer from Stepney called Stephen Donovan as a frontman for the deal. In January 1986, Meacock left her council flat near Elephant and Castle, south-east London, and moved into Turpington Farm. She embraced the country lifestyle, spending lavishly on the house, while buying two Rottweiler guard dogs. The names Meacock gave the dogs would later play an unlikely role in the police investigation.

Whether Meacock and her neighbour Jacqueline McAvoy ever had any contact is not known. What is known is that, with the purchase of these two houses, together with the Aachen border incident, the seeds had been planted for the downfall of the money-laundering operation.

• • •

In early 1985, Detective Inspector Tony Brightwell found himself reading a strange report. Not long before, a car had been stopped in Aachen, West Germany with over £700,000 that largely consisted of new £50 notes with consecutive numbering beginning A24. If it wasn't for the German police diligently including this detail in the report that eventually made it to Brightwell's desk, he would have taken little notice. But Brightwell knew that police had recently established that notes with the A24 prefix had been issued to Barclays Bedminster by Barclays Cash Centre and withdrawn by representatives of Scadlynn. He therefore endeavoured to look into the matter further, as soon as there was time in the constantly evolving Brink's-Mat enquiry, which at that point was focused on building the murder case against Noye and Reader and the ongoing inquiries into the gold-smelting operation.

By the spring of 1985, Brightwell had both more time and more information. Police had learned that Noye and others had paid large amounts of cash into various bank accounts, often in £50 notes, which they believed were those issued by Barclays to Scadlynn. 'Whenever you found an A24 £50 note,' Detective Sergeant Bill Miller recalled later, 'you knew you were onto somebody who was involved with the Brink's-Mat gold bullion robbery.' It was time to ask the Elcombes some questions. In June 1985, they were arrested, along with the last registered owner of the Mercedes, Gordon Parry. It is not known exactly what happened in these police interviews, but it appears that the Elcombes and Parry denied all knowledge of any criminal activity and were all released without charge. Perhaps the police did not have enough evidence – or they were released so they could be put under surveillance.

Either way, police were soon pursuing a new lead in their hunt for the Brink's-Mat money men. In December 1985, Detective Inspector David Sandlin of the Brink's-Mat task force received a tip from an underworld source. McAvoy's girlfriend, Kathleen Meacock, was moving to a house advertised in *Country Life* magazine. Sandlin embarked on an unusual piece of police investigation, searching through a year's worth of back issues of the magazine, before finding the advertisement for Turpington Farm, which matched some of the information he had been given. The police began to question whether McAvoy's wife was enjoying a similar change in fortune to his girlfriend. They soon discovered that she had moved from the family's modest flat in Herne Hill to her considerably grander new house in Kent.

The police felt it was highly likely that both houses in Kent had been bought with the proceeds of the Brink's-Mat gold. Sandlin began tracing the money used to buy the properties; in doing so, he became the first British police detective to use recent legislative changes that allowed police to examine bank accounts before making any arrests. Through painstaking detective work, Sandlin and his team began to piece together the convoluted financial processes that had been used to purchase the houses. With Turpington Farm, they worked their way past the Cayman Islands offshore company, past the frontman Stephen Donovan, to get to a numbered account in Switzerland controlled by Michael Relton. With Bird-in-Hand Lane, they got past Stephen Donovan and the complicated purchase, to get to a numbered account in Liechtenstein, again controlled by Michael Relton. When they looked into the false mortgage application, they found that Jacqueline McAvoy had listed her landlord as Gordon Parry, who was already on the task force's radar after the Aachen border stop. Around the same time, the task force was looking into Brian Perry following his involvement in the unsuccessful police negotiations with McAvoy concerning the possible return of his share of the gold for a reduced sentence. They found Perry was also living in a house bought with money transferred through accounts controlled by Relton.

The police had three names: Relton, Parry and Perry. That, the police were starting to suspect, was the laundering operation that was handling the criminal proceeds of the Brink's-Mat robbery.

Now they just had to catch them.

CHAPTER TWENTY-FOUR

Tortola

Shaun Murphy was born in Cheshire in 1953, before his family relocated to the Isle of Man. After school, he qualified as a chartered accountant, married a local girl and worked for a number of large corporate accountancy firms. His life might have remained on that unremarkable, traditional course if he hadn't been offered a job in the British Virgin Islands in 1977.

Murphy loved life on the island, with its white beaches, sunshine and a lax approach to financial regulation. In 1980, Murphy set up on his own, working from an office in a wooden building in front of the main church in Road Town, the capital of Tortola, the largest of the island chain. So ingrained was Murphy in the island's social and business networks just a few years after his arrival, that he persuaded Cyril Romney, the chief minister and minister of finance on the British Virgin Islands, to become a director of the firm.

Patrick Diamond spoke to the Brink's-Mat detectives with awe of Murphy's work and showed them a brochure for Murphy's firm, Financial Management and Trust Ltd. The brochure pitched the benefits of doing business in the British Virgin Islands, where clients were offered low taxes and a secure and secret home for their money. Diamond told his interviewers that Murphy was even more closely involved with Levine than he was.

Lundy concluded that Murphy should be searched and questioned before he learned that Levine was under investigation. On 7 April 1986, Lundy, Detective Inspector Tony Brightwell and Detective Inspector Ian Brown flew out to the British Virgin Islands. They established a base in the Treasure Island Hotel in Tortola and were sworn in as special constables – as they had been on the Isle of Man – to allow them to operate on the islands. They began their inquiries but when Levine was subpoenaed in the United States on 16 April, he tipped off Murphy that Diamond must have been turned, warning him to expect a police visit and to remove any incriminating material. At the same time, a report had appeared in the *The Times* about the Brink's-Mat task force's work in the British Virgin Islands and the Isle of Man. No names appeared but it was obvious to anyone who knew that the article contained references to Diamond and Scott Errico. One of Murphy's friends in London faxed a copy to him. After reading it, he removed an incriminating file on Levine from his office and hid it in a cupboard at the school in which his wife Jennifer taught.

At 5am on 22 April 1986, the Scotland Yard detectives and a local officer banged on Murphy's door. A sleepy Murphy opened it. He was petrified, fell into a chair and buried his face in his hands. He was taken for questioning by Lundy and one of the DEA agents, who persuaded him to tell all and cooperate with the DEA in exchange for immunity from prosecution. Within days, Murphy was in a safe house in Florida detailing the international laundering operation. It has never been revealed what role Murphy might have confessed to playing with regards the laundering of Brink's-Mat proceeds. A hint as to his possible involvement came in a 1987 BBC documentary, which claimed that Brink's-Mat money was moved from the Isle of Man to Tortola and on to Florida, where it funded a $1.5 million drugs syndicate.

The joint operation was a major success. Lundy told a conference, 'The scale of the problem is immense. It stretches from the United States to the Caribbean, London, the Channel Islands, the Isle of Man, Europe and the Far East. London, being one of the major money markets, is an important centre for the transfer of cash. The money ... represents the proceeds from armed robberies, drug dealing and every other aspect of criminal activity.' By 1987, £160 million of criminal money had been located. The operation received a great deal of publicity, a positive story to detract from the relatively poor results so far against the Brink's-Mat gang. But it was also a worrying sign for the police, as it showed how quickly the proceeds of the Brink's-Mat gold could slip out of Britain and become mixed up with criminal revenue streams around the world.

It was also not yet a victory. For them to prove that the money that went through Diamond came from the Brink's-Mat robbery, they had to prove the links all the way back to the robbery itself. Which meant they had to prove that John Fleming was one of the robbers.

• • •

While Lundy and his team pursued their inquiries in the Isle of Man, Florida and the Caribbean, in Spain, the surveillance operation on John Fleming had continued. Useful intelligence about British criminals was gathered, but no evidence that could be put before a court to prove Fleming was involved with the Brink's-Mat robbery or had handled the proceeds. Although he had long been suspected of being part of the robbery gang, the case against him was weak: only that he was closely associated with some of the convicted robbers and that his wealth had suddenly increased immediately after the robbery. At this point, the task force did not feel they had the evidence to attempt to seize Fleming in Spain. The Spanish, however, had other ideas.

The authorities in Spain had good reasons to want Fleming gone. Spanish police had narrowly missed catching him in connection with several loads of drugs they believed he had financed and, as seen with John Palmer, the Spanish government had a renewed wish at the time to rid itself of the British criminals who had set up home there. In November 1985, police raided Fleming's villa and established that he was living in Spain on a false passport and in possession of a false birth certificate. At the beginning of January 1986, police formally applied to a judge in Benidorm for him to be expelled from the country under Spain's tough new undesirable aliens law. Fleming was being flushed out, and the media soon picked up on it.

Tiempo, a Spanish news magazine, named Fleming as one of the Brink's-Mat robbers, leading Fleming to insist to local reporters that he had nothing to do with the robbery. He was soon tracked down by John Suchet of British Independent Television News. On 7 July 1986, an interview was filmed beside the pool on the terrace of Fleming's villa, that had striking similarities to the conversation in Tenerife a year before between Palmer and Kate Adie.

Casually dressed in a blue polo shirt and wearing his gold-framed Cartier sunglasses, a sun-tanned Fleming answered the reporter's questions about the Brink's-Mat robbery with a bottle of beer in his hand. 'Certain policemen seem to think I was involved,' he said. When asked by Suchet if he was, Fleming looked aghast. 'No,' he said, 'I had nothing to do with the robbery. I believe they know that.' Suchet pressed him on why he would not go back to England to clear his name if he was innocent. Fleming replied, 'I really fear that they will fabricate some evidence, verbal admissions. I could sit here now and say "I had nothing to do with this robbery" but I should think that one day in an English cell, a confession would appear.' Explaining his wealth, he said, 'I worked very hard. I've worked in pubs, clubs, I've started businesses, I've sold cars, I've bought houses, sold houses, I've done many things, but crime, I've not been involved in any crime.' At this point, Fleming had ten criminal convictions.

Agreeing to the interview may not have been a wise move. Noye had been convicted and Palmer had been found innocent. For the media, their stories had lost impetus. But now the press had a new Brink's-Mat angle to cover: the suspected robber hiding in the Spanish sunshine. And that was a story that was only going to get more dramatic.

CHAPTER TWENTY-FIVE

Relton

The arrests (and subsequent release) of the Elcombes and Parry alerted Relton, Parry and Perry that, while the police appeared to have very little to go on, they were certainly skirting around the edges of their money-laundering and investment operation. What the three men correctly assumed, however, was that though the police might have drawn loose links from the A24 notes through Noye to the Elcombes, the Brink's-Mat task force had no idea about the overseas bank accounts and shell companies. With no new cash entering the laundering system, and therefore at risk of detection, the money that was already in it felt safe. They therefore continued to energetically invest it in highly profitable property schemes, which proceeded to generate millions more in profits for themselves and others connected to them.

Relton and Parry's feeling of invincibility was shattered in summer 1986 when the Brink's-Mat task force had gathered enough information from their inquiries into the Kent houses to make a move. In coordinated raids, Kathleen Meacock, Jacqueline McAvoy and Brian Perry were arrested. Detective Inspector Tony Brightwell was part of the team that arrested Meacock at Turpington Farm. As he approached the door, Meacock's two Rottweilers bounded up to him. Meacock called them from inside the house and he was astounded to hear she had named the dogs 'Brinks' and 'Mat'. Over at the nearby Bird-in-Lane, Jacqueline McAvoy is said to have told detectives, 'It's what me and the kids deserve. Micky's given me fuck all, the bastard. We're living on egg and chips.'

Brian Perry, Jacqueline McAvoy and Kathleen Meacock were charged at Rochester Row police station on 13 August 1986 with dishonestly handling proceeds of the Brink's-Mat robbery. As detectives pieced together more about Perry's role, the charges against him increased. By December 1986, police believed he had played a much bigger part in handling the proceeds of the robbery. He was rearrested and charged with handling £6 million derived from the stolen gold.

The net was closing on Relton and Parry, and they knew it. Panic-stricken, they began a desperate attempt to distance themselves from the laundering operation. Relton sold his stake in his legal firm, Lynn Relton & Co. Both men left the country almost immediately and began taking steps to avoid arrest and retain the wealth they had accumulated. Relton wrote to close associates to tell them he would be going away and, at the end of August 1986, opened another secret account in Liechtenstein into which he transferred £300,000 from the Burton account. He named it 'Asbestos Stiftung' and joked that it was intended to be fireproof.

Relton went to Paris and it was there, on 6 September 1986, that a highly irregular meeting took place between Relton, Detective Inspector Peter Atkins, one of the officers drafted into the task force in spring 1985, and Relton's long-standing associate, the disgraced former detective Michael Ross, one of the Ross brothers whom Relton had once defended in court. Relton picked up the other two at the airport before the three men enjoyed a long £105 lunch at Relton's expense in a restaurant in Montmartre. It is likely that at this meeting, Relton had it confirmed that the task force was closing in on him and Parry. It was later said that Relton told Atkins and Ross that he knew McAvoy and Robinson had offered to return some of the gold in exchange for a reduction in their sentences and that he wanted to do something similar. A few days later, Relton fled with his wife to Spain, where he had property. Days after hosting a lavish christening party for his youngest daughter, Parry also went to Spain, leaving his new home in Westerham empty and his red Bentley in the drive.

In Spain, the two were anonymous and safe, certainly in the short term. All Relton and Parry needed was for the secretive banking systems of Switzerland and Liechtenstein to hold up to British police enquiries. They hadn't factored in the determination, and the contacts book, of Brian Boyce.

• • •

The police investigation into the purchase of Turpington Farm and the Bird-in-Hand Lane property had pointed towards money held in the Burton account in Switzerland and by the Moyet Foundation in Liechtenstein, but the banking regulations in both countries meant it was difficult for the task force to get any information about who controlled the source accounts.

Boyce, however, didn't give up that easily. Reasoning that the Swiss banks would not want to be seen as repositories of blood money, following the death of John Fordham, Boyce flew to Zurich to meet with the Swiss authorities. He took with him Detective Inspector Ron Smith, the Fraud Squad officer on the task force, and Detective Sergeant Rokoszynski, a task force officer with Polish heritage who was, crucially, a fluent German speaker. Meeting with Swiss police, Boyce persuaded the authorities to open the numbered accounts held in Switzerland by showing them photographs of Detective Constable

John Fordham's body after his violent death. Boyce was told that, under Swiss law, the requested information could only be shared if it had been authorised by a Swiss court in a closed hearing. A date was duly arranged and, with Rokoszynski subtly eavesdropping on proceedings, the British police learned that the Burton account was controlled by Parry and Relton. The task force was then able to make a request to the Swiss authorities for assistance in gathering evidence, which they accepted.

Once cooperation between the Swiss and the British police forces had been established, the Brink's-Mat task force was told by the Swiss police about Parry's visits to Zurich, and that he had hired a chauffeur-driven Mercedes to take him and three other people to Vaduz in Liechtenstein. The Moyet Foundation was established in Vaduz on the same day. The task force attention turned to Liechtenstein, where getting information from the authorities was even more difficult.

Once more, Boyce found a way. After being told that the identities of the beneficiaries of the Moyet foundation could not be divulged, Boyce called on a friend in the British intelligence services to help. Through him, the police were able to get the names of Parry, Relton and Perry. Secure in the knowledge that they were looking in the right place, a formal application for information was made through the Home Office to the bank in Liechtenstein and further incriminating information was gathered.

Around the same time, there was another development. Perry was charged and Parry had disappeared. Michael Relton, however, wanted to talk.

• • •

Relton had briefly been under task-force surveillance while police built the case against him, before slipping his observers and escaping to Europe. But, at the beginning of September 1986, Detective

Inspector Peter Atkins approached Detective Inspector Sandlin and told him that Relton was in Florida, scared out of his wits and keen to do a deal. Atkins explained that he had known Relton privately for several years, and that he had received the information from Michael Ross, who had been his best man. He said Relton had been helping invest money obtained from the sale of the Brink's-Mat gold and had fled after learning from someone on the task force that there was enough evidence to arrest him, and that the task force was looking into the Swiss accounts. Now, Atkins said, Relton wanted to save himself from prison by doing a deal in which he could return Krugerrands worth £6 million to the task force. With Boyce on holiday, Sandlin reported what Atkins had said to Lundy. Lundy was due to fly to Miami on 8 September 1986 to pursue inquiries connected to the Patrick Diamond–Shaun Murphy laundering investigation, so he told Sandlin to ask Atkins to arrange a meeting for him and Relton in Florida. While in America, Lundy repeatedly called Tintagel House to establish whether the meeting had been set up but returned home without having met Relton. According to Lundy, Sandlin reported that Atkins told him a meeting could not be arranged. It was never established whether Relton really was in Florida or not.

By October 1986, the task force had enough evidence to arrest Relton and be confident of a prosecution. A timetable was drawn up with the aim of finding Relton wherever he was in the world and arresting him within two weeks. After a task force briefing during which Sandlin outlined the progress of the inquiries into Relton and the money, the detectives gathered for a post-work drink in the Black Dog, a pub across the road from Tintagel House. While they were there, Sandlin approached Lundy looking visibly distressed; as Lundy noted in his subsequent report of the incident, this 'dedicated professional detective was obviously emotionally upset'. Sandlin told him that Atkins had approached him after the briefing and had offered him £100,000 to 'lay off' Relton. After a long conversation, Lundy and Sandlin left the pub and went home. Lundy was horrified and the next day reported the incident to Commander Phil Corbett. Sandlin was summoned to a meeting with Corbett and Lundy on 13 October 1986 and asked to repeat what he had said to Lundy at the Black Dog. He appeared upset that Lundy had reported the conversation and denied that he had been offered any money. Corbett later spoke with Sandlin alone and said the detective had confirmed the conversation but refused to give evidence against a fellow officer without anything to corroborate his statement. When questioned, Atkins claimed he had Relton as an informant, and said Sandlin had misunderstood – he had not been offered any money.

Around the same time, Corbett learned from a phone tap of the lunch meeting between Relton, Atkins and Michael Ross in Paris. It was, at best, highly inappropriate. Relton was being actively sought by the task force and yet Atkins had not told anyone about the meeting, even when Lundy had stressed the importance of finding and arresting Relton. Atkins had not mentioned it when he told Sandlin that Relton was in Florida and wanted to talk.

Corbett was furious. When he then learned of the meeting, Boyce was apoplectic. He demanded that Atkins be removed from the task force. Corbett reported his findings to Assistant Commissioner John Dellow, but without corroboration of what had been said between Sandlin and Atkins, no formal action was taken. Atkins had recently been selected for promotion to detective chief inspector and so was allowed to transfer out of the task force.

Despite facing complications from within their own ranks, the task force continued to build the case against Relton. They had uncovered details of his property deals in Spain and had requested legal assistance from the Spanish authorities. This link up with the Spanish police was to pay dividends when they were told that Relton was in Spain. Even better, he was on the move.

In mid-October 1986, Relton made the decision to slip back from Spain to London in order to wind up the remaining offshore companies and arrange for more getaway cash for him and Parry. Like so many decisions made by the protagonists of the Brink's-Mat story, it was likely motivated, at least in part, by greed. Like many of those decisions, it was one that would be regretted.

On 14 October 1986, Spanish police notified the task force that Relton was driving back to Britain and was due to arrive at an English Channel port. Surveillance officers from C11 and a team led by Detective Inspector Tony Brightwell spotted Relton at the port and kept him under observation as he returned to London. In the city, he was followed by a team directed by Detective Sergeant John Redgrave, one of the officers who arrested Tony White in 1983 and who had been involved in the surveillance on Noye and Reader in January 1985. Detectives watched as Relton visited addresses across the capital, made calls from telephone boxes and got progressively more drunk. At one point, Relton visited a bank to finalise a property deal. In an extraordinary coincidence, Sandlin was in the same bank branch, checking financial records.

To the watching detectives, Relton appeared to be 'a man at the end of his tether'. 'He was spooked,' Redgrave later recalled. 'My judgement was that he was going to do a runner because of the way he was acting.' The detectives had seen enough. Redgrave requested and was granted permission by Lundy to arrest the suspect. The detectives pulled over Relton close to Rochester Row police station, where a number of Brink's-Mat suspects had passed through. In the boot of Relton's car were two envelopes that Relton had originally posted from London to an address in Malaga in Spain, which he had now brought back with him. They contained dozens of incriminating financial documents, including a letter concerning Meacock's Turpington Farm, property plans, bank statements and details of the Burton account. More documents were found at a subsequent search of Relton's London home. Taken together, the paperwork gave the task force a detailed inventory of where much of the Brink's-Mat money had been hidden.

When Redgrave had walked to Relton's car and introduced himself, the former solicitor's response surprised the detective. 'I sensed,' Redgrave said later, 'an enormous relief on his face.'

• • •

At Rochester Row police station, Relton was greeted by Lundy, who explained that he had been arrested because he was suspected of handling money derived from the Brink's-Mat gold. With Relton heavily inebriated, he was placed in a police cell and left overnight. Waking up with a hangover and in surroundings which left him deeply uncomfortable, Relton was never going to be a difficult opponent for the Brink's-Mat detectives. Detective Sergeant Tony Curtis, the task force's exhibits officer, reported back to Boyce that Relton resembled a 'rabbit in the headlights'.

Tony Brightwell began his interview of Relton by asking, 'Why did you send all this material to Spain?' To the surprise of the police, Relton reacted by lifting his eyes from the documents before him and saying, 'I'll tell you everything.' It was a spectacular breakthrough for the task force. Relton began describing the money-laundering network, writing out explanations of more complicated aspects. Over a series of lengthy debriefings by Tony Brightwell, David Sandlin, Robert Suckling and Ron Smith, Relton would provide detailed information about the operation to launder the money that had been coming out of Scadlynn.

On 17 October 1986, Relton was formally charged with handling proceeds of the Brink's-Mat robbery at Horseferry magistrates' court, just a short walk from his former legal practice and a life that must, at that moment, have seemed very different. He appeared with Stephen Donovan, the frontman of the Kent house purchases, who had been arrested and charged with a similar offence.

Relton was granted bail under the unusual condition that he live at a police station. He was moved to a luxury, carpeted suite at New Malden police station, where he was held in a special unit. Relton had a living room, a colour television, a kitchen, bedroom and bathroom. He was allowed to have his own food sent in and could have regular visits from his wife Terri and his two grown-up children. Relton's solicitor, John Blackburn Gittings, told the curious press, 'The accommodation comprises a secure suite. I understand that under this arrangement, Mr Relton will not be allowed to leave the station unless accompanied by police officers, if it was thought necessary for him to leave in connection with the police inquiries.'

It was noted by the *Evening Standard* that 'the conditions of Relton's bail recall the treatment given to Scotland Yard's "super-grasses" of the 1970s'. It was a hint towards the danger that Relton was in. The supergrasses' accommodation might have been a step up from prison cells, but it came with bulletproof windows and armed guards. Relton's accommodation was not designed to keep him in. It was to keep others out.

For years, Relton had cultivated friendships with Scotland Yard detectives and now he charmed those guarding and interrogating him. Lundy soon heard that some officers were being over-friendly, soft-pedalling Relton and undermining pressure being put on him by other detectives. One officer complained to Lundy that he could not do any more interviews with another detective present because every time he tried to be hard on Relton, his colleague told Relton there was no need for concern and that everybody would look after him. Lundy later learned that the two men were both Freemasons. 'I gave this man a right dressing-down about him bending over backwards to help his friend,' Lundy told Martin Short later. 'I told him, if this had anything to do with Freemasonry, to keep out of it because Relton was going to be dealt with, whatever any secret society might think. I said he was in deep trouble and would be charged, so all this extra-niceness had to stop.' Lundy had the friendly officers removed from the interviews.

Relton admitted that he had received a tip-off from police sources that he was wanted and that was why he had decided to flee the country until things settled down. Under pressure, he told detectives that while he was in France, he made contact with Atkins to see if an offer to return the value of some of the stolen gold, or some other offer, would interest Boyce. While Relton's friendly relations with some police officers was a cause of concern to Boyce and Lundy, there was a greater issue at hand in Relton's less-than-friendly relations with his former criminal associates.

The task force had intelligence that a contract had been taken out on Relton's life. Initially, Relton did not take the threats seriously. However, at the end of November 1986, after helping the police for a month with their inquiries, Relton abruptly withdrew his cooperation. What happened to force that decision has never been clearly established, but detectives believed he had been threatened by the criminal gangs with whom he had become involved through his laundering of the Brink's-Mat money. There were later reports that Relton's wife had been visited at her home by the well-known

London gangland figure Mad Frankie Fraser, and that that she had found a listening device under the sink in her kitchen.

On 20 January 1987, Relton was back before the magistrate at Horseferry Road for his pre-trial remand hearing. This time, Relton was a tense, nervous presence who was keen to send a message that he was not cooperating with the Brink's-Mat task force. He specifically asked for reporting restrictions to be lifted so he could publicly refute claims he had become a supergrass. Alongside Relton was Brian Perry, who made the same request, showing similar concern that others may feel he was cooperating with police following his arrest. Also appearing at court were a number of those involved in the laundering operation, including John and Ann Elcombe, Kathleen Meacock and Jacqueline McAvoy. There was also a link to the other Brink's-Mat laundering route, as John Fleming's wife, Lesley, was also charged in the same proceedings.

Relton's withdrawal of cooperation meant he was sent to a normal prison. However, police feared that if he was let loose among the prison population he would be killed. Instead, Relton was placed in a special regime at Wormwood Scrubs prison. He made the best of it, enjoying meals of pheasant, smoked salmon and fine wine, brought to him by his loyal wife.

Meanwhile, the police continued to hunt his former partner Gordon Parry.

CHAPTER TWENTY-SIX

Manhunter

In early July 1986, Fleming was ordered to leave Spain within fifteen days. Under the conditions of the expulsion order, he was asked to tell local police his intended destination so it could be passed on to Scotland Yard. The request was ambitious. After two weeks of silence, other than the Suchet interview, Spanish police raided his house. It was deserted, though Fleming had left a note indicating that he had flown to South America. Friends told police he had flown to Brazil and was living in Rio. His Spanish lawyer told reporters, 'I can only say that he is not planning on returning to England.'

In fact, Fleming had booked a multiple-destination ticket from Madrid to a group of South American countries that did not have extradition treaties with Britain: Costa Rica, Cuba, Brazil and Panama. He made the travel arrangements on his American Express card, which Detective Inspector Tony Brightwell used to track him down to a hotel in San José, Costa Rica, where Fleming was holed up with £5,000 in cash and a Spanish girlfriend, Leocadia Aguilar. Brightwell was sent to Costa Rica to inform the authorities, with Scotland Yard fearing they had 'another Ronnie Biggs in the making' if Fleming was not extradited quickly. Brightwell did not know he was about to initiate an increasingly farcical chain of international events.

In Costa Rica, Brightwell persuaded the authorities to act, with Fleming arrested and Aguilar returning to Spain. All Fleming's possessions, including his Rolex watch and Cartier sunglasses, were seized at the request of Scotland Yard. Although Costa Rica did not have an extradition treaty with Britain, it had a policy of deporting undesirable foreigners. The authorities hoped to deport Fleming within days, but his lawyer submitted a writ of habeas corpus demanding his immediate release, citing the fact that Fleming had entered the country legally and had committed no crimes in Costa Rica. The appeal was taken to the country's supreme court, which confirmed Fleming's expulsion. All flights from Costa Rica to the UK or Spain connected in Miami, so Fleming was sent in the first place to the US. Brightwell went with him, as did the media. Fleming told reporters that his treatment was illegal, he was under 'constant surveillance' by British and Spanish authorities (which was true) and again denied he was involved with the Brink's-Mat robbery. Brightwell told a different story, later claiming that shortly before the flight, Fleming told him, 'The world and his fucking wife knows I had something to do with it, but you have fucking nothing. If you want me, you will have to drag me back in fucking chains.'

The British police's plan in Miami was that the DEA would immediately put Fleming on a flight back to London. It wasn't quite that simple. When Fleming arrived in Miami on 20 August 1986, he told reporters he would like to go to Panama, before being ushered away for questioning. Fleming began a legal argument as to whether he should be deported to Britain, insisting that he should be allowed to choose where he went. At a series of court hearings, Fleming appeared in bright orange prison dress and listened as the US immigration authorities and judge wrestled with an administrative nightmare. Perry Rivkind, the US Immigration

Service district director, said, 'The United States has nothing to do with Fleming – I question the appropriateness of him being sent to Miami from Costa Rica. He is an "excludable alien" because he has been convicted of crimes in other countries.' Fleming 'will not necessarily have to go back to Britain', he admitted. Judge Williams accepted that there were no grounds to extradite Fleming to Britain as British police had not issued an arrest warrant but warned that he would have to return Fleming to Britain if nowhere else would take him. Fleming was delighted; now all he had to do was find a country willing to accept him.

For Brightwell and the British authorities, it set up a difficult and faintly absurd challenge. They did not want to apply for Fleming's extradition from the United States or anywhere else as they did not have enough evidence to bring charges. Instead, they tried to ensure the American authorities would eventually have to deport him back to Britain because no other country could be found to take him in.

For the next eight months, while Fleming languished in a detention centre on the edge of the Everglades swamp, his lawyers travelled South America and the Caribbean trying to find somewhere that would accept him. Each time they found a country that looked likely to accede to the request, American immigration officers quietly informed Lundy and the task force's detectives, who then persuaded the country's diplomats how important it was for Scotland Yard that he come back to Britain. It was a long, drawn-out process, with each step doggedly followed by the British press.

By 29 August 1986, Fleming's lawyers had persuaded the Panamanian government to allow him into the country. British officials immediately began to put pressure on the Panamanian authorities. Fleming's lawyers chartered a private plane but were told by the American authorities that he needed to take a regular scheduled airline to be sure he went to the destination he had given. His lawyers duly booked a ticket, then gave it to the immigration services to make sure he was taken to the airport at the correct time. However, immediately after it was ruled that Fleming could leave the United States for a country of his choosing, a grand jury investigating money laundering and drug smuggling issued a subpoena for Fleming's passport, saying they wanted it for their inquiries. The passport was confiscated and, without it, Fleming could not take the Panama flight. Fleming's lawyers argued in federal court, possibly with some justification, that the American and British authorities were colluding in trying to stop him going to the country of his choice. The judge adjourned the case without a ruling, and by the time Fleming had his passport returned, the Panamanian authorities had decided they would not accept him.

Fleming's search continued. On 12 September 1986, victory was within his grasp. Fleming boarded an Eastern Airlines flight bound for the Dominican Republic, took a seat in the first-class section, and enjoyed two cans of Budweiser as he waited for the plane to take off. Minutes before departure, Fleming was ordered off the flight. He crushed his beer can, tore up a napkin in frustration, and shouted, 'Why won't the world leave me alone? Scotland Yard is behind all this.' The same three immigration officials who had driven him to the airport were waiting to take him back to the detention centre. When a cameraman asked what had happened, Fleming fired back with various degrees of expletive.

Fleming was right about the hidden hand of Scotland Yard. Lundy had lobbied the new Dominican consul in Miami, who called the airline and told them that the plane would not be allowed to land if Fleming was on board. Police told reporters that Fleming would be given a ticket back to Britain. Soon after, the immigration judge ruled that Fleming should be deported back to Britain, which Fleming's lawyers immediately appealed. Back in England, a British reporter tracked down Fleming's wife, Lesley, who said, 'I hope he never comes back, he'll be hounded by the police.' She doubted her husband would be treated fairly by the British system: 'He's innocent,' she told the reporter, 'but he'll never get a fair trial.' The reports that Fleming had been involved with the Brink's-Mat robbery made her fear for her young son: 'There are nuts around and I'm terrified he'll be snatched by people who think I'm sitting on a fortune.'

While the British press enjoyed every twist of the ongoing saga, Fleming remained behind the barbed wire of the Krome Detention Center, where his fellow inmates were largely Cubans and Haitians who had been refused entry to the United States. He grew increasingly depressed and, after almost three months in custody without being charged of any crime, made an appeal in the *Sunday Express* newspaper, saying, 'If the Yard takes Detective Superintendent Tony Lundy off my case I will come straight back home. I have nothing to hide and will answer all questions put to me. I hate being here – it's full of criminals – but I'd rather be here than having a noose put round my neck in Britain. I'm sure I can last longer than Mr Lundy. I have had Lundy on my back for eleven months. He's driving me crazy. I will never go back while he's in charge of the case, but I've got nothing to hide. I've got absolutely nothing to do with the Brink's-Mat job. The real robbers must be laughing at the way I'm being persecuted. I'm terrified of being stitched up if I go back on British soil. That's why I will continue to fight.'

Lundy was unrepentant and scornful in his reaction. 'It's not a question of him dictating who is dealing with his case. That's a matter for my bosses. I am carrying on with my duties.'

However, Lundy wouldn't be carrying on with those duties for long. *A World in Action* documentary programme called 'The Untouchable' was broadcast in November 1986, shortly after Lundy returned from Florida. The programme makers had investigated Lundy's relationship with Ray Garner, who had been one of Lundy's key informants, and alleged that Lundy had protected Garner from prosecution for a series of serious crimes, despite him being described in court as one of London's most dangerous criminals and a major cocaine trafficker. After the broadcast, two Labour MPs used parliamentary privilege to call for an investigation into Lundy's relationship with Garner. Lundy rejected the allegations and claimed he had already been investigated and exonerated. But the broadcast had come just a few months after Noye's handling trial ended in the acquittal of half the defendants. Whatever the truth, it did not reflect well upon the Brink's-Mat task force. After the broadcast, Lundy was taken off the Brink's-Mat case and subsequently suspended. South Yorkshire Police Force was appointed to investigate the allegations.

In June 1987, Garner was arrested by Customs officers and charged with importing $13.5 million of cocaine following a raid in Harley Street. In July 1987, probably as a result of Garner's arrest, Lundy was suspended for a 'recent breach of discipline'. Lundy retired in December 1988 with a doctor's note diagnosing him as suffering from acute stress. He ran a marathon shortly after. The result of any investigation was never made public. Whatever the truth of Tony Lundy's relationship with Ray Garner, the task force and the Metropolitan Police had lost a superlative detective.

In Florida, Fleming celebrated both his nemesis Lundy's removal from the case, and a new glimmer of hope. In December 1986, he obtained a visa to travel to Peru. A few hours before take-off, however, the visa was rescinded without explanation by the Peruvian consul-general after he was contacted by the British consul. The same day, Fleming's wife Lesley was arrested at her home in Herne Hill, south London, and appeared at Horseferry Road magistrates' court charged with dishonestly handling £100,000 from the robbery. Brian Perry appeared alongside her, charged with dishonestly handling £6 million. She was remanded on bail until February for £30,000; Perry was remanded in custody. The charges against Lesley Fleming were dismissed in June 1987.

In February 1987, a judge ruled that Fleming could be deported. A last-ditch appeal to the Eleventh Circuit, the regional appeals court, also failed and, in March, Fleming was finally placed on a flight to Britain, only to be removed at the last minute by American officials, who told him his lawyers had found a loophole and obtained a visa for Venezuela, only for this too to be rescinded at the last minute. In Britain, Fleming's travails were the subject of a lead story in *The Times* on 23 March 1987. It noted that British police had not formally applied for his extradition because they did not have enough to put against him. It concluded, 'The present comedy being enacted in Miami reflects badly on the law in either country and does the cause of justice no good.'

And still it wasn't over. In yet another last-ditch court appearance, Fleming's lawyers said they now had permission for Fleming to go to Nicaragua. Perry Rivkind, the director of the Immigration and Naturalization Service in Miami, declared enough was enough and told the judge he had authority to expel anyone he chose: 'I'm now going to use my discretion and deport Fleming back to Britain,' he said. The judge did not intervene. 'I somehow knew it would come to this, but I was prepared to fight them all the way,' Fleming said with a shrug and a smile.

Despite Scotland Yard never having made a formal request for his extradition and not issuing a warrant for his arrest, Fleming had to return home. He was said to be calm, spending his final hours in Miami reading Dickens's *A Tale of Two Cities* and sunbathing. Rivkind said, 'He seems to be a calm, strong individual. What's going on doesn't seem to faze him.' Fleming was placed on board Pan-Am flight 098 to Heathrow at 6.50pm local time on Wednesday 25 March 1987. He refused to speak with reporters as he was whisked through Miami Airport in handcuffs surrounded by immigration officers. One British consulate officer said, 'I won't believe that he's gone until I see the plane in the air.' He would soon get his wish, as photographers captured the plane lifting off into the sky. On board, Fleming followed the example of Palmer in engrossing himself in the in-flight movie. The film was *Manhunter*.

Over two years after the robbery, the Brink's-Mat task force had, in their minds, finally captured another of the robbers. Now they just needed to work out how to convict him.

CHAPTER TWENTY-SEVEN

Parry

Gordon Parry had been on the task force's radar since spring 1985, when he was interviewed after the Elcombes were stopped at the West German border. Sandlin's inquiries into the purchase of Turpington Farm and Bird-in-Hand Lane uncovered that Parry had played a role and now, from the inquiries in Switzerland and Liechtenstein, it seemed that he was linked to the wider laundering operation. By autumn 1986, Relton and Parry were prime suspects. In the period of Relton police cooperation following his arrest, he had confirmed police suspicion, explaining how Parry had persuaded Perry, who controlled McAvoy's share of the gold, to invest money generated from Brink's-Mat into property.

With Relton and Perry caught, Parry was now a key target of the task force. But, while Relton was sitting in Wormwood Scrubs eating smoked salmon, Parry was nowhere to be found. The police decided to go public, playing on the media's insatiable demand for Brink's-Mat stories. In March 1987, Scotland Yard stated publicly that it wanted to question Parry about the handling and laundering of the stolen Brink's-Mat gold. Parry became known in the press as a 'millionaire property dealer'. It was said he was thought to be on the Costa del Sol. On 3 April 1987, a warrant was issued for his arrest.

With the return of John Fleming to the UK on 26 March 1987, Parry became the task force's most prominent fugitive.

It was not until the autumn, almost exactly a year after Relton was arrested, that police had an opportunity to apprehend Parry. On the morning of 28 October 1987, he was caught in a task-force operation on the Trinity Estate in Deptford, south-east London. Parry was spotted being driven by his twenty-one-year-old son, John, in a red BMW convertible. Detectives cornered them and ordered Parry out of the car, but the car began to drive toward the line of plain-clothed police officers. Detective Sergeant Malcolm Baber reached in through the car window and tried to grab the keys from the ignition but was not quick enough. The car raced forward at the officers and sped off with Baber clinging to the bonnet. He was carried about fifty yards, but was eventually thrown off into the gutter, sustaining light injuries. The car raced off with detectives in hot pursuit. Police managed to head it off, but Parry leapt from the vehicle and fled through a maze of backstreets and tower-block walkways on an estate in Rotherhithe, south-east London. Scotland Yard denied that an ambush had been bungled, claiming – somewhat implausibly – that 'we chanced upon them and had to move in'.

The BMW was later found abandoned. John Parry was arrested and charged with preventing his father's arrest, two counts of causing actual bodily harm, while driving uninsured on a car without insurance. He would later be sentenced to two years, with twelve months suspended. In the wake of Parry's escape, a senior detective told a reporter, 'The hunt for Gordon Parry has gathered pace over the last few days. Our inquiries are even more intensified now.' Airports and ports were placed on alert and a photograph was widely distributed, but it was too late. Parry had gone, and remained gone, as his former associates faced justice.

They weren't alone.

CHAPTER TWENTY-EIGHT

The Last Robber

John Fleming's arrival back in the UK was a major event. At Heathrow Airport, about a dozen officers with a police truck and four escort vehicles waited on the tarmac for the plane to arrive. One passenger said, 'It looked like something out of a movie. He was under heavy escort. I think they had about thirty FBI and Justice people escorting him. He was grim-faced and … very stern-looking.' Fleming was formally arrested on the plane by Brink's-Mat task-force officers, and photographs of a handcuffed Fleming being led away across the Heathrow tarmac made the front pages and television news bulletins. In a final twist to Fleming's American saga, the following day, the FBI agents who accompanied him on the flight were caught up in a police raid on illegal after-hours drinking in a south London pub behind a police station and were arrested. Once their identities had been established, they were allowed to go.

Fleming was taken to Rochester Row police station, where he spent an hour with his solicitor, the familiar face of Henry Milner. It was a busy time for the task force. On the day that Fleming arrived back, eight people were remanded to appear at Lambeth magistrates court, charged with handling £11 million of the proceeds, including Michael Relton, Brian Perry, Kathleen Meacock and Jacqueline McAvoy.

Fleming was questioned for two days at Rochester Row police station before being charged with dishonestly handling £1.1 million of alleged proceeds from the stolen Brink's-Mat gold bullion and remanded in custody. If he was looking for reasons to be confident, it was just three days later that John Palmer, Fleming's fellow fugitive from justice, who shared the same solicitor, was cleared at the Old Bailey of involvement in the Brink's-Mat robbery.

Fleming's committal hearing offered more glimpses of what was becoming a recurring cast in the Brink's-Mat story. Once again, the prosecution case was put by Nicholas Purnell QC, while Fleming was represented by the same legal team that had been so successful in previous Brink's-Mat trials: Henry Milner, with John Mathew QC and Ronald Thwaites QC.

Purnell put the prosecution evidence before the court. Patrick Diamond refused to testify against Fleming, despite pleading guilty in the Isle of Man to receiving Brink's-Mat money from him. The court nevertheless heard about the transformation of Fleming's finances in the months immediately after the robbery. Purnell said Fleming met with Diamond at his Isle of Man offices in February 1984 and told him he wanted to buy a company. Diamond was paid £2,500 and later met Fleming at the Palace Hotel, where Fleming allegedly handed him a 'gift-wrapped' package that contained £100,000 in £50 notes. Purnell also said that on 28 March 1984, Fleming had Securicor deliver £100,000 in cash to pay an insurance broker to take out a unit trust policy in his wife's name. A commodity broker testified that in May and June 1984 Fleming had given him £50,000 in cash, including £30,000 in a Mothercare shopping bag. The broker had subsequently made a series of terrible investments that had lost Fleming's money.

The magistrate was told that Fleming was linked to Kenneth Noye. It was alleged that Noye had spent a night at Fleming's villa in

1984 and that his phone number was found among Fleming's possessions. Purnell told the court about Brightwell's claim that Fleming
had said about the Brink's-Mat robbery – 'The whole world and his
wife fucking knows I had something to do with it.' Purnell also told
the court of an alleged conversation between Fleming and Boyce
who had gone to his cell at Rochester Row police station after he
was returned to Britain. Fleming allegedly quipped to Boyce, referring to the alleged bribe that Noye had offered, 'This is where I am
supposed to offer you £1 million, isn't it?'

All this evidence against Fleming, however, was circumstantial.
As *The Times* had noted months before, the police 'lack sufficient
evidence to mount a prima facie against him'. At the end of the
first day's hearing, John Mathew QC submitted that there was no
evidence linking Fleming's money to the Brink's-Mat robbery and
asked for the defendant to be discharged. Henry Milner later said,
'It was a formality. It was a very slim case, but we didn't really expect
a magistrate to have the guts to throw it out at that stage after all
the publicity.' The stipendiary magistrate, Mrs Norma Negus, spent
the evening studying the evidence. The following morning, 25 June
1987, after just twenty-five seconds, she delivered her verdict: 'I have
had the time to consider the charge against Mr Fleming and I find
there is insufficient evidence. He is, therefore, discharged.'

Fleming showed no emotion, but as he walked from court,
free after almost a year, he told reporters, 'It's like a dream. It did
take me by surprise.' He went on, 'I feel a relief. It has been a bad
year. Justice seems to have been done. The case was expensive and
unnecessary. I will probably celebrate with a quiet drink with my
family.' He blamed the press for starting 'the whole ball rolling' and
castigated the police for fabricating quotes from 'corridor conversations which did not exist' and pressuring him to explain his wealth.

'It's private,' Fleming said about his money, 'but I'll probably have to tell the taxman.' Fleming offered his own summary of his legal adventures: 'It was an incredible case, full of scheming and dirty tricks by the governments of Costa Rica, Spain, Britain and the United States. It was full of illegal acts and they broke all the rules to get me. They threw the rule book out of the window.'

There was some truth to his statement. If the Brink's-Mat detectives had the evidence for the extradition, they would likely have had the evidence for a conviction. Instead, they achieved neither. Scotland Yard refused to comment on the verdict and in private, detectives greeted it with resignation and some internal tension. Boyce later said Lundy ignored his order not to pursue Fleming. It has been suggested that Boyce was 'under instructions' from British intelligence to leave Fleming in Brazil or the United States.

The Brink's-Mat task force's conduct over Fleming was criticised by the press, MPs, the American Immigration authorities and British officials in Miami. Perhaps the detectives' biggest regret was seeing their last chance of convicting another Brink's-Mat robber end in failure. For the police, the collapse of the Fleming prosecution was in many ways the last act of the original robbery, ensuring that they would only ever convict two of the six robbers. For Fleming, it was a Pyrrhic victory. His finances had been depleted and his new-found notoriety would bring unwelcome attention. After the Brink's-Mat charges were thrown out, he returned to Spain, but in April 1988 the authorities detained him and expelled him for a second time. In the early 1990s, he and others found themselves ensnared in legal action in America around Brink's-Mat money laundering that bankrupted him. In later years, he was said to have been conned out of his remaining money and was living on a barge in south-east London.

CHAPTER TWENTY-NINE

Farewell to
The Old Bailey

In early April 1988, the Brink's-Mat saga returned to Court Twelve of the Old Bailey for the laundering trial. It was the start of a trilogy of trials, which would be the last of the many Brink's-Mat trials at the Old Bailey and wrap up the criminal investigations of the Brink's-Mat task force. Brian Perry, Michael Relton, Joseph Medayil, Stephen Donovan, Michael Osborn, John and Ann Elcombe, Kathleen Meacock and Jacqueline McAvoy were together accused of dishonestly handling £7.5 million of the proceeds of the stolen Brink's-Mat gold and converting it into a property empire worth £18 million. All of the defendants pleaded not guilty.

Judge Richard Lowry QC presided over the proceedings, like he had done at Noye's handling trial two years previously. As with previous trials, security was intense and the judge ordered police surveillance for the jury. Detective Sergeant John Redgrave prepared a report for senior Scotland Yard management arguing that the trial should not be held in London. He pointed to Relton's relationships with a coterie of former and serving police officers, the Ross brothers and other disgraced detectives. There was a danger, argued

Redgrave, that the trial could be brought down from the inside. Boyce and Corbett endorsed Redgrave's recommendations. In a note on the report, Corbett wrote that he was 'convinced that serious and concerted attempts to pervert and impede the course of justice will be made' in the trial; 'indeed it is likely that they have already commenced'. Despite this police fear, the trial remained in London.

Kathleen Meacock was newly married; she and McAvoy had wed in the gymnasium of Leicester jail on 2 June 1987. Afterwards, the bride was photographed leaving through the heavy doors of the Victorian prison. As the newspapers noted, she had shown considerable commitment and loyalty to McAvoy, and would have up to twenty years to wait for the honeymoon. For many, it seemed as though McAvoy was also making a statement about the future. He would not be broken by his long sentence and there would be a life after Brink's-Mat.

At the Old Bailey, Parry was named as a co-conspirator and was a notable presence despite his absence from the proceedings. Opening the prosecution, the familiar presence of Nicholas Purnell QC described Parry as 'a figurehead … intimately involved', who set up property companies to launder the money. It was reported during the trial that Parry had been spotted in Spain and that he was thought to be enjoying his millions on the Costa del Crime. Jonathan Goldberg QC, one of the defence barristers, described Parry as 'a confidence trickster with great charm and charisma, a Mr Fixit at the centre of the web'. The trial without him, he said, was 'like *Hamlet* without the Prince of Denmark'.

For his part, Relton felt he had identified an alternative conspiracy unfolding. Arriving outside court, he held up a large handwritten sign to the gathered press: 'Chief Supt Boyce scripted book "BULLION" to Pervert Justice'. The book, *Bullion*, which was published in February 1988, was the first major journalistic investigation of the robbery and its aftermath, and was written by the Insight team at the *Sunday Times*. Boyce had been interviewed for the book, which covered the police inquiry. It said very little about the money-laundering ring around Relton as the case had not yet come up in court at the time of publication.

Setting out the case for the prosecution, Purnell told the court that the operation by the defendants to launder more than £10 million in cash acquired from smelting and selling the Brink's-Mat bullion began soon after the robbery. It was claimed that Parry and Relton had invested money generated by the sale of McAvoy's share of the stolen gold, which Perry had appropriated without McAvoy's knowledge. The letter found at Kathleen McAvoy's house was read to the jury, where Micky McAvoy wrote that he thought 'one of our own' was using the gold for his own purposes. Perry was described as a 'secret partner, or silent director' who represented the interests of McAvoy and Robinson and acted as a 'figurehead' in the property deals. Purnell said Relton was the business brain behind the operation, the 'paymaster general or chancellor of the exchequer', who managed the money and planned how it would be brought back to Britain. Together, Relton and Parry planned to invest money from the robbery with a view to giving back the original stolen sum and keeping the massive profits.

Purnell outlined how great lengths were taken to disguise the true origins of the money when purchasing property and revealed how it was used to purchase lavish homes for many of those involved. The prosecution used photographs to contrast the old flats of Kathleen McAvoy and Jacqueline McAvoy with their new homes in Bickley. Purnell described how Turpington Farm had been bought for Kathleen 'financed by Brink's-Mat money. She was being physically cared for by Brink's-Mat money.' He read out a letter from McAvoy that had been sent to Kathleen from prison: 'Whatever happens to our relationship, and even if it breaks up because of the twenty-five years I have to serve, the house is yours. Everything in the house is yours.'

Purnell described how Relton had provided the task force with crucial evidence before he stopped cooperating and tried to withdraw his admissions, including telling police that he knew the money had come from the stolen gold, and describing the formation of front companies registered in Panama with Parry and their illicit property deals. Relton, like all the other defendants, denied the charges against him. Choosing to appear as a witness in his defence, he spent nine days answering questions and stuck resolutely to his new position, furiously back-pedalling on his period of cooperation with the police. He admitted working with Parry, but claimed that neither he nor Parry had any knowledge that the money came from the robbery, and that his confessions had been made under duress and should not be admitted as evidence. 'There is no way,' Relton gravely told the court, 'I would connect Mr Parry with the Brink's-Mat robbery. He was a man of considerable ability and substance … who came back from adversity and proved himself in business.'

Partway through the trial, following a submission from her defence team, the judge directed the jury to acquit Ann Elcombe of the charge against her, because 'suspicion is not enough'. The fact that she had been with her husband when the money was driven to Europe and present when it was paid in was not sufficient proof of her involvement in the conspiracy. On the stand, her husband admitted to having transported large sums of money to Switzerland and Liechtenstein, and to paying money into accounts there and elsewhere. Parry, he said, told him the money had been 'skimmed off' his businesses and had to be taken out in cash so that it could be repatriated and invested without coming to the notice of the Inland Revenue.

After three months listening to complex evidence, the jury deliberated for six days before returning a verdict on 2 July 1988. They acquitted John Elcombe, Joseph Medayil, Stephen Donovan, and Michael Osborn. The jury was unable to reach verdicts on Perry and Jacqueline McAvoy, so a retrial was ordered. They did, however, reach a unanimous guilty verdict against Kathleen McAvoy and found Relton guilty by a ten-to-one majority. The new Mrs McAvoy got off relatively lightly, with Lowry telling her, 'The lure of good living constituted your criminality,' before sentencing her to eighteen months imprisonment, suspended for two years. Afterwards, Kathleen was pictured grinning outside the court, laughing with friends as they drove off.

There was no such relief for Relton. Of the three main players in the laundering ring, he was the only one who had been caught and convicted, and justice landed heavily upon him. Relton was white-faced as he stood to hear his sentence. Judges do not traditionally look favourably on fellow lawyers who commit crimes and Lowry was no exception, saying, 'Far from serving the community as a lawyer, you aspired to live as a rich parasite. You are not a man who has been led into crime by others. You were grossly dishonest. You were too keen to mix with persons you knew were linked to organised crime.' He sentenced Relton to twelve years imprisonment.

After the verdict, Relton's wife Terri was furious: 'I can't believe it. Mike has been set up by a man who should have been in the dock.' She continued, 'We didn't need the Brink's-Mat money. We were happy enough.' She claimed Relton had been misjudged: 'What's been said against him is all lies. I don't know why he's been singled out. He's a good man. My husband is not corrupt. The judge doesn't know him … Mike's been left carrying the can.' She then asked a question that she wasn't alone in wondering: 'But where is Gordon John Parry? He should be in the dock.'

After the trial, Scotland Yard investigated suggestions that the jury had been intimidated. Reports came out that the jury foreman had refused to deliver the verdicts in protest at events that had taken place in the jury room during the long period of deliberation. His place was taken by another juror who needed to be prompted in the verdicts. At least one woman was heard sobbing as she returned to the jury room. Police believed that money was offered to at least one member of the jury before the end of the trial.

During the trial, while being questioned as a witness, Boyce made some controversial claims. He told the court that he believed 'there were corrupt solicitors who were assisting some or all of the likely prisoners that I would have'. He said that suspicions became so acute that in August 1986, an unprecedented blanket order was made that all people arrested in connection with the inquiry would be denied their normal right to immediate legal representation. The order was made, he said, because police feared lawyers were passing information to the criminals, who would use it to hinder the police's efforts to arrest and charge them.

He said the police had discovered video tapes during the search of Noye's home that suggested Henry Milner 'was likely either to be unprofessional or possibly corrupt'. One of the home videos, Boyce said, showed 'a wedding party involving a man who I suspected of being a leading member of the robbery gang who has not been charged. On that video tape, Mr Milner was at the party, Mr and Mrs Noye, and Mr and Mrs John Fleming, and it was my view that this was a purely social occasion which indicated to me that what the solicitor, Mr Milner, had with the persons I suspected was much deeper than a simple client–solicitor relationship.' He said Milner was also suspected of smuggling letters from Micky McAvoy out of prison. Police had found a letter from McAvoy during the search of Kathleen's house and a letter from her had been found in McAvoy's prison cell. Boyce went on to name two other solicitors who he believed were improperly passing information they gleaned from police interviews to other suspects.

Boyce's evidence had been given in the absence of a jury and it was not until the trial had concluded that reporting restrictions were lifted by the judge. It caused a sensation. The Law Society reacted angrily to the allegations, which reignited a row from earlier in the year when it emerged that the Flying Squad was compiling a list of lawyers who were thought to help criminals illegally. The accused solicitors all vigorously denied that they had acted improperly or illegally. From his office in Hatton Garden, Henry Milner told reporters, 'Over four years ago, I attended a client's wedding in a public hall. To this day, the client has never been arrested, interviewed or charged with any offence connected with the robbery.' Of the smuggling claims, he declared, 'To suggest I have ever taken a letter into or out of prison is nonsense.'

When the dust settled on these multiple controversies that marked the end of the trial of the laundering ring, the police returned to work. High in their priorities was a wish to answer the question asked by Terri Relton and many others. Where was Gordon Parry?

• • •

Parry was found as a result of international policing links formed by multiple Brink's-Mat investigations. The burgeoning relationship between the Brink's-Mat task force and Spanish police, forged often through failure, had a major success when they worked together to track down Parry to a luxury apartment in Carvajal, near Fuengirola on the Costa del Sol. When armed Spanish police raided the apartment during the evening of 7 April 1989, Parry attempted to escape but was arrested in nearby bushes by police, including Brink's-Mat detectives David Sandlin and Bill Miller. Flanked by six armed officers, Parry was bundled into a police car and driven at speed to a local police station.

The British authorities issued an extradition warrant, which Parry spent the rest of the year fighting while being held in a jail near Madrid. Parry claimed that a contract had been taken on his life because he 'knew too much'. By January 1990, he had had enough, gave up and agreed to return to Britain voluntarily, saying he feared for his life.

Miserable and depressed, on 6 April, Parry flew back to London accompanied by two Spanish detectives. On the plane, he complained to a reporter about the conditions he claimed to have faced in Spain: '80 per cent AIDS in the prison, hepatitis, bugs that bite you, horrific. If I was the Pope, I'd kiss the ground. I've been trying for weeks to get out of those rotten Spanish jails.' Parry said he was ready to face the Brink's-Mat detectives: 'I have an answer to anything they want to throw at me.' Like Palmer and Fleming before him, Parry was arrested as soon as the plane touched down at Heathrow. Giving a wave to the waiting press photographers, he was led away in handcuffs by Detective Sergeants Bill Miller and Tony Curtis. The following day, he appeared before Horseferry Road magistrates to be charged with handling more than £16 million of the proceeds of the Brink's-Mat robbery and remanded in custody. As he stood down from the dock, he shook hands with the detective who arrested him. At his later committal hearing, Parry wore two yellow rosebuds in the buttonhole of his grey suit. By the time Parry's case came to trial, at the Old Bailey on 1 July 1991, he had some company.

• • •

Jean Savage had been a person of interest since the very start of the investigation and her significance only seemed to grow as the inquiry progressed. She lived as the common-law wife of John Lloyd in a bungalow on Hever Avenue in West Kingsdown previously owned by Kenneth Noye, whom Savage and Lloyd were known to be acquainted with.

Police had long suspected that Lloyd could be one of the Brink's-Mat robbers. Certain actions caught by their surveillance operations suggested he could have been involved with Noye's handling of the stolen bullion. They wanted to interview Lloyd after Noye was arrested, but he vanished, some thought to Florida. Meanwhile, Savage publicly distanced herself from Noye. When the *Daily Mail* printed a photograph of her bungalow and incorrectly identified it as belonging to Noye's sister, she got the newspaper to print a correction stating she had 'no connection with Mr Kenneth Noye or his family'.

The bungalow on Hever Avenue was searched. Two cake stands from the stolen Darnely porcelain collection were found, other items of which had been discovered at Noye's house. Detectives established that some more of the stolen porcelain had been entrusted by Savage to a carpenter from Bethnal Green, east London, who was doing work for her and Noye. Police found the stolen porcelain in his van. Savage's fingerprints were found on the porcelain in the van and at Noye's home. She and Noye were both charged with dishonestly handling stolen property. After an Old Bailey trial in May 1987, Noye was found guilty and sentenced to four years – which ran concurrently with his sentence for the Brink's-Mat handling offences – while Savage, who admitted assisting Noye, was given a £500 fine.

During Noye's trial in November 1985 for the murder of John Fordham, Jean Savage appeared with Brenda Noye in a photograph taken at a disco that was shown to Noye by the prosecution. Otherwise, despite being a known associate of several men intimately connected with the robbery, the police had nothing on Savage. On paper, she was simply the owner of the Silk Cut newsagent and tobacconist on Walworth Road in south-east London. Her partner Lloyd remained at large, even after the Brink's-Mat insurers offered a reward for information that led to his arrest.

What the police did not know was that Savage deposited millions of pounds in cash on behalf of Noye into the Bank of Ireland during 1984. Following Noye's arrest, that money remained untouched, generating huge amounts of interest, while Savage kept her head down. When news arrived of Gordon Parry's arrest in April 1989, however, it is thought that Savage panicked.

On 15 May 1989, she travelled to Dublin and visited the head office of Bank of Ireland Finance in Burlington Road. She was with an associate, a financial criminal known to the Noyes and Patrick and Stephen Clarke. Savage and the associate arranged to open a new account in the associate's name and to transfer into it the entire contents of another account – £4.1 million – held in the name of Savage and her daughter. The emptied account was then closed. The following day, the associate transferred £1 million of that to an account he held with an associate in Abu Dhabi. News of Savage's finances somehow filtered out through the underworld and from there was picked up by Brink's-Mat task-force officers.

A few weeks later, at the beginning of July 1989, an injunction was taken out in Dublin at the instigation of the solicitors representing Brink's Ltd to freeze the account. Detectives and financial investigators established that between March 1984 and November 1984, Savage had paid over £2.5 million into the Bank of Ireland branch in Croydon. On 12 October 1989, Savage was arrested by armed officers of the task force in a dawn raid. Patrick and Stephen Clarke were arrested as part of the same coordinated operation, which involved sixty officers located at nine addresses in London, Kent and Surrey. Lloyd and the associate would have been arrested but both had vanished.

The following day, Savage and the Clarkes were charged with conspiring with Noye, Perry, Relton and others to dishonestly handle the proceeds of the stolen Brink's-Mat gold. Savage's solicitor was Henry Milner, who applied for her to be bailed. Shortly before Christmas 1989, Savage was granted bail for £300,000 with a surety of £30,000 lodged with Milner. It was the largest bail amount in British legal history for a female defendant.

• • •

The second major Brink's-Mat laundering trial began in Court Sixteen at the Old Bailey on 1 July 1991. With Judge Henry Pownall QC presiding, Brian Perry, Jacqueline McAvoy, Gordon Parry, Jean Savage, Patrick Clarke and Stephen Clarke stood accused of laundering around £14.5 million of the proceeds from the Brink's-Mat robbery. This trial was essentially the bundling together of the retrial of Perry and Jacqueline McAvoy, the trial of the captured Parry and the addition of the newly caught suspected money launderers Savage and the Clarkes.

It was a massive undertaking. The prosecution statements took up five volumes estimated at a total of 2,000 pages, and there were twelve volumes of exhibits. Two computer terminals were installed in the court room and were connected to nineteen screens to help guide the jury through the mass of complex financial evidence. Seven QCs and eight junior barristers were involved.

Opening the prosecution, Michael Austin-Smith QC explained 'It is all very well to have £26 million worth of gold, but it is another thing altogether to use that gold in a way that does not cause instant suspicion.' He explained to the jury that the defendants were essentially split into two laundering teams, each disposing of around £7 million.

For one team, Austin-Smith explained, Perry was the 'unofficial director on the board of governors', who acted as an 'agent' for Jacqueline McAvoy and Robinson. Austin-Smith outlined the familiar roles of Perry, Parry and Relton in this laundering route. On the other team, Kenneth Noye was 'the link man', responsible for smelting and selling the stolen gold, with Savage and the Clarkes then paying 'a fountain of cash' into bank accounts. McAvoy was 'on the fringe' of the plot, Austin-Smith said, but had benefited from the robbery.

The trial ground along. The prosecution evidence continued through the summer into the autumn. Proceedings were laborious and slow-moving until 11 November 1991, when, after a private meeting with the prosecution and defence barristers, Judge Pownall suddenly announced that the jury were to be dismissed, the trial aborted and a retrial ordered. Pownall declared there was 'a very good reason' for his decision. 'Believe me,' he said, 'it is a proper reason.' That reason would never be disclosed publicly, in order not to prejudice the retrial, but it has been reported to centre around a concern that there was an attempt being made to nobble the jury.

By the time it was stopped, the trial had already become one of the longest in British legal history and was estimated to have cost the taxpayer £2.5 million, a fact highlighted in newspaper coverage of its collapse. The *Daily Mail* pointed out that the hire of the computer equipment alone had cost £45,000, more than it would have cost to buy it outright. For the police, it was a depressing development. 'It is so much work down the drain', said one officer. 'We have got piles and piles of documents and now we are back where we started.'

The retrial began at the Old Bailey in January 1992. The charges against Jacqueline McAvoy were set aside to be dealt with in a separate trial, presumably to simplify the case presented to the jury. Brian Perry, Gordon Parry, Jean Savage and Patrick and Stephen Clarke were left standing, once again, as co-defendants. After the nobbling scare that had brought the previous trial to an abrupt halt, a team of seventy-two police officers provided the new jury with round-the-clock protection.

Michael Austin-Smith QC once again began setting out the case for the prosecution. The story was by now a familiar one. The plot to disguise where the gold had come from was, he said, 'little short of brilliant' and inspired a 'grudging admiration'. Perry had acted as an agent for the convicted robbers, watching over their interests, but had 'set about feathering his own nest'. Austin-Smith, perhaps seeking new colour for an old story, told the court that above the desk in his cab office, Perry had hung a plaque that read: 'Remember the golden rule: whoever has the gold makes the rules.'

The court was told that Parry and Relton's investment of the laundered Brink's-Mat money had been made 'much in Docklands during the mid-1980s boom', and that Savage and the Clarkes were linked to 'robbers who have not been identified and have not been brought to justice'. Austin-Smith accused the Clarkes of laundering about £4 million in cash. Of Savage, Austin-Smith asked the jury, 'What is a lady tobacconist doing with £2.5 million in a Dublin account?'

Once again, proceedings took an unusual turn. On 22 April 1992, with no explanation, the court went into chambers, with the press, public, solicitors, Crown Prosecution Service and the defendants all excluded. This unusual step could only be justified if it was felt publicity would defeat the object of the hearing, if the case involved matters of national security or if the judge had received critical information. It wasn't until 19 May that the court sat in public again. The judge apologised for the long delay and explained that an anonymous letter had been sent to him. Although he did not reveal the contents, he discharged a young juror, telling her not to worry, that he did not think she had done or said anything wrong, but offering no further explanation. The woman broke down in tears. The letter purported to come from the spouse of one of the jurors, but the judge later said he thought it came from a known trouble-maker.

The defendants all pleaded not guilty. Parry chose not to give evidence. Perry, however, took to the witness stand where he defended himself against accusations that he had stolen McAvoy's stolen gold. 'The reality, unknown to poor old McAvoy on the inside, is that the gold had been traded – had it not?' he was asked by Austin-Smith. 'No, it hadn't,' Perry replied. 'That's why McAvoy got so cross with you,' continued Austin-Smith, 'and said there was "some lowlife" as he described it, on the outside. That was referring to you, was it not?' Perry denied this.

The trial dragged on until 10 August 1992, when the jury finally retired to consider its verdicts. On Saturday 15 August, after over thirty-three hours of deliberations, the jury came to a decision on Parry and the Clarks. Parry and Patrick Clarke were found guilty; Stephen Clarke was found not guilty. The jury had not yet been able to come to a decision on Savage and Perry. At this point, there was another twist in proceedings, when one of the jurors was told that her seven-year-old son had fallen off a cliff while on a family holiday in Cornwall and that he was fighting for his life. The judge sent her in a helicopter to be by the boy's bedside in Truro hospital. He told the other jurors, some of whom were sobbing, that they should spend the rest of the weekend in their hotel and resume work on the Monday morning.

When the jury returned to its deliberations, they found Perry guilty but could still not reach a verdict on Savage. Pownall told them he would be prepared to accept a majority nine-to-one verdict. Shortly after, the jury returned with a guilty verdict. Savage, who was wearing a black and gold suit, looked visibly shocked when the verdict was announced, and relatives in the public gallery wept.

Sentencing the convicted defendants, Judge Pownall said, 'You were playing for very high stakes indeed. There can hardly have been a more serious case of handling than this.' Parry received ten years. Smartly dressed in a dark suit, blue shirt and red tie, he showed no emotion as the sentence was read out. Patrick Clarke received six years. Savage received five years. She looked shaken upon hearing the sentence. Perry was jailed for nine years, with police believing he felt dire dread that he would be placed in the same prison as McAvoy. A month later, Jacqueline McAvoy walked free from the Old Bailey, after the prosecution decided not to proceed with the case against her.

In the 1980s, the British press had lapped up every Brink's-Mat story they could get their hands on. The robbery, and what happened next, was a perfect encapsulation of the time, reflecting the extravagant consumerism, booming property market and rush of financial opportunity that the public saw all around them. But the Brink's-Mat story had now intruded into the early 1990s recession, and the reaction to the latest trial showed a changed public appetite and attitude towards the story. The details of unlimited money and profligate spending seemed like something from an already distant era and most press reports at the trial's conclusion chose to highlight its great cost to the taxpayer. The jury protection operation was the longest ever undertaken by the Metropolitan Police and was estimated to have cost £1 million. The trial itself was said to have cost £8 million, which brough total estimates for the Brink's-Mat trials to £14 million.

This wasn't the end of the Brink's-Mat story, but it was the last of the criminal trials under the direction of the Brink's-Mat task force.

By the time this final criminal trial had finished, Michael Relton, who had had his sentence reduced on appeal, was free, as was Brian Reader. Kenneth Noye was enjoying day release from prison. Tony Black and many of the others involved in the gold-smelting and laundering operations had long been free. Matteo Constantino was dead. The police inquiry, which at one time had had over two hundred officers working on it, had been reduced to just Detective Sergeants Bill Miller and Tony Curtis.

The Brink's-Mat robbery was already becoming popular folk-lore, with myths and legends growing around it. That autumn, ITV screened a dramatisation of the robbery that starred Sean Bean as Micky McAvoy. It was called *Fool's Gold*.

CHAPTER THIRTY

The Loss Adjusters

In Geneva on a summer's day, shade is hard to find. Children play in public pools while parents huddle under parasols. The wide streets bake in the heat, the restaurants stretch awnings over their outside tables and offer the *menu du jour*.

Geneva is a city that runs on money. Through commodity trading, it creates new money. Through wealth management, the city minds and nurtures a reserve of old money that could fund a nation. With money comes the laws to protect it. In a street in central Geneva sits a gleaming office block. Up the elevator, past the receptionist, down a corridor and into a grand executive office, there is a solicitor who has spent decades helping clients protect their money and their assets. In particular, he has helped them get it back.

Bob McCunn is an Englishman in his sixties, a bookish, cerebral presence, and studiously careful in manner from a career in intricate litigation. Initially, he is measured and precise, correcting and chiding where he sees gaps in our knowledge. After a while, McCunn relaxes. There are laughs and anecdotes, and perhaps a wistfulness for the decade or so of his life which offered a novel unpredictability and exposure to a very different world.

On a summer's day in Geneva, Bob McCunn talks of Kenneth
Noye, John Palmer, Micky McAvoy and Brian Boyce. He talks of danger,
adventure and an oil well in Kansas. He talks of the Brink's-Mat gold,
but he talks more about the Brink's-Mat money. Bob McCunn knows
more than anyone in the world about the Brink's-Mat money.

Because he found it.

• • •

Robbery is never a victimless crime. In the case of the theft of the
Brink's-Mat gold, the victim is often wrongly identified as the gold's
owners, the metal dealer Johnson Matthey. That is inaccurate. The
stolen gold was insured by a consortium of underwriters at Lloyds of
London. The victim of the Brink's-Mat robbery was that consortium
and the loss was devastating. 'In insurance terms,' one insurance
expert told a reporter the day after the robbery, 'it's equivalent to
the loss of a supertanker.' In the weeks after the robbery, Stewart
Wrightson, the broking group, handed cheques worth almost £26
million to the owners of the missing gold and valuables. Within a
month, all the insurance claims had been settled.

The insurers might have paid up promptly, but that was only one
half of their response. The other was a determination to get their
money back. They immediately appointed a private investigations
firm, Robert Bishop and Co., to try to trace the stolen property and
within two days, offered a record-breaking £2 million reward for any
information that led to convictions and the recovery of the stolen
bullion. It wasn't enough to shake any information from the criminal underworld, but when £1 million in gold, cash and other assets
were discovered following the arrests of Noye and others involved in
smelting the stolen bullion, the insurers saw a glint of hope.

Led by Stephen Merrett, one of the leading underwriters at
Lloyds, they instructed Shaw and Croft, a firm of London solicitors,

to represent them in the legal case to recover the stolen property once the police had finished using it as evidence. Bob McCunn, a partner at Shaw and Croft, took on the case. Then a young, ambitious solicitor, McCunn took a look at the case and came back with a proposal. 'We felt,' he would recall later, 'that we could do a bit better than that.'

McCunn and his colleague told the underwriters that they felt they could follow leads of investigation thrown up by the court proceedings to trace and reclaim vastly more of the proceeds of the Brink's-Mat robbery than £1 million. What they were proposing was highly ambitious. By working with investigators to gather evidence, the solicitors could prepare a case to sue anyone involved in the crime, whether knowingly or not, in the civil courts for compensation. It would effectively create a second private investigation that would run parallel to the police inquiry and a civil legal case separate to the one in the criminal courts.

When McCunn and Peter Steger, the lead investigator at Robert Bishop and Co., put their daring plan to the insurance companies, they were excited by the response. 'The insurance companies were furious about the robbery, the scale of it and the violence,' said Steger. 'A decision was taken to deliver a message to the underworld that no one would be allowed to get away with something like this.'

Now that McCunn had the backing of the insurers, he had to work out how to go about tracing a vast criminal fortune and asking those criminals to pay it back. McCunn had been a commercial litigation solicitor since the early 1970s. Much of his work involved maritime fraud, looking at ships that had sunk in mysterious circumstances and chasing money around the world. McCunn viewed the Brink's-Mat case in the same way as his other work: it was simply a case of tracing assets and getting court judgements against people to

enable them to be returned to their rightful owner. The only significant differences were the scale of the work that would be necessary
to attempt to trace almost £26 million of stolen gold and valuables,
the publicity that the case was attracting and the very real, and very
frightening, security risks.

McCunn and his team began work in spring 1985, with little
to go on. The only leads were details that the police made public
about discoveries at Hollywood Cottage, the Coach House and
other properties searched after Noye was arrested. McCunn's team
were effectively working from news reports. McCunn approached
Scotland Yard to establish whether they could work together and
if the police could share further evidence. The reply was a definite
no. Scotland Yard's duty was to the public interest. They could not
be seen to be working with the insurers because it would allow Noye
and others to accuse them of being in the pocket of outside interests.
The two investigations would proceed separately.

The legal team looked for other sources of evidence. McCunn
spent a day reading through the piles of letters at the investigators'
offices that the reward had attracted. As he said later, the reward had
'produced files and files and files and files of the most bizarre claims:
neighbours were complaining about their neighbours digging in the
garden in the dead of night and they thought they were burying the
gold; people were coming along with lode stones and pendulums and
maps and saying they could point to where the gold was; even down
to one person claiming extra-terrestrials were telling him where the
gold was.' The team followed the leads. It went nowhere.

Kenneth Noye's trial for the murder of John Fordham was the
first opportunity for McCunn's team to hear detailed information
about the case and those involved. McCunn sat through some of
the proceedings but there was little to be gathered from a recovery

perspective, with the trial focusing on Fordham's death and not the handling of the stolen gold. McCunn employed a young barrister to sit in the public gallery and quietly note anything of financial interest. She did the same in summer 1986 when Noye and the other suspects were tried for handling the stolen gold. This time, it paid off.

Making detailed notes, the barrister kept McCunn and his small team informed of relevant information. She also befriended key figures, including defence and prosecution counsels and the occasional witness. Perhaps flattered by the attention of a young woman and not realising her motives, the largely middle-aged and elderly men shared useful details. As the handling trial drew a conclusion, McCunn made his first move.

As the jury began to consider its verdicts, McCunn applied to the High Court to issue a writ that would begin the process of civil action. McCunn's writ named Noye and his six co-defendants, plus those involved in the robbery and the innocent parties who had inadvertently been involved in handling the proceeds of the robbery. Because there were so many defendants and because there was the potential for huge publicity, McCunn took the paperwork to the High Court himself. It was quickly followed by an injunction that froze the financial assets of Noye and other defendants. Their property was also seized. Noye had boasted in court of the millions he had stashed in various bank accounts; now he had no way of accessing them. More ancillary applications followed as the legal team worked in secret to get orders against the banks to disclose information about the defendants' bank accounts. McCunn began the painstaking work of sifting through financial records to put together the civil case against those involved with the robbery. Negotiations began to recover money from some of the innocent parties caught up in the case.

As the summer of 1986 turned to autumn, McCunn and investigators secured a second major breakthrough. In the form of
Michael Relton.

• • •

After Relton's arrest, when he was cooperating with police, he also
asked to speak with the insurers. Lead investigator Peter Steger had
enjoyed a twenty-eight-year career in the Metropolitan Police, serving
in the Flying Squad, anti-terrorism and the organised and international crime branch before retiring as a detective sergeant in 1984.
At his leaving party at Harry's Bar in the basement of the Central
Park Hotel in Bayswater, fellow detectives, senior police officers and
lawyers rubbed shoulders. Among those present were Detective
Constable John Fordham and Michael Relton. Steger was in a unique
position, trusted by Relton and by the police investigating the case.

Steger was allowed to question Relton. 'That was a real piece of
luck,' he said later. 'We were able to sift through documents, accounts
and look at money transfers. We were looking at corporate entities
and acquisitions.' Early one Sunday morning, he called McCunn
and told him he was going to collect him from home. He warned
him that secrecy was paramount and that no one, not even his wife,
could be told about where they were going. The two men made their
way to the New Malden police station, where Relton was being held
in the custody suite. Steger later said that the confident, affable solicitor he had known was now white-faced and sweaty-palmed, and had
acquired a nervous twitch, though McCunn felt that Relton calmed
as the conversation entered familiar legal discussion.

McCunn and Steger began to debrief Relton, gathering a mass
of detailed financial information. Steger said later that Relton 'sat
drawing out diagrams on pads in the custody suite. He provided
codenames for the accounts and, even more importantly, written

authority for us to serve letters on the banks concerned, letting us see the accounts.' The debriefing continued until Relton received a phone call. It was the phone call that saw Relton stop all cooperation. He attempted to withdraw his confession from the police. But with McCunn and Steger, it was too late for that.

Armed with documents, bank statements and the authority to look at bank accounts in Switzerland, McCunn and Steger got to work. 'I was able to get all the account details and circumvent normal police channels,' Steger said later. 'What we were getting the next day the police would have taken eighteen months to lay their hands on. I basically spent the next year of my life at 33,000 feet accessing the accounts and sorting out the details.' For the next few years, as McCunn said later, 'We investigated any company, any thing or person that might have a bearing on the case.' A civil action was started against Relton in mid-November 1986, with a High Court injunction freezing his and others' assets granted a few days later.

The legal team buried themselves in financial schedules, tracking how money had flowed between various different bank accounts, through cash withdrawals, bankers' drafts and shell companies. By following the money, they gradually amassed a clear and accurate picture of how proceeds from the gold had been distributed and spent. McCunn also embraced new technology. In 1986 he became the first in his firm to have a personal computer on his desk. An American information technology expert created software that would enable McCunn and the investigators to make sense of the mass of evidence that they were gathering. The hand-typed transcripts of the first Noye trial were sent to the United States and re-typed into a format that could be put into a database and searched. At a time when personal and business computing in Britain was still in its infancy, it was a groundbreaking move.

McCunn and the private investigators were soon moving ahead of the police. They had independently sourced so much evidence that not working with the police became an impossible position for either party to defend. When they met with the police, usually Brian Boyce or Tony Brightwell, very little was put in writing. Those meetings were convivial. Fortunately, they all shared an appreciation of wine and often met in pubs, which were hard to bug.

As cooperation increased, the police began to ask the investigators to find information for them, especially about properties held overseas. It was much easier for McCunn and Steger to gather information than it was for the police, who had to go through official channels, the Foreign Office and other administrative hoops to conduct investigations overseas. It would not always go smoothly. On one occasion, a member of McCunn's team was leaving a building after serving documents on a target when they walked into a police-surveillance operation on the same individual.

The insurance investigators followed the proceeds of the Brink's-Mat robbery around the world. They tracked down money in accounts in Switzerland, Liechtenstein, Hong Kong, Ireland, the Isle of Man, South Africa and the British Virgin Islands, and followed leads that took them as far as Australia. It was Steger who found the Kansas oil well bought for John Fleming with some of his share of the Brink's-Mat money. On a hot day in Kansas, a bewildered Steger found himself looking not at the 'bustling concern filled with men in Stetsons and cowboy boots' that he expected, but rather at a 'a tiny nodding donkey in the middle of a desert, trying to extract oil from a dry oil field'. The investigators discovered many such examples of the Brink's-Mat criminals being relieved of their money by other criminals.

The investigators looked at a host of people, from wildly differing backgrounds, linked to the robbery. In most cases, the evidence needed to initiate a civil case could not be found and, in some cases, it didn't make financial sense to pursue them. In the case of Fleming, poor investments, his briefly extravagant lifestyle, the legal bills from his failed attempt to find sanctuary in South America and falling victim to other criminals had left him virtually penniless.

The freezing actions brought unexpected consequences. When Brenda Noye decided that she wanted to make some alterations to the kitchen at Hollywood Cottage, she had to negotiate with McCunn because the house had been placed under the freezing order, a situation that led to the unlikely situation of the litigator travelling out to West Kingsdown to check the plans. When Jacqueline McAvoy suffered a water leak at Bird-in-Hand Lane she called McCunn and asked what she should do. He told her to get a contractor in to fix it and altered the freezing order to pay for it.

Relations were not always so cordial. McCunn and the legal team were concerned about security. McCunn kept his team small to avoid leaks and Steger strictly controlled any sharing of information. It wasn't enough. Steger was working undercover in Fuengirola, Spain, when the criminals came for him. He was looking at a development allegedly bought by Relton with Brink's-Mat money, posing as a British businessman interested in buying a property. The former police detective was recognised. He was followed back to his hotel, drugs were placed in his room and a local magistrate was bribed to jail him for six months. The trap was set. Fortunately, Steger's connections ran just as deeply as the criminals'. He was given a tip-off, rushed to the airport, boarded the first flight out and returned to Britain in beach shorts and flip-flops, suntanned and shaken. Later, the team would learn that a contract had been taken out on the life of one of their number.

When the Brink's-Mat criminal trials came to an end in the early 1990s, McCunn and the investigators could no longer rely on information being thrown up by the criminal investigations and spent more money and effort in pursuing assets. They faced another challenge on Friday 10 April 1992, when the IRA detonated the largest bomb on mainland Britain since the Second World War. The bomb was contained in a truck parked directly outside the Shaw and Croft offices on St Mary Axe in the City of London. When it exploded at 9.20pm, the blast passed through the building's underground car park and out the other side. The glass façade of the building was shattered. Reorganising and re-indexing the Brink's-Mat papers, and removing all the shards of glass, was a massive job for the legal team.

The huge civil cases that McCunn and Steger were working towards were pencilled in for 1995, with civil actions to be taken against up to fifty individuals. McCunn's hope, however, was that none of these cases would ever be heard. Now that they had the evidence, and now that the criminals knew that legal action was pending, McCunn went looking for settlements. These were tense affairs, conducted through secret meetings held in venues including hotel foyers, prisons and the back rooms of south London pubs, where McCunn and his team would be watched over by security guards as deals were thrashed out. McCunn knew that there would be a ripple effect. If he could strike a deal with the biggest criminals involved, the message would go out that he and his team were to be taken seriously.

He started, therefore, with Kenny Noye.

• • •

In 1994, McCunn began negotiations with Noye, who had recently been released from prison, along with Brenda Noye. McCunn met Noye in his solicitor's office and talked through how a deal might work. Noye looked, to McCunn, far older than a famous photograph of him in a tuxedo that had circulated in the press. Initially, Noye was aggressive, but once McCunn had explained that he was simply seeking compensation for the insurers, that he was not trying to re-prosecute Noye or any of the other defendants, and simply wanted to do a deal, Noye became more accommodating. Ultimately, Noye was a businessman. He recognised that this was a financial deal and approached it as a business transaction. 'There was no suggestion I was talking to a major criminal or anything; we just sat down and talked about it,' McCunn remembered later. 'We simply wanted to recover the money, as much as we economically could.'

The investigators had traced £2,858,066 from the raid to bank accounts in Britain and Ireland that Noye controlled. They also wanted ownership of the eleven gold bars found at his house. Finally, after insurers agreed that they would make no claim against Hollywood Cottage, the secret discussions ended with an out-of-court settlement in which Noye agreed to hand over £3 million. After agreeing the deal, Noye left on holiday for several weeks in Tenerife, perhaps not coincidentally where Palmer was based. For McCunn and his team, it was a major breakthrough. 'Noye was an important stage in getting other people to talk,' recalls McCunn.

From then on, they didn't encounter much trouble, even with the more hardened end of the criminal spectrum. Although, McCunn said, 'We did have occasional slightly heavy language and slightly heavy people hanging around, and one occasion, somebody opened a jacket and revealed a fairly hefty lump underneath his arm.' Noye's decision to settle sparked a merry-go-round of out-of-court settlements. McCunn had meetings with a cast of Brink's-Mat characters, from the robbery and the smelting and laundering operations, some of whom had not been found guilty in the criminal trials.

McCunn met with John Palmer's former partner Garth Chappell in Long Lartin prison and listened to Chappell deny all involvement with the Brink's-Mat gold. He found Gordon Parry 'quite likeable, friendly and could exchange a joke' and met with Jean Savage, who was 'a good old Cockney type'. When McCunn met Brian Perry, he realised that the two had history. When he was a young solicitor, McCunn had been contacted by a haulage company about a consignment of handbags stolen while in the possession of a courier company run by Perry. The young McCunn had gone to Perry's office to serve the writ in person, only to be met by several intimidating men and a lot of 'muscle lying around'. An incident which led McCunn to serve future papers by post.

McCunn struck some remarkable deals. Settlements were reached with John Palmer and Patrick Clarke. He reached settlements with five individuals who were not convicted of any criminal involvement with the Brink's-Mat gold, and one who was not even charged in connection with the crime. Perhaps the most unlikely settlement was agreed with John Lloyd. Lloyd, the common-law husband of Jean Savage, had long been suspected of being part of the original robbery gang but disappeared shortly after Noye was arrested in January 1985. It was thought he had gone to live in Florida. A warrant was issued for his arrest in connection with handling £17.3 million of the robbery proceeds and in May 1991, Lloyd was named on the *America's Most Wanted* television programme as one of the ten most wanted international fugitives. Despite there being a reward of £10,000 for his capture, he lived for some of this time in east London, an indication of his high standing in criminal circles. In 1994, he returned to Britain and gave himself up. With the civil case pending, the Crown Prosecution Service decided not to charge him. In June 1995, he came to an out-of-court settlement with McCunn and his team. Despite having never been charged with involvement with the Brink's-Mat robbery, Lloyd is said to have agreed to pay £4.2 million. After settling, Lloyd went back to his bungalow in West Kingsdown, and his business of hiring out cars and vans.

For McCunn, the defendants could be divided into three categories. First were the villains, the criminals who had been involved with the initial robbery. Many of them thought the civil action was another form of prosecution and that McCunn was after a conviction. Second were the fences and money launderers involved in converting the gold into cash and investing the proceeds. These were businesspeople involved in illegal acts who understood McCunn was only after a financial settlement to be reached through a process of negotiation. The third were the banks and other institutions caught up in the case who had handled the proceeds innocently. There was no question of criminal action against any of them, with the possible exception of Barclays in Bedminster, but they had a legal obligation to return the money. Soon, the investigation became self-funding, with McCunn sending cheques back to the insurers. By June 1995, McCunn had recovered £14 million. And he hadn't finished yet.

The civil trial process eventually started in April 1995, once the appeals linked to the criminal convictions had been concluded. The civil case had begun with fifty-seven plaintiffs. Settlements were eventually reached out of court with fifty-three. Four plaintiffs went to court. Two were swiftly successful. That left only the once-suspected Brink's-Mat robber, Tony White, and his wife.

Perhaps emboldened by his earlier success in being found innocent of involvement with the Brink's-Mat robbery itself, the defiant White decided to take the civil claim to trial. However, the burden of proof required in a civil trial is different from in a criminal case. In a criminal case, prosecutors must prove the case 'beyond all reasonable doubt'. In a civil case, the requirements are less onerous. The claimant only needs to prove their case based on the balance of probabilities, that their case is more likely than not to be correct.

The trial, McCunn remembered, was 'a good show'. White had been arrested on drugs charges and was on remand in prison as a Category A prisoner. He arrived at the High Court every day in an armoured van, with police sharpshooters stationed on the roofs of neighbouring buildings. Inside the building, he was covered by an armed guard and stood in a section of the courtroom covered by iron bars. The civil court had seen nothing like it.

Having been found innocent of being one of the Brink's-Mat robbers alongside Micky McAvoy and Brian Robinson, White might have thought he was past the repercussions of the robbery over a decade before. He was apparently angered by Noye's decision to settle with McCunn and his team. The strength of the investigators' case would not have pleased him any more. They methodically demonstrated the substantial wealth that White came into after his acquittal and revealed lavish spending. By 1987, White had invested around £450,000 in property in south-east London and in November 1986, he moved to Marbella in Spain, where he bought a town house and cruised around town in a midnight-blue BMW convertible.

In Spain, White was suspected of involvement in drug smuggling. When he was arrested in October 1989 for his alleged involvement in a plot to kill two Spanish undercover policemen, police found in his house jewellery worth about £108,000 and around £100,000 in British, French, Belgian and German currency, all of which White claimed he had acquired legitimately. In 1989, irritated by police surveillance, White returned to Britain, bought a house in Catford, south-east London, as well a shoe shop and a wine bar, which he named Blanco's Tapas Bar. In 1991, White was charged and acquitted in connection to a ton of hashish found hidden in a cargo of frozen chips on a lorry in Dover. Moving back to Spain, he acquired a home between Marbella and Fuengirola, and began making regular trips to Tangier.

The prosecution diligently traced White's wealth and spending since the robbery. They recorded that over £1 million was paid into his bank accounts and that in 1986, he withdrew over £1 million in cash from the same account. The prosecution claimed that this wealth was funded by the proceeds of the Brink's-Mat robbery. On 1 August 1995, Mr Justice Rimmer agreed with them and ruled in favour of the insurers. He told White that his acquittal at the Old Bailey did not mean that the jury had been satisfied that he was innocent, only that they had not been satisfied he was guilty, according to the standard of proof required for a criminal trial. Rimmer said, 'Mr White is a dishonest man with an appalling criminal record,' and that White's wealth was 'the fruit of a major crime' with 'a compelling inference that it was derived from the Brink's-Mat robbery'.

White was ordered to repay £26,369,778, the full value of the robbery, plus a further £2,188,600 in compensation. His wife was ordered to pay £1,084,344. The couple's home in Catford, their Spanish property, jewellery and other assets bought with the proceeds of the robbery all became the property of the insurers. He would go bankrupt shortly after, with only a small portion of the order ever paid, but it was a significant symbolic victory.

For McCunn and his team it was 'a good day', as he recalled. For Scotland Yard, it was a moment of vindication. Detectives had always believed that White had been part of the original robbery gang and that his acquittal in 1984 was a mistake. The verdict in the civil case provided confirmation that what they believed had been correct all along. McCunn recalls that the police 'were absolutely over the moon', and that he was able 'to get a free beer whenever the police were in the vicinity for quite a long time'.

After the White verdict, McCunn told reporters, 'I am realistically optimistic of recovering a total of £20 million for the underwriters. So far, we have about £16 million under lock and key. But, of course, at today's prices, the £26 million stolen would be worth at least double, if not treble.'

The last point is important. Bob McCunn and his team would eventually recover around £27 million for the insurers, more than the value of gold stolen in the robbery itself. It was an extraordinary endeavour and certainly the most remarkable piece of insurance recovery in British legal history. But the proceeds of the Brink's-Mat robbery were invested around the world in highly profitable criminal and legal enterprises. Even McCunn himself believes that the £27 million recovered is, at best, only half of the proceeds and profits of the original robbery.

McCunn's work was largely completed in 1995. It was over a decade since the robbery and most of the police involved in the original inquiry were retired or dead. In terms of the investigations that the robbery had produced, McCunn was one of the last men standing.

One day, towards the end of his work, McCunn found himself dealing with a number of the A24 £50 notes issued through Scadlynn. McCunn had seized them as part of a settlement and wasn't sure what to do with them. He took them to a Barclays bank, which felt fitting, and told the teller that the notes were part of the proceeds of the Brink's-Mat robbery. The young teller, recalls McCunn, 'had absolutely no idea what I was talking about'.

CHAPTER THIRTY-ONE

The Rise and Fall of John Palmer

Detective Chief Superintendent Brian Boyce retired from the Metropolitan Police at the end of June 1989. He could claim some clear successes from his leadership of the Brink's-Mat inquiry. The Gold Chain had been broken and Kenneth Noye, Brian Reader, Garth Chappell and Matteo Constantino had been convicted for their part in smelting and selling the gold. Michael Relton had been convicted for his role in laundering and investing the proceeds, and, at the time of Boyce's retirement, Brian Perry was awaiting a retrial in which he would be found guilty. Gordon Parry had also recently been arrested on the Costa del Sol and would later also be found guilty. In the Isle of Man, Patrick Diamond had been found guilty of helping to launder other Brink's-Mat proceeds, dismantling another laundering route. The money movements that brought Jean Savage and others to the attention of the task force had been detected, and the police were well on their way to arrest those involved.

Boyce had injected energy and drive into a fading investigation and delivered a string of convictions in often highly complicated jury cases, while battling challenges that included allegations of

corruption within his own ranks. He had forged new investigative alliances, such as with Her Majesty's Customs and Excise,
and encouraged his team to operate in new and innovative areas
of policing. After his retirement, Boyce was presented by Bob
McCunn with a framed A24 £50 note, one of many drawn from
the Scaddlynn bank account in Bristol, in recognition of their work
together, which had occurred both publicly and privately, in bringing the laundering operation to justice.

However, there had also been notable failures for the police. The
robbery was thought to have been conducted by six robbers, plus Black
as the inside man. Four of those seven individuals had been charged
and three had been convicted – McAvoy, Robinson and Black. Tony
White had been found not guilty of involvement with the robbery,
while the case brought against John Fleming for his alleged role was
thrown out before trial. John Lloyd, despite being wanted for questioning, was still on the run, while charges had never been brought against
the sixth suspected robber.

Twenty-nine people were charged with handling offences related
to the robbery, but by the time of Boyce's retirement only seven
had been convicted – Noye, Perry, Reader, Chappell, Constantino,
Relton, Kathleen McAvoy (for her minor role in accepting a house
bought with Brink's-Mat proceeds) and Diamond in the Isle of Man.
Parry, Savage and Patrick Clarke would ultimately offer three further
convictions. A number of individuals that police were confident were
involved in the plot to launder and invest the proceeds of the robbery
were acquitted, didn't make it to trial or were never charged at all.

As some in the press were fond of observing, despite all the
money spent on the inquiry and court cases, aside from the eleven
bars of gold found at Noye's house, none of the gold and valuables
stolen from Unit 7 had ever been recovered. And there is no doubt

that the police felt huge disappointment over the failure to prosecute Noye and Reader for some level of criminal culpability with regards to the tragic death of John Fordham.

The investigation into the Brink's-Mat robbery had become the longest-running continuous inquiry in a hundred years of Scotland Yard, and it wasn't finished yet. Boyce left behind a small team of trusted officers to help get the last of the ongoing criminal cases over the line. For some of the police involved, there was one other lingering task that they weren't yet ready to let go.

At some point, someone had to do something about John Palmer.

• • •

When Palmer returned to Tenerife after his acquittal on Brink's-Mat charges, he had already begun to build what would become an empire. Island Village Club, a collection of holiday homes dug into an arid Tenerife hillside, was Palmer's first commercial venture on the island. The construction is said to have been partially funded by Palmer's Brink's-Mat proceeds, along with bank loans and local investors, with the development supported by Tenerife's tourist authority, who thought it would bring more visitors to the island. They were right. Palmer's new company, registered in the Isle of Man, soon developed into a multi-million-pound business, helped by a sales approach that could kindly be described as aggressive. Timeshare lets were sold by Palmer's gang of largely British touts, who patrolled the streets and beaches of Las Americas most mornings, lured tourists to the Island Village development with promises of prizes and alcohol, then subjected them to an array of hard-sell tactics.

The financial success of Island Village led to Palmer embarking on further developments, but his burgeoning business soon attracted attention from an array of authorities. Questions were raised about the financial management of Island Village, which Palmer ran with the same looseness he had applied to his English jewellery shops, with huge cash transfers being made to his personal bank account and countless stories of unpaid bills. The company's sales tactics were becoming notorious, and Island Village was fined by authorities for 'aggressive' street sales. The fine was never paid.

Palmer's timeshare business was soon being investigated by the European parliament's ombudsman, Spanish authorities, disgruntled investors and an MEP, while Bob McCunn and his team investigated Palmer's activities in the UK and froze his British assets.

Palmer might have been a man under pressure from multiple sources but he didn't appear to show it. Through the late 1980s and into the 1990s, he concentrated on making a huge amount of money – and spending it freely. In 1988, Palmer bought a $3 million Learjet, which he used to fly between Tenerife and Bristol, and would replace with a bigger Gulfstream jet. At Bristol airport, Palmer left by a side gate to avoid passport control and would later buy a helicopter to take him straight from the tarmac to his home. In Tenerife, Palmer bought a string of impressive properties, along with a private yacht called *Brave Goose of Essex* and a large collection of classic cars.

Meanwhile, Palmer's personal life became increasingly complicated. While on the run from the Brink's-Mat enquiry in Tenerife, with his family back in England, Palmer had begun a relationship with Christina Ketley, who worked at his new timeshare company. On the morning after Palmer's acquittal, Marnie visited a local shop and saw a tabloid front page that revealed the affair with the headline: 'Mistress and Wife Fight Over Mr Gold'. On his return to Tenerife, Palmer continued the relationship. Ketley, who was from a middle-class Kent background and spoke with a clipped accent, was a meticulous business operative who was soon playing a major role in helping manage Palmer's growing timeshare empire.

Never a man to rest on his laurels, in the late 1980s Palmer also began a relationship with a German student called Saskia Mundinger, who was working as a sales rep for his organisation. Mundinger became pregnant and returned to Germany to have the child. Palmer flew to Germany for the birth of the child, made his brother godfather, paid £60,000 in child support and managed to keep the entire arrangement secret from both Marnie and Christina Ketley.

As he became more established on Tenerife, Palmer's business interests diversified and darkened. Initially, he concentrated on expanding the timeshare business, bribing local authorities so he could buy wasteland and build more resorts. He built the island's first and biggest water park, which he joked was used to wash money. Palmer is then said to have moved into drug trafficking. He reportedly used members of the island's police force, with whom he already had a corrupt relationship, to ensure that shipments of cocaine could pass through the island unhindered, taking a percentage on every shipment. The money he received was laundered through Tenerife banks and reinvested through other enterprises.

Palmer employed an intimidating security team led by Mohammed Durbur, reportedly known as both 'Tel' and 'Mo', who was a Lebanese ex-militiaman. It has been suggested that Mo was sent to protect Palmer by Charles Taylor, a civil servant in Liberia from whom Palmer bought some diamonds who would rise to become Liberian president. Western Africa was not the only place Palmer is said to have sought alliances. After the fall of the Soviet Union, it's claimed Palmer developed links with Russian organised crime, taking Russian investment and employing a Russian bodyguard whom Spanish security sources believed was an ex-KGB colonel.

Palmer became so adept at money laundering that he is said to have offered the service to other criminals. This reportedly attracted an unlikely would-be customer. The journalist Wesley Clarkson has written that on 3 November 1991, the disgraced newspaper tycoon Robert Maxwell docked his yacht in Tenerife, approached Palmer and asked him to change £10 million in cash into dollars. Palmer refused and Maxwell was found dead two days later, having fallen into the sea from his yacht. But Palmer's money-laundering services would soon become the cause of a very public embarrassment.

By the early 1990s, Palmer's activities in Tenerife were beginning to attract the attention of British investigative journalists. In early 1993, Adam Holloway and Kate Stone reported on the web of corruption and terror that lay behind Palmer's apparent success in Tenerife for an ITV Granada documentary series called *Disguises*, in an episode called 'A Little Piece of Eldorado'. Using hidden cameras, they revealed to viewers in Britain how Palmer's touts lured unsuspecting holiday-makers into complex timeshare cons.

Worse was to come for Palmer in 1994, when he became the focus of the prominent investigative journalist Roger Cook and his television show *The Cook Report*. In a six-month investigation, an undercover team filmed Palmer making a string of eye-catching statements, including offering to sell arms from the Russian mafia and asking if he could be supplied with foreign hitmen to use in Britain. Via an undercover reporter posing as one of the world's biggest opium producers, *The Cook Report* captured conversations in which Palmer offered to launder £75 million, through the mixing of clean and dirty money, in return for 25 per cent commission, explaining 'I'm not cheap, but I am very good' and that he had police and judges in Tenerife in his pocket. At the end of the programme, which was broadcast in June 1994, millions of British viewers watched as Cook confronted Palmer, who denied all knowledge of the meetings the programme-makers had filmed and ultimately fled in a taxi from Cook and his cameras.

Other than a charge of mortgage fraud in 1988, for which he later received a suspended sentence, the police had been unable to lay a glove on Palmer. However, Scotland Yard had been secretly liaising with *The Cook Report* and, shortly before the programme was aired, officers from Scotland Yard's international and organised crime branch coordinated raids on ten addresses linked to Palmer in London, the West Midlands, the south-west and Essex. Palmer, however, could not be found. His Learjet was thought to have flown from London to Faro before the raids took place, and he subsequently went into hiding. Dangers were gathering for Palmer, which would soon include a name from the past.

• • •

When Kenneth Noye was released from prison on licence in 1994, one of his first moves was to go on holiday to Tenerife. It's hard not to imagine that the trip involved a meeting with Palmer. Two years later, on 19 May 1996, Noye became involved in an altercation with another motorist, twenty-one-year-old Stephen Cameron, on a slip road off the M25 near Swanley in Kent. The incident ended with Noye stabbing Cameron to death. In the nine hours afterwards, Noye made seventeen calls on his mobile phone. Some were to arrange for the destruction of evidence, including his Range Rover, while others were to tie up loose business ends. Likely the most important call of all was to Palmer. Soon after, Noye is said to have collected a suitcase of money from his Kent home and driven along the M4 to Palmer's Somerset home.

Noye, wearing a cloth cap in an attempt to conceal his identity, was then flown in Palmer's helicopter to a golf course that Palmer owned in Caen, Normandy, where Palmer was said to be waiting. From there, the two men travelled by train to Paris. The next day, Palmer's private Learjet arrived at the city's Charles de Gaulle airport. Using a false passport in the name of Alan Green, Noye was flown to Madrid, and then the two men flew on to Tenerife where the trail went cold. Although they did not know any of that detail at the time, the police spoke to Palmer in 1996 due to his status as a 'close associate' of Noye. Palmer told them that he couldn't help. After a huge manhunt, in which British police were assisted by GCHQ, Noye was found more than two years later living in the Spanish resort of Barbate. Cameron's girlfriend, Danielle Cable, who had witnessed the killing, was secretly flown out to positively identify Noye in a Spanish restaurant. The following day, Noye was arrested and would later receive a life sentence for the murder.

Meanwhile, Scotland Yard's Organised Crimes Squad continued their inquiries into Palmer's activities in Tenerife. By early 1997, they had gathered enough evidence of fraud to arrest and charge Palmer. He was contacted by police and on 7 April 1997, almost exactly ten years after his acquittal at the Old Bailey, Palmer walked into Holborn police station in central London accompanied by his solicitor and was arrested along with his now partner Christina Ketley. Palmer was charged with eight counts of conspiring to defraud others and freed on a £1 million bail, which he paid in cash. He was photographed leaving the court flanked by burly minders.

The police were desperate to make these charges stick. Palmer had become a very public embarrassment, having recently been included in the *Sunday Times* Rich List as the fifty-first wealthiest person in Britain, with an estimated fortune of £300 million, which the newspaper said was derived from a 'large and lucrative timeshare operation in Tenerife'. Palmer's annual appearance in the Rich List from this point on would become a yearly reminder to the police of their failure to convict him.

In Tenerife, there were also those who hoped that Palmer would be brought to heel. Palmer had shown no signs of toning down the more nefarious side of his operations. In 1999, the Russian newspaper *Kommersant* reported that Palmer's plane flew to Russia practically every week from Tenerife or Bristol. It was never checked at customs and very heavy boxes were unloaded from it.

Palmer's trial began at the Old Bailey in September 1999. Alongside him were Christina Ketley and five of his managers. The jury was told that Palmer was 'the biggest shark in the water' in Tenerife and that, over a period of seven years, 17,000 couples had been 'systematically tricked' out of large sums of money that they could not afford. The prosecution calculated that over £30 million had been paid to Palmer's resorts between 1990 and 1997 as a result of a variety of fraudulent practices. Not for the first time in the Brink's-Mat story, it was a false start. The trial was halted after eight months when Palmer successfully argued, through his solicitor, the ever-present Henry Milner, that press publicity had prevented him from getting a fair trial. Palmer, who had enjoyed the press attention the Brink's-Mat story had brought him in the 1980s, was now benefiting over a decade later from the heightened public profile he had as a result.

By the time Palmer's retrial began on 2 October 2000, he had made the highly unusual decision to dispense with the services of Milner and to instead defend himself in court. Though he had struggled with literacy as a child and did not have a single academic qualification to his name, Palmer took charge of a major, complicated case at the Old Bailey. Where this decision came from is unclear. Roy Ramm, a Scotland Yard detective who led the timeshare-fraud investigation against Palmer, and who had assisted the Brink's-Mat task force in their negotiations with Micky McAvoy over the possible return of some of the Brink's-Mat gold, recalled that Palmer had by this point become 'an incredibly arrogant bloke'.

At the Old Bailey, Palmer opened his defence case by telling the jury: 'I have been portrayed as a gangster. I am not a gangster or ever have been a gangster.' The trial then saw the unlikely sight of Palmer questioning witnesses but, as the defendant, conducting that questioning from the dock.

There was a series of bitter exchanges between Palmer and Ramm. 'He made some ludicrous mistakes,' recalled Ramm. 'The judge was trying to persuade him not to ask me questions that would cause me to call him a member of an organised crime syndicate and I did so on three or four occasions, and the judge said, "Mr Palmer … do you really want to continue with this?"'

The judge, Gerald Gordon, also had to intervene several times when Palmer began shouting and wagging his finger at police witnesses. When a procession of senior officers gave evidence against him, Palmer accused them of corruption. Palmer told the jury that he accepted that fraud had gone on but that it had taken place behind his back. He claimed that the police had had a vendetta against him ever since they failed to convict him for involvement in the Brink's-Mat robbery. 'They have done anything to try and get me and have spent millions and millions of pounds of public money to get me,' he said. At one point, Palmer shouted 'I am not guilty!' at the jury.

From the dock, Palmer flaunted his wealth. He suggested that the prosecution could have spared the taxpayer by simply suing him for £50 million, as he could comfortably afford the loss, before taunting one witness with his lack of knowledge of his assets. 'You didn't know how rich I am,' Palmer declared. 'Were you aware of my private plane and my two helicopters?' Palmer was so confident of success that during breaks in proceedings he showed the prosecuting team brochures for a £10 million leisure complex and a £40 million hotel that were under construction in Tenerife.

The jury spent nearly six weeks deliberating its verdict. When they came back into court and delivered a guilty verdict, *The Times'* court correspondent noted that Palmer 'looked as though he was going to faint in the dock as he slowly took off his expensive wristwatch and handed it to his solicitor before being led to the cells'. Ketley was also found guilty but escaped prison. She was given a two-year suspended sentence, the judge saying she acted under Palmer's 'malign influence'.

When Palmer was brought back to the Old Bailey for sentencing, he opened with a complaint, that he had unfairly been treated as a Category A prisoner, before growing emotional as he pleaded for leniency. 'I acknowledge I have a very strong, dominant personality, probably from my background, and have always relied on my wits to provide for those near and dear to me,' Palmer said. 'You cannot set up this level of business by running a Mickey Mouse con. I have worked all my life and always will.' He claimed he had 'never imagined' that he would be the subject of British court proceedings and that all the big timeshare companies engaged in similar practices. He added, perhaps reflecting on his cataclysmic decision to defend himself, 'The biggest lesson I have learned is that I cannot do it all myself and should delegate to others.'

Unmoved, Judge Gordon sentenced Palmer to eight years, noting: 'The jury has heard from elderly witnesses, many of whom have been through periods of extreme anxiety and whose retirement has been ruined by the financial state they were left in as a result of this fraud.' Palmer was also ordered to pay £266,367 costs, and detectives and Crown lawyers began looking into how to seize his assets. There were plenty of them. Palmer's *Sunday Times* Rich List residency had reached an embarrassing nadir for the police in 2001, when Palmer, now said to be worth £300 million, was named in joint

105th spot on the list of the richest people in the world. He shared the position with the Queen.

By April 2002, the police and Crown solicitors had worked their way through Palmer's assets. Palmer, the richest inmate of the British prison system, looked 'a grey and drawn figure with a prison haircut, prison pallor, and spare figure', as he was summoned from Long Lartin jail to attend another Old Bailey hearing. Judge Gordon told a grim-faced Palmer that he must pay £33,243,811 under a confiscation order, plus £2,039,899 compensation to his victims and £342,429 in legal costs. The sum was a British legal record, three times higher than anything previously ordered by a British court. Judge Gordon gave Palmer two years to pay the first £20 million or spend an extra eight years in prison. If he defaulted completely, Palmer would face a total of nineteen years in jail. The man who had undoubtedly made the most money following his involvement in the Brink's-Mat story looked to be ruined. But the Brink's-Mat story is rarely that simple.

Palmer's lawyers were granted an appeal on a legal technicality surrounding the notice of confiscation. A few months later, three Court of Appeal judges threw out the confiscation order because of a clerical error, with the paper served on Palmer having referred to the wrong section of an Act. In May 2003, the Lord Chief Justice ruled that the appeal judges had 'misunderstood and misapplied' the law, but he was unable to reinstate the confiscation order as it had been rejected. The Crown Prosecution Service had no way to resurrect the order and Palmer did not have to repay a penny.

It was a remarkable piece of good fortune for Palmer but luck had become a rarity for him. It was reported that his Russian partners had taken over his timeshare businesses as he became ensnared within the British legal system. In May 2005, Palmer was made bankrupt. A few months later, he was released on parole after serving just four years in jail to find that many of his Tenerife assets had been frozen by Spanish authorities and he owed at least £4 million in tax to the Spanish government. Palmer had creditors swarming all around him, including former girlfriends, as he split his time between Tenerife and a large house near Brentwood in Essex. At least his domestic life now offered security, with Palmer living happily with Ketley and their son.

Palmer's situation worsened further when the Spanish police made a move that they had been working towards for nearly two decades. Judge Baltasar Garzón was one of Spain's most celebrated investigating magistrates. Unbeknown to Palmer, Garzón's investigators had been secretly looking into his Tenerife activities since the late 1980s. Now that Scotland Yard had flushed Palmer out, Garzón made contact with the British police and together they began planning a pincer movement, codenamed Operation Beryk, focusing on his timeshare empire. Due to concerns over Palmer's police contacts in both Spain and the UK, information on Operation Beryk was tightly controlled.

In summer 2007, Palmer flew from London to Tenerife, unaware that he was being tailed by undercover Spanish police. As soon as he set foot on Spanish soil, he was arrested on the orders of Spain's national court and accused of being the kingpin of an international criminal organisation operating out of Tenerife that was allegedly responsible for crimes that included timeshare fraud, money laundering, credit card counterfeiting, bribing officials, production of false passports, possession of firearms and committing 'crimes against the physical integrity and liberty of persons'.

According to the journalist Wensley Clarkson, Garzón visited Palmer in prison to show him a dossier of the crimes he was to be charged with and evidence that Palmer had continued to run his criminal enterprise while in prison. Palmer refused to cooperate. In 2009, after two years without charge in a high-security Spanish jail, he was released on bail.

Following his release from Spanish prison, there is little doubt that Palmer continued to operate at a high level of international crime, with a corresponding level of police attention. Roy Ramm recalls that at this stage, Palmer was 'one of the most dangerous members of organised crime in the UK'. It was later revealed that British police had run an intelligence operation on Palmer from RAF Spadeadam in Cumbria since 1999, with Palmer under electronic surveillance by a secret police intelligence unit for the following sixteen years. The Serious and Organised Crime Agency (now the National Crime Agency) gathered intelligence on Palmer in an operation codenamed Alpine and kept highly confidential because of concerns of corruption in the Metropolitan Police. In 2015, it was alleged by *The Times* from files leaked from Operation Tiberius, an internal Metropolitan Police corruption investigation, that Palmer was protected from arrest and investigation by a clique of high-ranking corrupt Metropolitan Police officers. He was identified in the report as 'a top echelon figure in UK organised crime'.

Palmer had come a long way from the Bristol jeweller who became involved with the Brink's-Mat gold over thirty years earlier. Of all those who had played a part in the Brink's-Mat case, he had accrued the most wealth, the most infamy and, possibly, the most enemies.

• • •

On 24 June 2015, a bright, sunny day, John Palmer was tending to the garden of his home near Brentwood, Essex. Later, a CCTV clip would be released of Palmer that day, older and greyer than in his 1980s pomp, behind the wheel of a small green tractor, driving around the grounds of the property dressed in a white T-shirt and jeans.

Around half past five in the afternoon, Palmer was shot six times in the chest in the one area of the garden not covered by CCTV. A mortally wounded Palmer managed to walk a short distance towards his house before collapsing. He was found by relatives who called for help, but Palmer died shortly after. Police would later find what they felt was a spy hole in the exterior fence and said that they suspected that Palmer's killer was a professional hitman who had been observing him for some time. A distraught Christina Ketley said later, 'It haunts us every day to think that whoever was responsible was clearly watching John, stalking him like an animal before brutally and callously ending his life.' Palmer's estranged wife Marnie voiced her anger that the cause of Palmer's death was initially missed, with paramedics and police somehow failing to identify the bullet wounds and suspecting that Palmer had suffered a heart attack, meaning valuable investigatory time was lost. Despite the subsequent police investigation pursuing 700 lines of inquiry, the killer was never found.

Competing theories emerged in the wake of Palmer's death. His Spanish trial was finally approaching and there was speculation in some quarters that he may have been seeking a deal with prosecutors. Then there was the vast range of criminal organisations that Palmer was said to have dealings with. But for some, the roots of Palmer's death lay a lot earlier than that. Former Scotland Yard detective Roy Ramm said he has 'no doubt' that Palmer's murder was 'directly linked' to the Brink's-Mat robbery.

CHAPTER THIRTY-TWO

The Search for an Ending

Coverage of John Palmer's death contained mentions of what some had termed the curse of the Brink's-Mat gold. There is no doubt that a significant proportion of those involved in the Brink's-Mat story met untimely deaths, but drawing a clear narrative thread through lives lived in the opaque world of professional criminality is a difficult task. Like much of the Brink's-Mat story, different explanations are available, with some seeing a clear pattern, which to others is significantly overstated. The killings took place throughout the 1990s and included a member of the Great Train Robbery gang murdered at his Spanish poolside, a Hatton Garden jeweller shot on his doorstep and a suited property investor gunned down in daylight on Marylebone High Street.

And then there was Brian Perry. After his release from prison in 2001, Perry returned to his old habits. Three mornings a week, he drove in his Mercedes from his home in Kent to the offices of Blue Cars in South Bermondsey where he parked in the same spot every time. On Friday 16 November 2001, Perry arrived around 1pm. As he stepped from the car, a man wearing dark clothing and a dark balaclava ran up and shot him three times at close range. Perry died instantly. Witnesses saw a man running to a waiting Ford Escort, which was driven off by a person in dark clothing. Two men were seen abandoning the car at around 1.15pm. It was clearly a professional hit.

After a lengthy police enquiry, two men from east London went on trial for the murder, with the prosecution claiming that they were hitmen hired to execute Perry, which 'may or may not' have been linked to Perry's involvement with the Brink's-Mat robbery but was 'part of the background to this case'. The case was weak, based on circumstantial evidence and debatable forensic links and the trial was soon abandoned. No further prosecutions were ever brought but detectives remained convinced the murder was connected to the Brink's-Mat robbery.

Others departed the story less violently. Michael Relton was said by the late 1990s to be living in Mayfair, dining regularly at Quaglino's, a fashionable restaurant in Bury Street, and overseeing business interests in South Africa funded by some lingering remnants of the Brink's-Mat proceeds. His former partner Gordon Parry quietly returned to legitimate business pursuits. John Fleming died in 2008, his occupation given on the death certificate as lighterman, a historical task performed by Thames boatsmen. Others can be found easily enough. They have new lives, new businesses, new families. Some are dead. Some are ailing. Some are living in healthy retirement.

In tracking down the characters involved in the Brink's-Mat story, there is one who has proved more elusive than the rest. The presence at the heart of the narrative, inanimate and yet endlessly dynamic. We are, at least, not alone in having failed to find the Brink's-Mat gold.

• • •

At the second Brink's-Mat laundering trial, the prosecuting QC Michael Austin-Smith said, 'The full story of what happened to the gold may never be known. For all we know, one of us in court who bought jewellery since 1984 might have some of the Brink's-Mat gold in it.' It was an arresting idea, first used by the journalist Andrew Jennings back in 1986, that so much of the stolen Brink's-Mat gold had been sold back into the market, it would have infiltrated much of the gold jewellery made in the UK ever since.

The police tracked around half of the Brink's-Mat gold through the Gold Chain and Scadlynn. What happened to the rest has become a rich source of conjecture and conspiracy. An early police theory was that the Brink's-Mat robbery was a sequel. Earlier in the same year of 1983, there had been a markedly similar armed robbery of £7 million in cash from a Security Express depot in east London. Police believed that there was a hidden hand controlling the two robberies and that the first robbery helped finance the second.

Among the suspects for both robberies named in a Spanish news magazine at the time were five men – Ronnie Knight, John Everett, John Mason, Freddie Foreman and Clifford Saxe – all of whom were now living in Spain. Although the men denied it, detectives believed they had been involved in planning and financing the raids, and had received some of the proceeds. Ronnie Knight ran Artistes and Repertoire Club on Charing Cross Road, which was where John Fleming was introduced to Patrick Diamond. But as this was before the extradition treaty with Spain was agreed, there was little Scotland Yard could do to reach the men.

By 1986, Scotland Yard detectives had a new theory of what had happened to the half of the Brink's-Mat gold that was not smelted by Noye and Palmer. The police believed that the gold was smuggled out of Britain to Spain, where it was smelted and sold back into the legit-imate market. They knew that a sophisticated mechanism had been used to dispose of the travellers' cheques stolen from the Brink's-Mat depot outside Britain, and thought a similar international operation had been mounted for the gold. They suspected that the vehicles used for this were international ambulances sent out to Spain by insurance companies to collect Britons who had fallen sick and wanted treatment at home, which crossed the Channel with the gold hidden inside. In a joint operation with Spanish police in summer 1986, dozens of pre-dawn raids were mounted and searches carried out. Thirty-six Britons in Spain were held and questioned. Spanish police were hoping to find the middleman who was thought to have handled the stolen bullion. But the raids came to nothing, with no charges brought and no gold found. Despite this setback, the police felt the theory remained valid.

And then there are the rumours that arrive mob-handed in the Brink's-Mat story – that the missing gold was hidden up a chimney in Kent, or had been smelted by the travelling community, or hidden in the house of a terminally ill pensioner in east London, or tucked away to this day in some dusty, distant vault. The tips kept coming to the police for decades. In 1995, the *Evening Standard* reported that between £10 and £12 million of gold was said to be languishing down a Cornish tin mine, untouched by the robbers since 1983, and 'defying helicopters full of investigators'. In 2001, police dug up a building merchant's land in Kent after receiving 'credible information' that the gold was buried there. It wasn't.

And so the Brink's-Mat story ends, by trailing off into uncertainty and conjecture, with even the end point itself the subject of debate. Or so we thought. Late in the day, with this book written and publication approaching, an email was received. It seemed unlikely but, following checks and double-checks, its provenance was assured. We had a new lead and we had a new ending. The story would end where it began. At the Heathrow trading estate, on a cold November morning in 1983.

Because Micky McAvoy wanted to talk.

CHAPTER THIRTY-THREE

Two Ton of Yella

Since the day of the Brink's-Mat robbery to now, thirty-nine years later, Micky McAvoy has never granted a public interview. But, he says, the time has come. He doesn't want the same mistakes, or, specifically, the same 'bullshit', to be told this time round. A phone interview is arranged. On the day, there is a nervous wait and a growing silence, until the line crackles and Micky McAvoy announces himself in a Cockney accent undimmed by age.

We start where McAvoy started, with the planning of the robbery. It is the first of several areas where McAvoy wants to right the record, as he answers our questions firmly and without prevarication. McAvoy is scathing at the suggestion of hidden hands, evil overlords and the robbery being financed by an earlier armed robbery. 'The only financing for the Brink's-Mat robbery,' laughs McAvoy, 'was the money for a set of number plates.' What would be the largest robbery in the world came about, according to the man who organised it, from his opportunistic hard work.

McAvoy says he met the corrupted Brink's-Mat security guard Tony Black with 'two other men', not named by McAvoy but likely to be Brian Robinson and Tony White, every Friday for 'around three months'. Black told McAvoy about the mounting riches being stored at the depot. It is here that McAvoy makes his most startling revelation. 'It's been coming up to nearly forty years of the same story being dished out,' he says, 'and none of it is true.' A central plank of the Brink's-Mat story has usually been that McAvoy and his fellow robbers had no idea such a vast amount of gold was in the depot when they broke in. According to McAvoy, 'nothing could be further from the truth'.

'This wasn't "Oh, we just got in the doors, stumbled in there",' says McAvoy. 'It wasn't that at all. We got ready every week, every Friday. We would have two vans, the cars, a place where we used … and then the place we went back to was separate, so it was clean. I used to meet Black every Friday night after he finished work down the Heathrow area and he'd say "there's two million, there's three million", 'cos he could see roughly. Then he started off giving me four million, six million. Ten. In gold. And then the night of 25 November, I met him at Heathrow and he told me there's two ton of yella. Which means gold.'

On learning there were two tons of gold, or yellow, in the Brink's-Mat depot, McAvoy worked out the street value of 'about seventeen million' and told the rest of the robbery gang. 'I said, "We're going tomorrow."' That was the reason that the robbers took two Transit vans, he explains: 'You can't put two ton of gold in one van. The wheels would be down on the floor. It's crazy!'

On the day of the robbery, there were not two tons of gold but three. When Black finished work around 6pm, there is likely to have been roughly two tons of gold in the depot, with another ton arriving without his knowledge after his departure.

McAvoy disputes the suggestion, made by the prosecution in court and reported in the press, that Black told the robbers there was 'a normal amount, somewhere between £1 million and £2 million' in cash and valuables in the depot on the day of the robbery, rather than two tons of gold. 'It's in the court documents that he said "two ton of yella",' insists McAvoy.

McAvoy bristles at the common conception of how the robbery played out. 'We stumbled on some tarpaulin and the gold was underneath it,' he says drily, 'absolutely fucking crazy. When we went in on a Saturday morning, we knew there was two tons of gold, but there were three tons, there was a million pound in cash in the safe inside the vault. But all the combinations got changed on the Friday. So, we didn't get the money out the safe inside the vault, but we went in there for the gold.' There is some supporting evidence for this version of events buried in the witness statement of the security guard Robin Riseley, who insisted that the robbers started removing the boxes of gold from the vault as soon as they got in and that they continued to do that while he attempted to remember the codes for the safes.

Not only did the robbers know that a large amount of gold was there, says McAvoy, but they had a clear plan of what to do with it. He confirms the belief that there were six robbers as 'absolutely accurate'. After the robbery, the six men took the gold to a hiding place where it was 'cut into two parcels'. The following day, 'One and a half ton went with me, and I took it somewhere. And to this day, no one's ever been in there. It was safe. And a fellow I know, he took one and half ton. He was involved in the robbery as well. And that was it.'

The plan was that 'one person' would handle the sale of the gold. 'Not people running off doing their own share. One person would have the control and it wouldn't go to certain people.' Those involved would 'get fed off of' what was sold and 'would know where that's going' with the gold sold in parcels of 'six hundredweight or three hundredweight at a time' (0.3 and 0.15 tons). That, at least, was the plan.

In the week between the robbery and his arrest, McAvoy returned to his outwardly normal life. 'I had a building company, so I would just go there. Our mother was in hospital. She had a couple of heart attacks, so I was going up to the hospital every day.' He was going to sit tight 'till it settled down'. The problem was Tony Black, the compromised, and now regretful, security guard.

'When I first met him,' recalls McAvoy, 'I said, "I don't trust you. There's something about you." I said, "I won't ever betray you. Don't betray me. The only way you're gonna get arrested is if you open your mouth. No one's gonna betray you." And no one did; he just betrayed himself.' McAvoy notes ruefully, 'Within the week, he was cooperating with the police.'

McAvoy doesn't deny his role in the robbery. He does, however, cast serious aspersions on how the police built their case against him. He notes that the guards gave multiple statements, which appeared to become progressively more damning. 'I looked at Riseley's first statements, it was "they come in with balaclavas on". Then they changed their stories. He remembered something: "he's got blue eyes, they had even white front teeth, about thirty-two years old, fair hair. Cockney accent." If you'd have seen their first statements, they never said none of that.'

It is true that the guards all made several statements; Robin Riseley alone made five. In their initial statements, the guards did not give details of McAvoy or the other robbers' appearance. At the trial, it was revealed that the guards got together to try to remember the robbers' appearances. McAvoy is particularly scornful of Black's ever clearer memory of the robbery once in police custody. 'Black decided, "I'm gonna give evidence to the police." And he said exactly how it all happened, but he never put me in the building. He said it was very quick, they had balaclavas on. And then he talks to Frank Cater, to the commander, on his own. And then he said, "Someone come in, lifted my hood up" – meaning me – and said, "We got all the gold."'

It is likely accurate that Black's initial statement, and confession that he took part in the robbery, did not put McAvoy in the building. After meeting with Commander Frank Cater, then in charge of the Flying Squad, Black is believed to have then added that during the robbery, McAvoy had come up to him while he was bound on the floor, raised his hood, taken off his mask and said, 'We got the lot.' Black's new, additional memory was noted by the defence during McAvoy's trial as being 'convenient' for the prosecution. McAvoy is scathing: 'Never went near him. Never went near this kid. We got charged because Black's put me in the building. We went back into police custody and then I get picked out by three guards.'

It is unusual to hear a criminal happily confess to a crime while complaining bitterly as to how he was convicted. But justice is not served by a rightful conviction achieved wrongly and McAvoy claims that pressure on the police drove them into questionable areas of conduct: 'Their job was "we've gotta put you away, we've gotta put you away". That's it. It was a big case.' He strongly disputes the police suggestion that he made a verbal admission while reading Black's statement. 'Their case was that I read Black's statement … and as I read it, I went, "Oh, we're in fucking trouble now". I never came out my cell and I never touched that statement.' At his trial, McAvoy's lawyers asked to see the custody-suite records, which would have shown if he had left his cell for interview, and the statement he was alleged to have touched, but neither was produced. The statement was said to have been destroyed by a police officer for 'security reasons'. When McAvoy and Robinson were convicted and sentenced to twenty-five years, they received their sentences politely, with McAvoy thanking the judge. 'We was never gonna change it,' explains McAvoy simply. 'We was gonna be a benchmark. You steal a lot of money, you're gonna do a lot of time.'

We ask McAvoy about the suggestion that there was an escape attempt foiled when he was on remand in Brixton prison. He confirms that the escape was to be organised by his former criminal associates after McAvoy had passed them control of his half of the Brink's-Mat gold. 'I was holding … one and half of this gold out of the three tons,' he says. 'So then, I was getting messages, can you hand the one and a half ton of gold to us to look after? I agreed, but it was also agreed that there was going to be an escape from Brixton prison.'

The prison authorities were tipped off about the daring escape plan, which was to involve a helicopter plucking McAvoy from the prison yard, and he was hurriedly moved at 5am to the higher-security Winchester prison. 'And that was it. I can't escape from Winchester, so I went on this hunger strike for thirty-six days to force 'em to move me back to London. All my security then just elevated. They said you're not gonna escape in a helicopter or anything else, hence why I spent the next eleven years in a special wing.'

After his conviction, McAvoy was moved to Leicester prison. That there were negotiations during McAvoy's time at Leicester over the return of his share of the gold is well recorded, including in this book. As is the suggestion that, somewhere during those negotiations, McAvoy finally lost control of the gold to his fellow robbers and others. On both points, McAvoy offers confirmation. 'I never asked for any deal for my sentence, I never asked for a trade, I never asked anything,' he clarifies, insisting it was the police who came to him. McAvoy says the first approach was from a detective whom he suspected was corrupt, and who told McAvoy that if he and Robinson returned their share of the gold, then the police could help get their sentences cut in exchange. McAvoy claims to have sent him packing. When McAvoy was approached by other detectives whom he concedes were 'down the middle' and more trustworthy, he took the offer more seriously. Not that there wasn't tension. McAvoy recalls an exchange with Brian Boyce. 'He went, "It's not your fucking gold." I said, "It's not yours either."'

When the police suggested that McAvoy could return some of the gold in exchange for a reduction to his sentence, while keeping a sizeable amount of it, McAvoy told his fellow robbers the plan. 'I sent a message outside: "This is what they wanna do." And people outside went, "Yes, call it on, you just do the negotiating,"' he recalls. 'I then put a message outside to people, they're saying, we put the shares back … we can get our sentence cut and we can still cut the rest of the money out between us. And they agreed,' he says.

McAvoy's position is that he ultimately agreed to give back 'six hundredweight', as did Robinson, meaning the police would recover just over half a ton of the Brink's-Mat gold. That would leave over two tons, worth over £20 million at the time, that the police would not seek to recover. In return, McAvoy and Robinson's sentences would be reduced from twenty-five years to eighteen years. 'Our share was gonna go back because we were going to take that trade,' said McAvoy. 'And the rest would've been cut up between the people involved in it.'

McAvoy says that at this point senior officers got involved along with 'the DPP's office, someone from the attorney general's office, our QC, [the] QC for the police all sitting there and working out the details. We was booked to go into the High Court in the spring.' The deal was: 'If you both put your shares back you'll get down to eighteen years and that's it.' But, McAvoy repeats, 'I never asked for any deal; that was offered to us. That's how this word "trade" started. By them, not me.'

The deal never happened. When asked why, McAvoy tenses. 'Greed,' he says, more than once.

Micky McAvoy was a convicted, sometime violent armed robber. He was also a man who believed in what he saw as the traditional criminal code. 'I know a lot of people would've just gone, I'll put people in it, [give] evidence against them,' he says about the period following his arrest, when he saw twenty-five years of imprisonment looming. 'That's not me. That's not how I was brought up.'

When McAvoy asked his criminal associates to pass the agreed 12 hundredweight to the police, word came back that the gold had gone. McAvoy belatedly realised that he had walked into a trap the moment he handed over the gold. The betrayal had begun with the tip-off that cost him his escape. 'You've been asked to hand over the one and a half tons for "we'll get you out, we're gonna help you escape", and all of a sudden Scotland Yard got involved,' he recalls bitterly.

Even worse, claims McAvoy, was what happened to the gold. Once they got hold of it, the others began to sell it off through the criminal underworld. The agreed plan that the gold would be sold slowly through one trusted source was abandoned. McAvoy says the process 'just went completely haywire; they involved everybody and their dog. They went to every Tom, Dick and Harry who wouldn't have got a bar of soap'. For McAvoy and Robinson, their shared ownership of the gold had been inadvertently relinquished when it left McAvoy's control.

McAvoy had been betrayed by his fellow robbers, his fellow south Londoners, and nearly forty years later, his outrage remains. He explains it was 'treachery by your own; they were worse than the grass, they were worse than Black. You've done it all really, you've planned it, you sorted it all out. Three of 'em come in just on the fucking day and they get the lion's share, and then leave you for the next fifteen years. They got what they wanted. I was in the prison doing the twenty-five years and they just kind of had a good life.' McAvoy won't name names, instead saying, 'Just look through court cases and what's come out in their cases and what they said about them and they're not far from the truth. Everyone ... tried to portray themselves as good and loyal people and they're just a bunch of shit-bags.'

McAvoy feels that it was his belief in the criminal code, to not implicate others, that made him an easy target for treachery. 'They knew that you would never betray 'em and give evidence against 'em. They knew that. They wouldn't have done it to someone else who they might've thought, "Oh, fuck me, he'll give us up." Because they knew your history, your background, you was never gonna do that. So, yeah, you got hung by your code. What they done, they left just a big knife in your back.'

It might have been some of his fellow robbers who took his gold, but it was others who sold it. We ask McAvoy if he knew Kenneth Noye or John Palmer. 'Never met Noye in my life,' he says. 'Never met Palmer in my life.' We ask if he was surprised to read their names in the newspaper when they were charged with handling the gold. 'Absolutely, I was surprised ... I see these names coming up and I just couldn't believe it.' When ask about Gordon Parry and Michael Relton he says, 'I knew their names. Friends knew Relton.' He observes of this growing cast of characters: 'It seems the people who was on the edge, not the main people, they got more than anyone.' McAvoy believes it was his half of the gold that went through Palmer and Scaddlyn. 'It probably did, yeah. I wasn't there, but it probably did. You know, I knew of this Palmer. I mean, I've only heard of this character.'

And as for the other half of the gold, about which endless theories have been offered, McAvoy says the situation is far more straight-forward. 'The gold did go,' he says simply, then repeats, 'the gold did go.' He knows enough about the money made by others to be confident that the vast majority, if not all, of the Brink's-Mat gold was sold back into the market. 'I knew one person who was involved with us at the time. He took eight million. Eight fucking million pound from that gold that was done. And other people, four million, five million, three million. The gold went,' he says in summary.

Talking to McAvoy, the robbery feels both very near and very far away. His memories are clear and his anger at those who wronged him is undiluted by the decades, but this is not the thirty-two-year-old professional armed robber who had a fearsome reputation, embodied by his Mad Micky nickname. This is a seventy-one-year-old widower, who is concerned that his late wife Kathleen McAvoy is treated with respect by those who choose to tell the Brink's-Mat story. Often her role, as the girlfriend of the married McAvoy at the time of the robbery, has been presented with titillation. In fact, McAvoy clarifies, after they married in Leicester prison, Kathy was his second wife for nearly forty years, a commitment that began with her loyally visiting him in prison for sixteen years 'when everyone else left me for dead'. After his release in 1999, McAvoy and Kathy lived in Spain for a long period before returning to England. He is, he says, 'cut off from everybody'.

When asked if there is anything he has left to say, McAvoy returns to Unit 7 at the Heathrow trading estate and the morning of 26 November 1983. The man who organised the biggest robbery in the world wants the world to know that it wasn't an accident. 'A lot of work went into that,' he says. 'Don't make it look cheap.'

And with that, Micky McAvoy is gone.

KEY PEOPLE

Robbers
CONVICTED
Michael McAvoy

Brian Robinson

SUSPECTED
John Fleming

John Lloyd

Brian Perry

Anthony White

Guards
Peter Bentley

Tony Black*

Ron Clarke

Richard Holliday

Robin Riseley

Michael Scouse

* *Also convicted of involvement with the robbery*

The Gold Chain

CONVICTED

Kenneth Noye

Brian Reader

Garth Chappell

Matteo Constantino

Patrick Diamond

Michael Relton

Kathleen McAvoy (Meacock)

Brian Perry

Gordon Parry

Patrick Clarke

Jean Savage

ACQUITTED

Thomas Adams

Michael Lawson

Terence Patch

Brenda Noye

John Palmer

Christopher Weyman

Hilary Wilder

Richard Wilder

Lesley Fleming

John Fleming

Stephen Donovan

Ann Elcombe

John Elcombe

Joseph Medayil

Michael Osborn

Stephen Clarke

Jacqueline McAvoy

KEY PEOPLE

Key police officers

Assistant Commissioner John Dellow

Deputy Assistant Commissioner Brian Worth

Commander Frank Cater

Commander Phillip Corbett

Detective Chief Superintendent Brian Boyce

Detective Superintendent Tony Lundy

Detective Chief Inspector Ken John

Detective Chief Inspector Roy Ramm

Detective Inspector Peter Atkins

Detective Inspector Tony Brightwell

Detective Inspector Ian Brown

Detective Inspector Tom Glendinning

Detective Sergeant Robert Gurr

Detective Inspector David Sandlin

Detective Inspector Ron Smith

Detective Sergeant Tony Curtis

Detective Sergeant Bill Miller

Detective Sergeant John Redgrave

Detective Sergeant Robert Suckling

Detective Sergeant Anthony Yeoman

Detective Constable Bruce Finlayson

Detective Constable John Fordham

Detective Constable Neil Murphy

Key HM Customs and Excise officers

Jim McGregor

Mike Newscombe

Insurers' lawyer and private investigator
Bob McCunn

Peter Steger

Lawyers
DEFENCE

John Mathew QC

Henry Milner

Ronald Thwaites QC

PROSECUTION

Michael Austin-Smith QC

Michael Corkery QC

Nicholas Purnell QC

Police outside the Brink's-Mat depot, Unit 7 of the Heathrow International Trading Estate, in the days after the robbery.

Michael McAvoy

Anthony Black

Brian Robinson

Kenneth Noye

John Palmer and his wife, Marnie, posing for press photographs in Tenerife, February 1985.

The smelting works installed in the garden of John Palmer's home, the Coach House, in Lansdown, Bath.

Detective Constable John Fordham

Police search the grounds of
Kenneth Noye's home, Hollywood
Cottage, in West Kingsdown,
Kent, following the death of
Detective Constable John
Fordham, 27 January 1985.

John Palmer escorted by police at Heathrow Airport following his return to Britain from Tenerife via Brazil, 2 July 1986.

John Fleming (centre) escorted by police at Heathrow Airport following his return to Britain from the United States, 26 March 1987.

Detective Chief Superintendent Brian Boyce (*centre*) and Detective Sergeant Bill Miller (*right*) deliver evidence files to Lambeth Magistrates' Court, 8 June 1987.

Detective Superintendent Tony Lundy

Kathleen McAvoy (Meacock), with guard dogs Brinks and Mat, at Turpington Farm in Bickley, Kent, 1988.

Michael Relton arriving at the
Old Bailey, London, 4 July 1988.

Gordon Parry (centre) escorted
by Detective Sergeant Bill Miller
(left) and Detective Sergeant
Tony Curtis (right) at Heathrow
Airport following his return to
Britain after his arrest in Spain,
6 April 1990.

Brian Perry (left) and Jean
Savage (right) outside the Old
Bailey, London, 17 August 1992.

ACKNOWLEDGEMENTS

This book is based on unpublished archive records, court transcripts, hundreds of contemporary media and press reports, interviews with those involved, and the many later accounts in television, radio and book form. Much of the personal testimony quoted in the book is taken from interviews published and broadcast over the years in newspapers, magazines, books and on television. The book therefore builds on the work of many others, not least the determined and illuminating police and crime reporting of several journalists.

We would particularly like to highlight the work of Peter Burden, Duncan Campbell, Michael Horsnell, Andrew Jennings, Paul Keel, Paul Lashmar, David Leigh, John McLeod, Tim Miles, Gareth Parry, Nigel Rosser, Adrian Shaw, Christine Smith, Stewart Tendler, Rosemary Urquhart and David Williams. Their reporting was invaluable in understanding the twists and turns of the Brink's-Mat saga. Our task was made easier by the many books that deal with the case. *Bullion*, the 1988 account by the *Sunday Times* journalists Andrew Hogg, Jim McDougall and Robin Morgan, provided a crucial guide to the early years of the Brink's-Mat inquiry. We would like to thank Andrew Hogg for being an encouraging and informative contact. Will Pearson's *Death Warrant* was instructive on the inquiry's later development. *Lundy* by Martin Short and *Scotland Yard's Cocaine Connection* by Andrew Jennings, Paul Lashmar and Vyv

Simson when taken together illuminated Tony Lundy's role in the inquiry and the controversies surrounding him. Michael Gillard and Laurie Flynn's *Untouchables* shed more light on the corruption that dogged the Brink's-Mat investigations and Scotland Yard more generally. Ian Brown's memoir, *From the Krays to the Drug Busts in the Caribbean*, provided detail on the identification of Noye and the inquiry's expansion overseas. Wensley Clarkson's *The Curse of Brink's-Mat*, *Kenny Noye: Public Enemy Number 1* and *Killing Goldfinger* provided insight into the robbery and the wider lives and connections between the criminals linked with it. Marnie Palmer's account of her life with Palmer, *Goldfinger And Me*, offered similar insight, while Henry Milner's memoir, *No Lawyers In Heaven*, provided the perspective of the legal defence team. Paul Lashmar's articles on Hatton Garden and VAT fraud using gold highlighted the broader criminal context against which the robbery took place. Filmed accounts were equally revelatory. In particular, Blast Films' 2003 two-part Channel 4 documentary *Brinks Mat: The Greatest Heist* and Crimefellas Media's 2019 film *The Brink's-Mat Robbery* contained extensive interviews with key individuals who are no longer alive. Adam Fenn from Bohemia Films shared several important archive documents.

We were fortunate in being able to speak with several people with intimate knowledge of the case. Brian Boyce kindly granted us multiple interviews. We thank him for his hospitality, his good humour and for access to both his memories and written recollections of his career. We would like to thank John Fordham Jr, who was an approachable and understanding presence, for sharing his memories and insight into his late father. We are very grateful to Bob McCunn, who sat for interviews and shared detailed information that was highly instructive. We also thank Bob Fenton, Roy Ramm, Ian Brown and Jackie Malton, the former police officers, and others

ACKNOWLEDGEMENTS

who spoke to us on condition of anonymity. We would like to note our gratitude to Micky McAvoy for choosing to give us his first public interview, which was granted without caveats or requests.

Our grateful thanks also go to this book's copy editor Liz Marvin; David Riding; and Sara Cywinski, Michelle Warner, Jessica Anderson and everyone at Ebury. Finally, Neil would like to thank Rhiannon, for her support and keen editorial eye.

LIST OF SELECTED SOURCES

Newspaper archives consulted

The Times, Guardian, Observer, Daily Telegraph, Sunday Telegraph, Independent, Daily Mail, People, Sunday People, Daily Mirror, Sunday Mirror, Sun, Daily Record, Evening Standard, Sevenoaks Chronicle and *Bristol Evening Post*, plus several other local British and North American titles and BBC online news.

Books and articles

Ian Brown, *From the Krays to the Drug Busts in the Caribbean: A Thirty Year Journey*, Pen & Sword: Barnsley, 2017.

Duncan Campbell, *That Was Business, This is Personal: The Changing Faces of Professional Crime*, Secker and Warburg: London, 1991.

Duncan Campbell, *Underworld: The Definitive History of Britain's Organised Crime*, Ebury Press: London, 2019.

Wensley Clarkson, *Kenny Noye: Public Enemy Number 1*, John Blake: London, 2006.

Wensley Clarkson, *The Curse of Brink's-Mat: Twenty-Five Years of Murder and Mayhem*, Quercus: London, 2012.

Wensley Clarkson, *Killing Goldfinger: The Secret, Bullet-Riddled Life and Death of Britain's Gangster Number One*, Quercus: London, 2018.

Michael Gillard and Laurie Flynn, *Untouchables: Dirty Cops, Bent Justice and Racism in Scotland Yard*, Bloomsbury: London, 2012.

Dick Hobbs, *Doing the Business: Entrepreneurship, The Working Class, and Detectives in the East End of London*, Oxford University Press: Oxford, 1988.

Dick Hobbs, *Bad Business: Professional Crime in Modern Britain*, Oxford University Press: Oxford, 1995.

Andrew Hogg, Jim McDougall and Robin Morgan, *Bullion: Brink's-Mat: The Story of Britain's Biggest Gold Robbery*, Penguin: London, 1988.

Andrew Jennings, Paul Lashmar and Vyv Simson, *Scotland Yard's Cocaine Connection*, Jonathan Cape: London, 1990.

Dick Kirby, *Scotland Yard's Flying Squad: 100 Years of Crime Fighting*, Pen & Sword: Barnsley, 2019.

Paul Lashmar, 'The Great Gold Fraud', *Esquire*, February 1993.

Paul Lashmar and Dick Hobbs, 'Diamonds, gold and crime displacement: Hatton Garden, and the evolution of organised crime in the UK', *Trends in Organized Crime*, vol. 21, 2018, pp. 104–25.

Duncan MacLaughlin with William Hall, *The Filth: The Explosive Inside Story of Scotland Yard's Top Undercover Cop*, Mainstream Publishing: Edinburgh, 2002.

Henry Milner, *No Lawyers in Heaven: A Life Defending Serious Crime*, Biteback Publishing: London, 2020.

James Morton, *Gangland: The Lawyers*, Virgin Books: London, 2001.

Mike Nevile, *Crime and the Craft: Masonic Involvement in Murder, Treason and Scandal*, Fonthill Media: Stroud, 2017.

Marnie Palmer with Tom Morgan, *Goldfinger and Me: Bullets, Bullion and Betrayal: John Palmer's True Story*, The History Press: Stroud, 2018.

Will Pearson, *Death Warrant: Kenneth Noye, the Brink's-Mat Robbery and the Gold*, Orion: London, 2006.

LIST OF SELECTED SOURCES

Tom Pettifor and Nick Sommerlad, *One Last Job: The Life of Brian Reader, Mastermind of the Hatton Garden Heist*, Mirror Books: London, 2019.

Martin Short, *Lundy: The Destruction of Scotland Yard's Finest Detective*, Grafton Books: London, 1991.

Television

Artnes/Channel 4, *Dispatches: Corrupt Cops: What the Met Knew* (2022)

BBC, *Gold* (1987)

BBC, *Inside Out West: John Palmer* (2016)

Blast Films/Channel 4/Discovery, *Brinks Mat: The Greatest Heist*, two episodes (2003)

Channel 5, *Real Kenneth Noye: Britain's Most Wanted* (2000)

Crime and Investigation Network, *Crimes That Shook Britain: The Murder of Stephen Cameron* (2010)

Crimefellas Media, *The Brink's-Mat Robbery* (2019)

Granada/ITV, *World in Action: Treasure Islands* (1988)

Granada/ITV, *World in Action: Scotland Yard's Cocaine Connection* (1989)

Granada/ITV, *Real Crime: Kenneth Noye* (2005)

Granada/ITV *Disguises: A Little Piece of Eldorado* (1993)

ITV Studios, *Judge Rinder's Crime Stories: Kenneth Noye Road Rage Killer* (2017)

SW Media/Channel 5, *Britain's biggest Armed Robbery: Brink's-Mat* (2017)

Unknown, *Britain's Top Ten Heists*, www.youtube.com/watch?v=P8zFjTPnxfY

Plus archive footage from BBC and ITN news.

Radio and podcast

Sky News, *Storycast: The Hunt for the Brink's-Mat Gold* (2019)

    Episode 1: www.spreaker.com/user/skynews/the-hunt-for-the-brinks-mat-gold-part-1

    Episode 2: www.spreaker.com/user/skynews/the-hunt-for-the-brinks-mat-gold-part-tw

Sky News, *Storycast: Beyond the Hunt for the Brink's-Mat Gold* (2019) www.spreaker.com/user/skynews/beyond-brinks-mat-1

Plus archive radio from Independent Radio News held by British Universities Film and Video Council.